STUDY GUIDE
TO ACCOMPANY

Foundations of
MARKETING

STUDY GUIDE
TO ACCOMPANY

Foundations of
MARKETING
FIFTH CANADIAN EDITION

M. DALE BECKMAN
DAVID L. KURTZ
LOUIS E. BOONE

C.E. Greene
B.Comm., B.Ed., M.A. (Marketing), M.Sc. (Instructional Systems)
Lethbridge Community College

<u>DRYDEN</u>

Harcourt Brace & Company, Canada

Toronto   Montreal   Fort Worth   New York   Orlando
Philadelphia   San Diego   London   Sydney   Tokyo

Canadian Cataloguing in Publication Data

Greene, C.E. (Clark E.)
    Study guide to accompany Foundations of
marketing, fifth Canadian edition

Supplement to: Beckman, M. Dale, 1934–
Foundations of marketing.   5th Canadian ed.

ISBN 0-03-922785-5

1. Marketing – Problems, exercises, etc.
I. Beckman, M. Dale, 1934–   Foundations of
marketing.   5th Canadian ed.   II. Title.

HF5415.B432 1992   658.8   C91-095280-9

Editorial Director: Scott Duncan
Acquisitions Editor: Donna Muirhead
Developmental Editor: Cheryl Teelucksingh
Director of Publishing Services: Steve Lau
Editorial Manager: Liz Radojkovic
Editorial Co-ordinator: Sandy Walker
Production Manager: Sue-Ann Becker
Production Assistant: Denise Wake
Copy Editor: John Kneeland
Cover and Interior Design: Dave Peters
Typesetting and Assembly: True to Type Inc.
Printing and Binding: Webcom Limited

∞ This book was printed in Canada on acid-free paper.

4   5   96 95

Preface

This *Study Guide* is designed to provide a wide selection of activities to assist students in learning the material presented in an introductory marketing course. Cases, exercises, and study questions are intended not only to facilitate learning of the material, but also to involve the student in applying this knowledge to the many and varied situations in marketing. It will not be possible for students to complete all of the suggested activities in any particular chapter; thus, instructors or students should select those activities that are of particular interest. All will provide a meaningful as well as analytical study of the principles and practices of marketing.

Each chapter of the *Study Guide* corresponds to a chapter in *Foundations of Marketing*, Fifth Canadian Edition, and is organized in the following manner:

1. Chapter Objectives. The chapter objectives indicate what the student is expected to know upon successful completion of the course.
2. Vocabulary and Key Terms. Listed under this heading are the key terms and vocabulary that the student must know in order to follow the discussion in each chapter. An answer key to each of these sections can be found at the end of each chapter.
3. Practice Test. The practice test, composed of true-false and multiple-choice questions, gives the student a clear indication of whether or not the learning objectives for each chapter have been accomplished. An answer key to each practice test is provided following the questions in each chapter in the *Study Guide*.
4. Exercises. The exercises test the student's ability to apply marketing principles in more complex situations. Again, suggested answers are included in the *Instructor's Manual to Accompany Foundations of Marketing 5/E*.
5. Case Analysis. Real-life cases improve the student's analytical skills and ability to apply marketing knowledge. These cases are grouped at the end of each part. Suggested solutions are available in the *Instructor's Manual*.
6. Product Analysis. Product analysis is a major component of the course. The student is guided through the development and analysis of a marketable product. The product analysis culminates in a major report, for which the student's own synthesis of the elements of the marketing mix is required. An example of a completed project appears in the *Instructor's Manual*.

Publisher's Note to Students and Instructors

This textbook is a key component of your course. If you are the instructor of this course, you undoubtedly considered a number of texts carefully before choosing this as the one that would work best for your students and you. The authors and publishers spent considerable time and money to ensure its high quality, and we appreciate your recognition of this effort and accomplishment. Please note the copyright statement.

If you are a student, we are confident that this text will help you to meet the objectives of your course. It will also become a valuable addition to your personal library.

Since we want to hear what you think about this book, please be sure to send us the stamped reply card at the end of the text. Your input will help us to continue to publish high-quality books for your courses.

PERMISSIONS

Jacuzzi Brothers. Prepared by Scott Markham, University of Central Arkansas, from *Marketing*, 3rd ed., by David L. Kurtz and Louis F. Boone. © 1987 by the Dryden Press. Reprinted by permission.

Rowen Plastics and Manufacturing Company. From *Situations in Marketing* by James H. Sood. © 1976 by Business Corporations, Inc., a Subsidiary of Richard D. Irwin, Inc. Reprinted by permission of Business Publications, Inc.

Nova Scotia. Prepared by Arch G. Woodside and Ilkka A. Ronkainen, Georgetown University, from *International Marketing* by Michael Czinkota and Ilkka Ronkainen. © 1987 by the Dryden Press. Reprinted by permission.

Mountain Gallery of Art. Prepared by Professor Eric R. Pratt, New Mexico State University, and Professor W. Daniel Rountree, Midwestern State University. Reprinted by permission of Platt and Rountree.

Aqua-Craft Corporation. From *Cases in Consumer Behaviour* by Roger Blackwell, James Engel, and David Kollat. © 1969 by Holt, Rinehart and Winston, Inc. Reprinted by permission of the Dryden Press.

Leduc Manufacturing Company. Prepared by Harold W. Fox and George A. Ball, distinguished professor in marketing at Ball University, from *Foundations of Marketing 4/E* by M. Dale Beckman, Louis Boone, and David Kurtz. © 1988 by Holt, Rinehart and Winston of Canada, Ltd. Reprinted by permission.

Robitussin. Prepared by Professor Thomas D. Giese and Thomas J. Cosse, University of Richmond, from *Foundations of Marketing 4/E* by M. Dale Beckman, Louis Boone, and David Kurtz. © 1988 by Holt, Rinehart and Winston of Canada, Ltd. Reprinted by permission.

Tootsizer Canada. Prepared by M. Dale Beckman and R. Lederman from *Foundations of Marketing 4/E* by M. Dale Beckman, Louis Boone, and David Kurtz. © 1988 by Holt, Rinehart and Winston of Canada, Ltd. Reprinted by permission.

Jai Lai Restaurant. From *Cases for Analysis in Marketing 2/E* by W. Wayne Talarzyk. © 1980 by the Dryden Press. Reprinted by permission.

Dylex Ltd. Prepared by Michael Slater, "On the Rack," *The Report on Business Magazine*, February 1990, p. 54; and Jan Matthews and Greg Boyd, "Can Lionel Robins Rescue Dylex," *Canadian Business*, November 1990, p. 106. Reprinted by permission.

Murphy's Snack Foods. Prepared by Bill Crowe, St. Lawrence College, and Mark Slemonsen, marketing consultant, from *Marketing Today* by Ross Crain and David J. Rachman. © 1991 by Holt, Rinehart and Winston of Canada, Ltd. Reprinted by permission.

Lucas Foods. Prepared by John Fallows under the direction of Walter S. Good. © Case Development Program, Faculty of Management, University of Manitoba. Reprinted by permission.

Bounce-a-Roo, Inc. From *Cases and Exercises in Marketing* by W. Wayne Talarzyk. © 1987 by the Dryden Press. Reprinted by permission.

Advertising — Chinese Style. From *Marketing*, 3rd ed., by David L. Kurtz and Louis K. Boone. © 1987 by the Dryden Press. Reprinted by permission.

Live Aid. From *Marketing*, 3rd ed., by David L. Kurtz and Louis F. Boone. © 1987 by the Dryden Press. Reprinted by permission.

Kellogg's Corn Flakes. From *International Marketing* by Vern Terpstra and Ravi Sarathy. © 1991 by the Dryden Press. Reprinted by permission.

We wish to acknowledge the following advertisers for permission to reprint the advertisements that appear throughout the text:

Certified General Accountants' Association of Canada
Kraft General Foods Corporation
American Express Company
Pharmaceutical Manufacturers Association of Canada
Participaction
Canadian Gas Association
Foster Parents Plan of Canada
Canadian Pulp and Paper Association

Contents

PART ONE   MARKETING AND ITS ENVIRONMENT   1

Chapter 1   The Nature of Marketing   2
Chapter 2   The Environment for Marketing Decisions   11
   Case 1   The Jacuzzi Brothers: An American Business Odyssey   20
   Product-Analysis Report   23

PART TWO   FOUNDATIONS OF THE MARKETING PLAN   29

Chapter 3   Market Segmentation: Finding a Base to Start   30
Chapter 4   The Market Segmentation Process   39
Chapter 5   Obtaining Data for Marketing Decisions   47
Chapter 6   Marketing Strategy and the Marketing Plan   56
   Case 2   Rowen Plastics and Manufacturing Company   63
   Case 3   Nova Scotia   64
   Case 4   Mountain Gallery of Art   68

PART THREE   CONSUMER BEHAVIOUR   71

Chapter 7   Consumer Behaviour   72
Chapter 8   Industrial Buyer Behaviour   81
   Case 5   Aqua-Craft Corporation   89
   Case 6   Leduc Manufacturing Company   91

PART FOUR   PRODUCTS   95

Chapter 9   Product Strategy   96
Chapter 10   Product Management   105
Chapter 11   Services   115
   Case 7   Robitussin   121
   Case 8   Tootsizer Canada   124

PART FIVE   PRICING   129

Chapter 12   Price Determination   130
Chapter 13   Managing the Price Function   141
   Case 9   Jai Lai Restaurant   150
   Case 10   Dylex Ltd.   152

PART SIX   DISTRIBUTION   155

Chapter 14   Channel and Distribution Strategy   156
Chapter 15   Wholesaling   165
Chapter 16   Retailing   174
   Case 11   Murphy's Snack Foods   182
   Case 12   Lucas Foods   185

PART SEVEN   MARKETING COMMUNICATIONS   189

Chapter 17   Marketing Communications   190
Chapter 18   Applying Marketing Communications   199
   Case 13   Bounce-a-Roo, Inc.: New Product Advertising   213
   Case 14   Advertising — Chinese Style   215

PART EIGHT   ADDITIONAL MARKETING MANAGEMENT CONSIDERATIONS   217

Chapter 19   Global Marketing   218
Chapter 20   Not-for-Profit Marketing   227
Chapter 21   Total Quality Management in Marketing   234
   Case 15   Live Aid   241
   Case 16   Kellogg's Corn Flakes   242

PART ONE

Marketing and Its Environment

- CHAPTER 1 — THE NATURE OF MARKETING
- CHAPTER 2 — THE ENVIRONMENT FOR MARKETING DECISIONS

Case 1 — The Jacuzzi Brothers: An American Business Odyssey

CHAPTER 1

The Nature of Marketing

CHAPTER OBJECTIVES

1. Define, explain, or describe the key terms listed under "Vocabulary and Key Terms."
2. Define "utility"; list and discuss the four types of utility and identify those with which marketing is concerned.
3. Define marketing and describe its primary nature.
4. Examine the scope of marketing.
5. Contrast the activities involved in each of the three orientations of a business.
6. Explain the marketing concept in terms of its essential features.
7. Apply your knowledge of Chapter 1 to the various activities provided in this chapter of the study guide.

VOCABULARY AND KEY TERMS

From the lettered terms listed below, select the one that best matches the meaning of each of the numbered statements that follows. Write the letter of that choice in the space provided.

a) marketing
b) utility
c) production orientation
d) sales orientation
e) marketing orientation
f) marketing concept
g) exchange process
h) nonprofit marketing

1. _____ The process of planning and executing the conception, pricing, promotion, and distribution of ideas, goods, and services to create exchanges that satisfy individual and organizational objectives
2. _____ Focusing marketing efforts on developing a strong sales force to convince consumers to buy
3. _____ A company-wide consumer orientation with the objective of achieving long-run profits
4. _____ The want-satisfying power of a good or service
5. _____ The theory that a business should first stress the production of quality products and then look for people to purchase them
6. _____ The process by which two or more parties give something of value to each other to satisfy perceived needs
7. _____ The theory that all aspects of a business must be involved with assessing and then satisfying the customer's wants and needs
8. _____ A form of marketing in which something other than return on investment is the objective

PRACTICE TEST

True-False: In the space to the right of each statement, check the appropriate line to indicate whether the statement is true or false.

		True	False
1.	The author's definition of marketing is somewhat limiting, because it takes into account only the flow of products that have already been produced.		
2.	The first step in marketing is to create a quality product.		
3.	The marketing concept is based on the assumption that a quality product will sell itself and that an effective production function is a key prerequisite for high profits.		
4.	The strong consumerism movement of the last ten years indicates that the marketing concept has been less than successful.		
5.	Marketing does not take place in underdeveloped countries because they have a lower standard of living.		
6.	Form utility is created when a firm converts raw materials and component inputs into a finished product or service.		
7.	The four utilities of marketing are form, place, time, and awareness.		
8.	Identifying needs in the marketplace could also be described as "creating a customer."		
9.	A quality product will always sell itself.		
10.	Pizza Hut is an example of a nonprofit business.		
11.	The Canadian government is the leading advertiser in Canada.		
12.	If an organization sees itself as being dominated by others, it will be incapable of taking new initiatives even if it identifies major unsatisfied customer needs.		
13.	The exchange process does not concern itself with selling.		
14.	A company with a sales orientation can still be product-oriented.		
15.	The advantage of a market-oriented strategy is that it makes use of the best parts of the other two strategies and avoids their drawbacks.		
16.	In a market-oriented firm, the marketing function is tagged on at the end of the marketing process.		
17.	A sales orientation affects all aspects of a company's operations.		
18.	A production orientation is very limiting, for it assumes that the tastes and values of the producer are the same as those of the market.		
19.	The marketing process starts with the gathering of information about the customer.		
20.	There are six marketing functions in the marketing process.		

21. Utility is the want-satisfying power of a good or service. _____ _____

22. "Time utility" is defined as making a product available at the locations where customers would expect to buy the product. _____ _____

23. Marketing activities should be understood because we are consumers, but they have little impact on job potential. _____ _____

24. Henry Ford's statement that "You can buy any car you want as long as it's black" is a good example of a sales orientation. _____ _____

25. The only constant in marketing is change. _____ _____

Multiple Choice: Choose the expression that best answers the question or completes the sentence.

26. The want-satisfying power of a product or service is referred to as
a. wants
b. need
c. utility
d. desire
e. marketing

27. The four utilities created by marketing are
a. time, place, form, and awareness
b. time, place, form, and ownership
c. place, form, awareness, and ownership
d. time, form, awareness, and ownership

28. When labour converts raw materials into a finished product the utility that has been created is
a. place
b. form
c. ownership
d. time

29. The Flower Shoppe Company has an extra supply of roses available on February 14 (Valentine's Day). What utility is represented here?
a. time
b. place
c. ownership
d. form

30. When the Zebra Corporation sells goods to XYZ Wholesalers, title to these goods passes to the latter business. What utility is represented here?
a. time
b. place
c. ownership
d. form

31. Neilson's Ltd. tries to ensure that all retailers selling candy bars are carrying its brand, because if this brand is not available, customers will buy a competitor's brand. What utility is represented here?
a. time
b. place
c. ownership
d. form

32. "Essentially, creating a customer means identifying needs in the marketplace, finding out which needs the organization can profitably serve, and developing an offering to convert potential buyers into customers." This statement was made by
   a. Roy Thomson Hall
   b. Professors Beckman, Boone, and Kurtz
   c. Professors Guiltinan and Paul
   d. Peter Drucker
   e. Theodore Levitt

33. The essence of marketing is the
   a. production process
   b. sale process
   c. functions of business
   d. exchange process

34. The essence of marketing is the exchange process in which
   a. two individuals each have something of value but are not willing to trade
   b. two individuals each have something of value and are willing to trade
   c. two individuals each have nothing of value but are willing to trade
   d. one individual has something of value and is willing to trade
   e. neither individual has gained anything of value

35. The prevailing attitude that a good product will sell itself is held by firms that are
   a. production-oriented
   b. sales-oriented
   c. marketing-oriented
   d. believers in the marketing concept
   e. servicing the government market

36. The Marcos Company believes that it should focus on developing a strong sales force that can convince customers to buy its products. This attitude reflects a
   a. production orientation
   b. sales orientation
   c. marketing orientation
   d. customer orientation
   e. technological orientation

37. In a market-oriented firm, the marketing function is
   a. tagged on at the end of the process
   b. of primary importance from the beginning of the planning process
   c. entered into when the product is distributed to members of the marketing channel
   d. only considered when the product is advertised

38. A Rolls-Royce executive said, "We have never had to worry about sales or advertising. Our cars are the best in the world." It can be concluded that Rolls-Royce is
   a. an advocate of the marketing concept
   b. a production-oriented company
   c. a firm with a sales orientation
   d. unique in its analysis of target markets
   e. operating in a buyer's market

39. The marketing concept emphasizes
   a. achieving long-run profits
   b. achieving short-run profits

c. an organization-wide focus
d. marketers' running the company
e. a and c

40. Nonprofit organizations
a. are prohibited by law from making a profit on their operations
b. are numerous in the public sector but are rarely found in the private sector
c. have as their primary objective something other than returning a profit to their owners
d. seldom deal in tangible goods
e. generate over $750 billion in revenues annually

41. When a marketer provides standardization and grading, that marketer is
a. reducing the need for purchasers to inspect each item
b. gathering information about market conditions
c. providing services to fill a consumer need
d. developing channels through which to distribute products
e. setting the price of the product in foreign currencies

42. Which of the following is not a nonprofit organization?
a. the United Way
b. the Red Cross
c. Mothers Against Drunk Driving
d. the Government of Canada
e. none of the above

43. Effective marketing begins with
a. a creative advertising plan
b. the consumer
c. the product manager
d. the product designer
e. the president of the company

44. Which of the following is not one of the three questions that management must ask itself?
a. Who has these problems?
b. What problems do our customers have that our products or services can solve better than those of other suppliers?
c. What circumstances, actual or potential, would dictate modifications in our products, prices, distribution, or promotion?
d. Are our engineers convinced that this product or service will meet with customer approval?

45. Marketing activity was developed through
a. the exchange of production surpluses
b. primitive, subsistence-level surpluses
c. shortages of goods in modern society and intense consumer demand
d. improvements in manufacturing techniques
e. none of the above

46. Which of the following statements best describes a firm with a production orientation?
a. Our company is consumer oriented.
b. We have a first-rate sales organization that sells, at favourable prices, all the products we make.
c. We guarantee that, if our customers are not completely satisfied, we will refund their money.
d. Our basic function is to produce the highest-quality products possible.
e. Selling is only one component of marketing.

47. What is the basic idea behind the saying, "If you make a better mousetrap, the world will beat a path to your door"?
a. Research and development are the most important tasks of a firm.
b. A quality product will sell itself.
c. Price is not an important consideration.
d. a and c
e. b and c

48. Which of the following is the definition of marketing given in the text?
a. Marketing is the flow of goods and services from the producer to the consumer or user.
b. Marketing is the creation of utilities.
c. Marketing is the development and efficient distribution of goods and services for chosen consumer segments.
d. Marketing is the process of planning and executing the conception, pricing, promotion, and distribution of ideas, goods, and services to create exchanges that satisfy individual and organizational objectives.

49. Who said, "Marketing is as different from selling as chemistry is from alchemy, astronomy from astrology, chess from checkers."
a. Peter Drucker
b. Dale Beckman
c. Theodore Levitt
d. Henry Ford

50. Which area is associated with the marketing concept?
a. production
b. sales
c. marketing
d. product

ANSWER KEY: CHAPTER ONE

Vocabulary and Key Terms	True-False	Multiple Choice
1. a	1. F	26. c
2. d	2. F	27. b
3. f	3. F	28. b
4. b	4. F	29. a
5. c	5. F	30. c
6. g	6. T	31. b
7. e	7. F	32. c
8. h	8. T	33. d
	9. F	34. b
	10. F	35. a
	11. T	36. b
	12. T	37. b
	13. F	38. b
	14. T	39. e
	15. T	40. c
	16. F	41. a
	17. F	42. e
	18. T	43. b
	19. T	44. d
	20. F	45. a
	21. T	46. d
	22. F	47. b
	23. F	48. d
	24. F	49. c
	25. T	50. c

EXERCISE 1.1: THE CONSUMER IS KING

The prevailing attitude among manufacturers during the first half of the twentieth century was that a good product will sell itself. This attitude is reflected in Henry Ford's statement, "They [customers] can have any color they want, as long as it's black." Offering customer service was considered secondary to maintaining production efficiency, increasing mass production, cutting costs and — the bottom line — making profits.

In the 1950s General Motors tried to produce a car for every "purse, purpose, and personality." This was a change in philosophy in an industry previously driven by a production orientation. From 1950 to the 1970s the North American car industry had everything its own way. Whatever it produced, it could sell; thus, it concentrated on expanding dealerships, controlling costs, and gaining or maintaining market share. Thus immersed, North American car manufacturers failed to take notice of the coming trends in the industry.

Japanese and European manufacturers began to produce fuel-efficient compact and subcompact cars while North American manufacturers continued to offer oversized, gas-guzzling automobiles. As a result, North American manufacturers' market shares fell off. (Ford Motor Company's market share dropped from 24 percent in 1978 to 17 percent by 1980.)

In the 1980s the North American auto industry took action to meet the challenge of the small-car manufacturers. The March 12, 1990, issue of *Business Week* points out that:

> to develop the Taurus and Sable models, design engineers invited more consumers than ever before to evaluate prototypes. One result: When consumers complained that they were scuffing their shoes because the rear seats lacked foot room, Ford sloped the floor underneath the front seats, widened the space between the seat-adjustment tracks, and made the tracks out of smooth

plastic instead of metal. Buyers have rewarded Ford for such efforts by making it the best selling nameplate in California for the past five years. (p. 90)

North American car manufacturers had not yet solved all their problems, however; this article also noted that while it took the Japanese only four years to design and launch a new car, it took Ford twice that long just to incorporate consumer suggestions into developing a new model.

The automobile industry in North America continues to lag behind its Japanese counterpart. For example, millions of dollars are spent on developing state-of-the-art products; yet the servicing of these products is left to dealers with franchises that are not owned by the auto companies. Dealer service is one of the main sources of complaints by motorists; for example, many would prefer to have their car serviced at night, but few dealers provide night maintenance service. Furthermore, auto salespeople are not trained in the area of customer service. Once a car is sold, the customer rarely sees the salesperson. In contrast, every customer who buys a vehicle from a Nissan dealership receives a call from an outside research firm, which inquires as to how the customer was treated.

Questions

1. What types of orientation are illustrated in this exercise? Discuss.
2. What is the marketing concept? Has the North American auto industry finally adopted this concept?
3. As a prospective car buyer, what customer services would you like automobile dealerships or the auto companies to provide you with?
4. Speculate on what changes may occur in the auto industry in the 1990s.

Source: "King Consumer," *Business Week*, 12 March 1990, p. 90.

EXERCISE 1.2: IT'S NOT MY DEPARTMENT

What is a service? It is a product with no physical characteristics, a bundle of performance and symbolic attributes designed to produce consumer want satisfaction. On the goods–service continuum even manufacturers and retailers are service providers, although perhaps not to the extent that a hair stylist is. Service is an important aspect of the marketing concept because the economic and social justification of a firm's existence is customer-want satisfaction.

In January 1989, while on a trip to Hawaii, the author and his wife had some film developed. We picked up the pictures from a one-hour photo studio in Kona, where we had dropped off the film the day before. A half-hour out of the city, we realized that they had put the wrong pictures in the package. After returning to the photo kiosk, we waited for 5 minutes for the retail clerk to finish a personal phone call. We explained the mistake to her, only to have her respond that we had just ruined her day! Our pictures were found, but our confidence in that photo studio was lost. In the book, *It's Not My Department!*, Peter Glen provides many anecdotal accounts of both excellent and substandard customer service. The following excerpt describes salespeople who believe in what they are doing:

> The biggest problem in providing good service is that most employers never talk about it in the first place. Compare that with McDonald's Hamburger University or Disney's Casting Department. Or Stew Leonard being out in the parking lot with a retarded kid explaining to him how to stack up carts exactly the way they should be stacked. On your first day at Nordstrom in the shoe department it would be explained to you that when a customer asks to try on a pair of shoes, you must bring out three pairs: the pair the customer requested, a second pair in the same style but different color, and a pair of the hottest-selling shoes that week. (p. 139)

In a more humorous vein is the story of Mr. Lazarus, owner of Lazarus Department Store in Columbus, Ohio. This store had a policy of refunding customers' money at any time for whatever reason.

Unfortunately the managers had not informed the salespeople of this policy:

> One day Mr. Lazarus, the owner, overheard a salesperson saying to a customer, "We can't refund your money." Mr. Lazarus, who was very old, just about went psychotic when he heard this. He went over to the salesclerk and said, "Come with me."
>
> They walked out the doors and across Broad Street. There old Mr. Lazarus turned around, pointed up, and said, "You see that water tower up there?" pointing to a huge water tower on the roof of his store which had written across it, in very large letters, LAZARUS.
>
> "Now I'm going to tell you why you're going to give everyone their money back whenever they want it."
>
> The clerk started to go on about how the woman wasn't deserving of her money back and Mr. Lazarus cut him short.
>
> "That name says Lazarus and that's my name, too. And the reason we're going to give her her money back is because it's my money."
>
> In this case, the employees of Lazarus became informed from this action. After that, nobody working at Lazarus had to ask about the store's return policy. They had all been empowered to make the customer happy, no matter what. (p. 177)

Questions

1. If the consumer is really king, should he or she demand good service? Why is it in retailers' best interests to provide service that meets customers' expectations?
2. Examples have been provided of poor service. From your own personal experience give examples of both good and poor service. Do you have suggestions as to how those situations where poor service was provided should have been handled?
3. Relate the marketing concept to the providing of service by both goods and service businesses.

Source: Peter Glen, *It's Not My Department!* (New York: William Morrow and Company, 1990), pp. 139, 177. Reprinted by permission.

CHAPTER 2

The Environment for Marketing Decisions

CHAPTER OBJECTIVES

1. Define, explain, or describe the key terms listed under "Vocabulary and Key Terms."
2. Identify the environmental factors that affect marketing decisions.
3. Discuss how competitive strategies influence the marketplace and are, in turn, influenced by the counterstrategies of competitive firms.
4. Explain the effects of the legal environment on the marketer.
5. Explain some of the major provisions of the Combines Investigation Competition Act.
6. Describe how the economic environment affects marketing strategy.
7. Discuss the importance of the socio-cultural environment in making marketing decisions.
8. Illustrate the relationship between marketing strategies and the technological environment.
9. Apply your knowledge of Chapter 2 to a case analysis project.

VOCABULARY AND KEY TERMS

From the lettered terms listed below, select the one that best matches the meaning of each of the numbered statements that follows. Write the letter of that choice in the space provided.

a) Competition Act
b) Department of Consumer and Corporate Affairs
c) mergers
d) misleading advertising
e) inflation
f) stagflation
g) fiscal policy
h) monetary policy
i) demarketing
j) competitive environment
k) legal environment
l) economic environment
m) societal environment
n) technological environment

1. _____ The process of cutting consumer demand for a product back to a level that can reasonably be supplied by the firm
2. _____ The manipulation of the money supply and market rates of interest
3. _____ The interactive process that occurs in the marketplace

11

4. _____ A federal government structure that closely controls business practices and is responsible for consumers' interests

5. _____ A provision in the Combines Investigation Act that protects the consumer against false statements made to the public about products or services

6. _____ The laws and interpretations of laws that require firms to operate under competitive conditions and protect consumers' rights

7. _____ A situation where an economy has both high unemployment and a rising price level

8. _____ A complex milieu within which operate dynamic, cyclical business fluctuations

9. _____ A policy that concerns the receipts and expenditures of government

10. _____ The rising price level resulting in reduced purchasing power for the consumer

11. _____ Canada's major legislation regulating business relationships and business practices

12. _____ The application to marketing of knowledge based on discoveries, inventions, and innovations in science

13. _____ A provision in Competition Act for when competition is likely to be lessened over a substantial segment of the market

14. _____ The marketer's relationship with society in general

PRACTICE TEST

True-False: In the space to the right of each statement, check the appropriate line to indicate whether the statement is true or false.

	True	False
1. The Food and Drugs Act falls solely under the auspices of the Minister of Consumer and Corporate Affairs.	_____	_____
2. It is perfectly legal in Canada for a manufacturer to require a retailer to sell its products at a suggested retail price.	_____	_____
3. The legal environment attempts both to maintain competition and to regulate specific marketing practices.	_____	_____
4. Even modest shifts in one or more of the environmental elements can alter the results of marketing decisions.	_____	_____
5. The interactive process that occurs in the marketplace as competing organizations seek to satisfy markets is known as the socio-cultural environment.	_____	_____
6. The most direct form of competition is between products that can be substituted for one another.	_____	_____
7. Selecting a competitive strategy involves asking three questions: Who are our competitors? What is their strategy? Should we compete?	_____	_____
8. Making tactical decisions is tied to the third question in selecting a competitive strategy.	_____	_____
9. The Canadian government has tended to promote a competitive marketing system.	_____	_____
10. Consumer and Corporate Affairs Canada was established in the year 1976.	_____	_____
11. Of all the legislation affecting the consumer, the Competition Act has the most significance in the legal environment for marketing decisions.	_____	_____

12. The Competition Act regulates rather than prohibits certain acts on the part of companies.

13. The Competition Act contains two main provisions, covering mergers and restrictive trade practices.

14. Price discrimination is covered under the Deceptive Trade Practices section of the Competition Act.

15. Bid rigging and price fixing are covered under the Mergers section of the Competition Act.

16. False statements about products or services are prohibited.

17. Demarketing is a rising price level resulting in reduced purchasing power for the consumer.

18. In a period of stagflation, high unemployment and rising price levels occur at the same time.

19. A recession normally follows a depression in the business cycle.

20. Monetary policy concerns the receipts and expenditures of government.

21. Rebates on automobiles are most likely to be offered in prosperous times, when manufacturers can afford to offer them.

22. Videocassette recorders and low-cost satellite receiving stations may adversely affect concert attendance and movie ticket sales.

23. In the last two decades, the public has lost confidence in all public and private institutions.

24. Consumerism is an evolving aspect of marketing's social environment.

25. It is more difficult to advertise sensitive products on television today than it was in the 1970s.

Multiple Choice: Choose the expression that best answers the question or best completes the sentence.

26. Making false statements to the public about products is prohibited under the misleading advertising section of the
   a. Food and Drugs Act
   b. Competition Act
   c. Hazardous Products Act
   d. Canada Corporation Act

27. Which section of the Competition Act makes it an offence to deny goods to an outlet that refuses to maintain the manufacturer's suggested retail price?
   a. Predatory Price Cutting
   b. Price Discrimination
   c. Resale Price Maintenance
   d. Misleading Advertising

28. Changes in the international societal environment
   a. do not affect Canadian marketers
   b. mirror domestic societal changes
   c. demonstrate how reactionary other societies are when compared with our own
   d. are, with domestic societal changes, in the forefront of marketing thought

29. The most important change included under the Competition Act was one that
   a. allowed the tribunal to act for the courts
   b. provided one consolidated piece of legislation
   c. provided that mergers would be covered under civil rather than criminal law
   d. made combines and restraint of trade an offence under the act

30. The most highly regulated areas of marketing are
   a. wholesaling and retailing
   b. branding and labelling
   c. production and distribution
   d. promotion and pricing

31. Which of the following is not an example of fiscal policy?
   a. The government adds a goods and services tax to raise revenue.
   b. The government cuts government expenditures to reduce the deficit.
   c. The central bank raises the interest rate to combat inflation.
   d. The federal government eliminates the manufacturer's tax to help foster international trade.
   e. All of the above

32. Which of these is not one of the three types of competition discussed in the text?
   a. competition between marketers of similar products
   b. competition between products that are substitutable for each other
   c. competition between companies that are competing for the same consumer dollar
   d. competition between service companies for greater market share

33. Which of the following is not one of the five questions asked in developing a competitive strategy?
   a. Who are our competitors?
   b. What are our objectives?
   c. Should we compete?
   d. If we should compete, in what market should we do so?
   e. How should we compete?

34. Which of these questions is relevant to the tactical decisions that must be made by a firm?
   a. Who are our competitors?
   b. What are our objectives?
   c. Should we compete?
   d. If we should compete, in what market should we do so?
   e. How should we compete?

35. Price, discrimination, predatory pricing, referral selling, pyramid selling, and double ticketing are areas covered under the
   a. Mergers section of the Competition Act
   b. Combines and Restraint of Trade section of the Competition Act
   c. Deceptive Trade Practices section of the Competition Act
   d. Canada Corporation Act
   e. previous Combines Investigation Act but not under the Competition Act

36. The most common types of practices considered illegal under the Combines and Restraint of Trade section of the act are
   a. price fixing, bid rigging, market sharing, and group boycotting of competitors
   b. the exchange of statistics
   c. restrictions on advertising
   d. the co-operation of rival firms in doing research and development
   e. company mergers that are not in the public interest

37. In selling to wholesalers and retailers, a manufacturer cannot
   a. make a practice of discriminating in price among purchasers who are competing with one another and who are purchasing like quantities and quality of goods
   b. offer the same quality goods to different resellers
   c. offer discounts and allowances to these resellers
   d. deny supplies to an outlet that refuses to maintain the resale price
   e. a and d

38. Which store received the largest fine ever imposed on a company under the Restrictive Trade Practices section of the act?
   a. Eaton's
   b. Procter & Gamble
   c. Campbell Soup
   d. Canadian Airlines International
   e. Simpsons-Sears

39. What is the correct order of the business cycle?
   a. recession, recovery, depression, prosperity
   b. recovery, prosperity, recession, inflation, depression
   c. recession, depression, recovery, prosperity
   d. depression, prosperity, inflation, recession, recovery

40. The introduction of the Goods and Services Tax (GST) is 1990 by the Conservative government is an example of
   a. monetary policy
   b. fiscal policy
   c. another unsound Conservative government piece of legislation
   d. sound Conservative government judgment
   e. taxing the poor for the benefit of the rich

41. Some utility companies have encouraged homeowners to install more insulation to lower their heating bills. Builders are promoting new energy-efficient homes. These are examples of
   a. inflation
   b. subflation
   c. demarketing
   d. socio-cultural conditions
   e. competitor strategies

42. Which of the following is not one of the five marketing environments?
   a. competitive
   b. financial
   c. legal
   d. economic
   e. socio-cultural
   f. technological

43. Shell Oil is publicizing gas-saving tips through a series of advertisements and brochures. This is an example of
   a. corrective advertising
   b. demarketing
   c. institutional advertising
   d. a and b

44. The struggle among companies in the same industry or among substitutable products is known as
   a. traditional economics
   b. competition
   c. marketing
   d. two of the above
   e. all of the above

45. Which question states the legal test of whether a certain merger would create a harmful monopoly in Canada?
   a. Is it likely to discriminate in price between purchasers?
   b. Is it likely to practise misleading advertising?
   c. Is it likely to agree upon a restriction of advertising?
   d. Is competition likely to be lessened over a substantial segment of the market?

46. Creeping inflation is characterized by
   a. modest increases in the general price level that go largely unnoticed
   b. loss of jobs
   c. poor marketing practices
   d. a surge in the economy

47. Which of the following would not be considered a competitor of Odeon Theatres?
   a. Famous Players Theatres
   b. the local hockey team in your city
   c. the symphony orchestra in your city
   d. fast-food franchises such as Dairy Queen and Burger King

48. The Competition Act became law in 1986; it was formerly known as the
   a. Canadian Corporation Act
   b. Hazardous Products Act
   c. Co-operative Act
   d. Combines Investigation Act
   e. Mergers and Combines Act

49. The "activist watchdog" of marketing practices is the
   a. Restrictive Trade Practices Tribunal
   b. courts
   c. federal government
   d. Department of Consumer and Corporate Affairs
   e. board of health

50. Inflation has the effect of
   a. increasing the value of the dollar in the marketplace
   b. reducing the value of the dollar in the marketplace
   c. increasing the value of the dollar in the international market
   d. reducing the government deficit

ANSWER KEY: CHAPTER TWO

Vocabulary and Key Terms	True-False	Multiple Choice
1. i	1. F	26. b
2. h	2. F	27. c
3. j	3. F	28. d
4. b	4. T	29. c
5. d	5. F	30. d
6. k	6. F	31. c
7. f	7. F	32. d
8. l	8. F	33. b
9. g	9. T	34. e
10. e	10. F	35. c
11. a	11. T	36. a
12. n	12. F	37. e
13. c	13. F	38. e
14. m	14. T	39. c
	15. F	40. b
	16. T	41. c
	17. F	42. b
	18. T	43. b
	19. F	44. b
	20. F	45. d
	21. F	46. a
	22. T	47. d
	23. T	48. d
	24. T	49. d
	25. F	50. b

EXERCISE 2.1: THE COMPETITION ACT

The June 1989 Consumer and Corporate Affairs information bulletin states that the purpose of the Competition Act is

> to maintain and encourage competition in Canada in order to promote the efficiency and adaptability of the Canadian economy, in order to expand opportunities for Canadian participation in world markets while at the same time recognizing the role of foreign competition in Canada, in order to ensure that small and medium-sized enterprises have an equitable opportunity to participate in the Canadian economy and in order to provide consumers with competitive prices and product choices. (p.1)

In the 70-year history of the earlier Combines Investigation Act there were few, if any, convictions for unfair business practices. Under the new Competition Act, which came into effect in June 1986, the Competition Tribunal has the power to stop mergers that substantially lessen competition and/or are not in the public interest. The Director of Competition Policy will try to resolve a case of unfair competition by convincing all parties to the agreement to change the terms of the agreement. If a reasonable solution cannot be found, the Director will likely send the case to the Competition Tribunal for final and binding ruling.

A number of mergers took effect in 1989 that made the job of the Director more challenging. The first of these was the merger of two Canadian breweries, Molson and Carling O'Keefe. This merger in effect left two giants in the Canadian brewery industry, Molson and Labatt. Did this merger lessen competition to the detriment of the consumer or were gains in efficiency a sound justification for the joining together of these two breweries?

This merger was followed by the sale of Wardair to PWA Corp., the owner of Canadian Airlines International (the latter having been absorbed by PWA Corp. from Canadian Pacific only a few years prior to this more recent acquisition). This left only two large airlines in Canada, the PWA group and Air Canada. Factors such as deregulation of the airlines, stiff competition, and the increasing costs of operation all led to the current situation. Is the consumer better served with only two strong airlines? With the free-trade deal now in effect, international airlines such as American are now considering entering the Canadian market.

In 1989, Exxon, the world's largest oil company, acquired Texaco Canada for approximately $5 billion. The oil industry is still fairly diversified in Canada and this merger is unlikely to affect the balance of power or the competitive environment; nevertheless, any future mergers will likely be carefully scrutinized by the Competition Tribunal's Director as they may change the balance of power. (One probable future change in the industry will be the privatization of Petro-Canada.)

The aforementioned takeovers, as well as many others, occurred soon after the ratification of the Canada–U.S. Free Trade Agreement, which led some observers to speculate that the companies involved in these mergers might not be acting in the public interest. Others claimed that these mergers were necessary in order for these companies to compete internationally, which led to further speculation that the larger the company, the greater the chances that it would survive in the global marketplace. And if this were true, are small and medium-sized companies adequately protected under the Competition Act?

Questions

1. Identify the essential features of the Competition Act. Do you feel that the act serves the public interest? Defend your point of view.
2. Are all mergers contrary to the public interest? From a marketing viewpoint, under what circumstances would mergers be beneficial to society?
3. The text discusses other sections of the act besides the Merger section. Identify these sections and briefly discuss them.
4. Respond to the following hypothetical situation: The policy of Harlequin, a maker of high-priced, quality cameras, is that all resellers must sell its cameras at suggested retail prices. Any franchise that sells the cameras for less will be discontinued. Is this manufacturer's pricing policy in violation of the Competition Act? Explain.
5. "The Competition Act does not have any teeth. Fines are so small that corporations do not take very seriously the legislation contained within the act." Do you agree with this statement? Why or why not?

Source: *Information Bulletin* no. 3 (June 1989), Program of Compliance, Consumer and Corporate Affairs, p.1.

EXERCISE 2.2: THE IMPORTANCE OF THE ECONOMY TO THE MARKETER

Economic conditions present both problems and opportunities to the marketer. A prosperous economy makes it possible for manufacturers to increase their investment in capital equipment to produce goods to meet the increased demand from consumers. This demand is at first for necessities such as food, clothing, and shelter, and later expands to consumer durables, such as appliances, automobiles, and equipment. Increased spending on recreation is another feature of a growth economy. In contrast, a major slowdown or recession puts the market in reverse: consumers spend fewer dollars on goods and services. Generally the durable goods and housing industries are the hardest hit initially; these companies then cut back on capital investment. Unemployment in industry becomes commonplace, and bankruptcies increase as the economy tries to avoid a tailspin into a depression that represents an acceleration of the negative effects that have taken place during the recession.

Marketers look to the 1990s with both excitement and trepidation. In 1990 the economy was in recession; and the Canadian government's Goods and Services Tax (GST) added points to the inflation rate, even though the tax was imposed in order to eliminate the manufacturer's tax and help reduce the deficit.

Inflation significantly diminishes the purchasing power of a dollar over time; for example, with 5-percent annual inflation, a product selling for $1.00 in 1990 would be priced at $1.63 in the year 2000 and $2.65 in 2010. To keep pace with this rate of inflation, a salary of $30 000 in 1990 would have to increase to $48 900 by the year 2000 and to $79 500 by the year 2010.

In the 1960s and 1970s inflation increased at its fastest rate in many years as Canadians suffered from double-digit inflation. Inflation slowed during the second half of the 1980s and into the 1990s, then moved from 5 percent to 7 percent in the early months of 1990, mainly because of the GST.

Inflation can also decrease productivity, or output per labour hour worked. Inflation generally stimulates wage demands from both trade unions and nonunionized workers. If wages move up and businesses do not experience increased productivity from their workers, the price of goods and services will rise in the marketplace. This may become a spiralling action of wage and price increases that moves the country into a recession.

For years, productivity in Canada increased at an annual rate ranging from 2 to 3 percent. During the 1980s, productivity sometimes slipped below 2 percent and on occasion has been virtually flat. With increasing bankruptcies as well as companies closing shop and moving their operations to the United States, there is a danger that negative productivity will be experienced. With workers producing less, total output declines, and employers can increase wages only by raising prices. The net effect is that the worker does not gain and demand for goods and services drops off as consumers try to stretch their dollars to pay for goods that cost more. In the long run the economy can prosper only with productivity growth.

The business cycle is one of recession, depression, recovery, and prosperity. During prosperous times consumers have excess dollars to spend on goods and services. When demand is high, all the factors of a competitive economy come into play, and those marketers prosper who do the best job of meeting consumer wants and needs. In a recession economy the job of marketing is more difficult; as there is lessened demand, more imaginative marketing schemes may be necessary. (For example, the reduction in automobile sales in a recession economy stimulates the introduction of manufacturer rebates and financing schemes.)

Inflation may occur during any of the stages of the business cycle. The central bank will usually raise the prime rate or take money out of circulation to counter inflation. Nevertheless, inflation continues to be a problem; during the recession of 1989–90, businesses failed, productivity dropped off, many factories closed, and workers found themselves out of jobs.

Questions

1. Define inflation. What are the harmful effects of inflation?
2. Define productivity. How does productivity affect the economy?
3. What are the various stages of the business cycle? Describe how the economy is affected by each stage of the business cycle.
4. The text talks about stagflation. How does inflation differ from stagflation?
5. Can you tell, from reading newspapers and magazines and watching television news programs, what stage in the business cycle we are at right now? What are the characteristics of this stage of the business cycle? Is inflation a problem during this stage of the business cycle? If inflation is a current problem, what monetary or fiscal policies are being employed to counter inflation?

Case 1

THE JACUZZI BROTHERS: AN AMERICAN BUSINESS ODYSSEY

Background, Product, and Company

The Jacuzzis had a reputation for industriousness. Giovanni and Teresa were both born in the picturesque town of Casarsa della Delizia, Italy. They had thirteen children, seven boys and six girls. Giovanni was a farmer, but wanted something different for his children. Their eldest son, Rachel, studied engineering in Germany and then had an opportunity to move to America. He sent for his younger brothers, one at a time. Eventually all of the family, including Giovanni and Teresa, moved to the United States.

Settling in Oakland, California, the brothers first manufactured airplane propellers for the then fledgling U.S. Army Air Force. In 1917 the brothers enlarged their operation and moved to Berkeley. Rachel, being the oldest brother, and the one with the most formal training, was president of the original corporation, and supervised all major business functions. Candido and Giocondo were in charge of marketing and sales activities. Francesco was in charge of the machine shop and Giuseppe handled assembly. Valleriano and Gelindo assisted where they were needed.

By 1920 the firm incorporated and diversified into airplane repairing and remodelling. Environmental factors entered the picture in 1920. World War I finally drew to a close, ending most of the demand for their product. The brothers decided to enter private airplane manufacturing, first with a small, single-seater. They then designed and built the first multi-passenger, enclosed cabin, high-wing monoplane in the United States. One of the brothers, Giocondo, was killed testing the plane and the surviving brothers decided against further production.

As agriculture was, and is, a major industry in California, the brothers decided to combine their knowledge of propellers and wind currents with agricultural needs. Frost was killing many of the new plantings and damaging the fruit at times, so the brothers developed a "frost machine" to blow over the plants and trees, keeping the frost from forming. An oil-burning furnace was also developed at this time, and research was begun on steam and water injectors, or jets, as they would later become known.

Times were hard for the brothers during the middle 1920s. Only Rachel and Giuseppe were actively employed by the business, the other four brothers finding work where they could. Between odd jobs on repairing trucks and propellers, and occasional manufacturing of oil burners, radiator fans, and grape crushers, the brothers continued their experimentation, research, and product development.

By 1926 they were ready to test their water jet idea in connection with a one-horse-power, centrifugal pump, but could not find a pump meeting their specifications. They manufactured their own.

The purpose of the system was to pump water (or other liquids) from twenty to thirty feet below the level in which the pump and water jet were installed, something that had not been accomplished up to this time. The pumps would prove especially efficient in agricultural water wells, as they required no moving parts in the well itself.

Candido took off his "production hat," replacing it with his "marketing" one and hit the road, pushing the newly developed liquid-jet injector pumps. Forty units were sold and installed in a fairly short period of time. Requests began to come in for larger-capacity units. Three and five horse-power models were thus developed. Not able to keep up with demand themselves, the brothers began selecting dealers in large western cities to handle sales. Business was humming. Not ones to rest on their laurels, the brothers proceeded to test and develop other types of pumps, including those operated by turbines.

The company began printing price lists and specification sheets, along with one-year guarantee policies after their dealers began requesting them. At this time, due to unfavourable and untrue publicity generated by other pump companies on the "unproved" scientific principle on which Jacuzzi pumps were based, the sales force met strong opposition in some geographic locales. Lengthening the guarantee to four years following installation helped overcome much resistance.

Having survived their growing pains, the depression hit. Pump sales dropped drastically, and the propeller business was now almost nonexistent. The company managed to survive by trimming expenses and personnel wherever possible, continuing to research new product ideas. A sampling of these ideas included pumps for the then-developing "car wash" industry, filters for area wineries, propeller turbine pumps, solar-powered appliances, high-pressure pumps, and multi-stage horizontal pumps.

Pulling out of the depression with new lines of single and multi-stage pumps, in both vertical and horizontal models, the company was poised for major growth. Their expanded facilities included a large new plant in Richmond, California. The war effort for World War II found Jacuzzi manufacturing valves for submarines, as well as continuing with their main pump lines.

The booming economy in Southern California following World War II, coupled with the swimming pool craze, was another growth opportunity for Jacuzzi — being in the right place at the right time with the right product at the right price. Their pumps and filters were ideal for swimming pools. The marketer's delight!

While working on the swimming pool equipment line, Candido's youngest son, Kenneth, was stricken with rheumatoid arthritis. Again the Jacuzzis' inventive minds turned to the drawing boards, this time developing, originally for Kenny, what has become the world-famous Jacuzzi Whirlpool Bath.

The 60s found the company developing another product from their research with water jets: the Marine Jet Drive for power boats, omitting the need for a propeller, and giving a smoother ride. These propulsion units were installed on both commercial and private craft. Additional product introductions around this time included gas cooking grills for the residential market as well as several sizes of air compressors, primarily targeted to the small manufacturing and service markets.

After several years of profitable operation, the air-compressors and jet-propulsion units began to lose volume and the company discontinued these two lines.

Prosperity continued during the 1970s as the company expanded into all areas of the United States and into many international markets as well. By the middle 70s plants were located in Arkansas and California in the United States and in Canada, Brazil, Italy, and Chile. Currently, manufacturing locations include Little Rock (International Headquarters) and Lonoke, Arkansas; Walnut Creek, San Leandro, Anaheim, Santa Ana, Costa Mesa, and Benecia, California; Monterey, Mexico; Toronto, Canada; São Paulo, Brazil; Valvasone, Italy; and Santiago, Chile.

The Whirlpool line continues to be the company's most recognized product by the end-consumer, but the pumps and accessories, swimming pool equipment and gas grills also continue to increase in volume, with profitability remaining encouraging. The pumps and accessories are marketed to end-consumer, industrial and agricultural customers, with the bulk of the sales in end-consumer products. Many sales are directly related to new-housing starts.

Pumps for homes, industrial use, farms, and irrigation purposes represent about 40% of the company's volume. The whirlpool spas would account for another 40%, with swimming pool equipment and accessories and gas grills contributing the remaining 20%.

Financial

In 1978 the firm began exploring the possibility of selling out. A deal was initially struck with Textron, Inc., in 1979 but it fell through. Later that same year Walter Kidde and Company offered about $70 million on the condition that at least 60% of Jacuzzi's approximately 4.6 million shares be tendered. Kidde offered $15.35 per share. This time the deal was completed, with 100% of the shares being tendered.

Major changes took place after the purchase. The company moved from a family-owned business to an operating subsidiary of a large conglomerate. Theoretically there should have been little difference in the day-to-day operation of the plant and the actions of most of management. The shareholder relationship, however, became very different. Whereas the operation previously answered to the Jacuzzis, now it had to answer to thousands of Kidde stockholders.

Another major change was financial. Previously, outside financing was a major concern; now it was not. Demonstration of earnings and accelerated growth were of concern in the past, but they did not have the emphasis that were now placed on them by the new ownership.

Sales volume for Jacuzzi when the deal was consumated was about $89 million, with earnings not being disclosed. Sales for Kidde were $1.9 billion with earnings of $68.7 million.

By the early 1980s, Jacuzzi, Inc. (previously Jacuzzi Brothers, Inc.), was smoothly operating as a wholly owned subsidiary of Kidde, Inc. (previously

Walter Kidde & Company). Ray Horan, President of Jacuzzi, Inc., in the 80s reported that the company "has shown growth every year since its establishment in 1920. In the last 10 years the company's sales have grown by an average of 15% compounded annually with net after-tax profits in the 5–10% range." Volume in the 1980s is not projected to be as rapid as the growth of the 60s and 70s. Sales in the $100 million–$150 million range are expected. The decade of the 1990s is expected to bring the company sales into the $175 million–$200 million+ range. Net after-tax profits are projected to continue in the 5–10% range.

Percentage of company sales volume, divided by country, would be approximately as follows:

	%	
Brazil	2	
Canada	25	
Chile	2	
Italy	3	
Mexico	3	
United States	65	(about 40% from the California operations and 25% from Arkansas)

Pricing

As previously mentioned, the pump lines are divided between end-consumer, or residential usage, industrial, and agricultural applications. For pricing purposes the company divides the pumps between residential and all other applications. $150 to $180 would be the range for the residential units, with $1000 to $5000 being the range for the industrial, commercial, and agricultural markets. Prices can reach above the high end of these ranges for special orders.

The swimming pool equipment and accessories, including filters, cover a wide price spectrum. Prices can be as low as $5 or $10 for a brass fitting to near $1000 for a Filter Pac.

The whirlpools, or whirlpool spas, sell for between $2000 and $4000 plus installation. The Jacuzzi units can be ordered in a moulded fiberglass form for indoor or outdoor installation, or in a wooden format, popularly known as a hot tub.

$150 to $450 would be the approximate price ranges for the backyard gas grills.

Distribution and Market Share

Pumps for residential use are channelled from Jacuzzi to wholesale plumbing and wholesale hardware outlets. The pumps then continue down the traditional channel to various retailers. Jacuzzi maintains from 10% to 12% of the U.S. market in this product line.

Pumps for commercial, industrial, and agricultural uses are sold direct to builder's supply houses and plumbing supply houses, primarily in the well-drilling and specialty pump lines. Jacuzzi maintains from 10% to 12% of the U.S. market in this product line.

Swimming pool equipment and accessories are channelled to the same or similar outlets that sell the residential pumps, i.e., wholesale plumbing and wholesale hardware outlets. Jacuzzi maintains about 8% of the U.S. market in this product line.

Whirlpool Spas are a real growth area for this firm. They continue to increase in annual sales as well as market share. The old adage "the firstest in the market gets the mostest" is truly exemplified in this example. In addition to wholesale plumbing outlets, Jacuzzi also markets the spas through "hot water specialty" retail outlet channels; retailers specializing in hot tubs and similar items. Jacuzzi maintains about 35% of the U.S. market in this product line.

Backyard Gas Grills are profitable for the company even though they do not maintain as large a market share for this line as they do for their other products. A primary reason for this is due to the larger industry volume of sales in this area and a larger number of competitors. The grills are marketed through mass merchandiser/discounters such as Kmart, as well as through independent natural gas companies. Jacuzzi maintains about 2% of the U.S. market in this product line.

Even though this case concentrates on the U.S. market, it should be mentioned that the firm's international operations are also growing and profitable, with Canada and Chile being the fastest growing of the international operations.

Promotion

The majority of Jacuzzi's promotional dollars are spent on the personal selling effort. Jacuzzi employs several hundred salesreps worldwide, with almost 90% of their promotional dollars going for sales salaries, commissions, and expenses. The remaining dollars are primarily spent in trade journals which consist of the following: *Hardware Age,*

Wholesale Plumbing Monthly, Groundwater Age, The Wholesaler Magazine, Swimming Pool Age, and *Swimming Pool Weekly.* Other magazines include *Architectural Digest, Better Homes and Gardens, Southern Living, The Merchandise Magazine, SPA and Sauna,* and the *American Gas Association Journal.* Much of the retail advertising is co-oped with Jacuzzi dealers on an even 50–50 split.

Questions

1. Outline Jacuzzi's marketing program. Analyze the firm's marketing strengths and weaknesses.
2. Discuss Jacuzzi's competitive environment.
3. Would you have sold the firm? Why, or why not?

Source: This case was prepared by Scott Markham of the University of Central Arkansas as a basis for class discussion. Reprinted by permission.

PRODUCT-ANALYSIS REPORT

This project is based on the new-product development process discussed in the product chapters of the text. The first three stages in this process (i.e., the idea, the screening, and the business analysis stage) form the basis for this product-analysis project. Also, this project involves developing a marketing plan for a new product; hence, Chapter 6 (Marketing Strategy and the Marketing Plan) will be a useful reference.

This project could be an individual or team course assignment. (The depth of analysis involved will depend on the objectives of your instructor.) It is also a progressive assignment, beginning with the conception of the product idea in the product chapters, developing through the coverage of the other elements of the marketing program, and culminating in a class presentation of the completed project (perhaps during the final week of the course).

The best time to start this project is after you have completed parts One and Two of the text. Either working on your own or as a member of a team, you will decide on the product that will form the focus of this project. To do this, you will need to complete the first two stages of the product development process, that is, generate ideas on new products and discard those product ideas that do not meet your company's objectives (screening). Your product may be completely new or it may be simply a more effective or innovative version of one that is currently on the market.

Product Analysis — Development of New Products

As discussed in Chapter 10 of the text, new product development in a company is a five-step process; however, as the product analysis will be conducted within the confines of the classroom, the first three stages should be emphasized. You will engage in a product-analysis project that requires you to come up with ideas for a new product (Stage I, new product development process) and to screen those ideas (Stage II) down to the one product or service on which you wish to concentrate. In Stage III (business analysis) you will examine the market for your proposed product in order to determine its feasibility and desirability. If your research (generally very limited in a student project) is positive and you decide to market the product of choice, you will then conduct a detailed analysis, synthesis, and evaluation of the marketing mix (the proper blending of product, price, promotion, and place). Marketing mix programs must take into account the wants and needs of the consumer, the characteristics of the market, and so on.

As Figure 1 shows, the product-analysis project deals with the first three stages of the product development process. In Stage III (business analysis) you will define the market target for your product of choice and determine your market objectives and strategies. At this point a number of inputs will enter the transformation process. The demographic, socio-cultural, and economic characteristics of the consumers that represent the market target will be analyzed. The final outputs from market research you conduct will provide a useful description of the market target for your next product.

From Figure 1 it will be noted that the next step in Stage III is to analyze the marketing mix for the product of choice. You will need to make a final decision on your product of choice to be

FIGURE 1 PRODUCT ANALYSIS

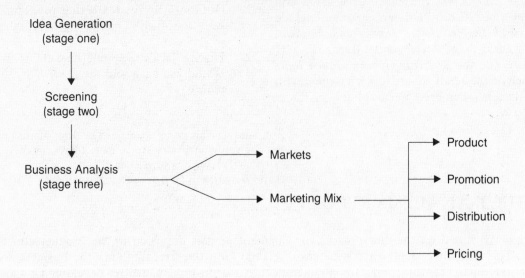

developed in the product analysis. This choice was made possible from the analysis that was conducted during the idea-generation and screening stage. Once this decision is made, product objectives and strategies can be planned. Determine the product's physical configuration, and either sketch the product or produce a mock model of it. Decisions can then be made regarding brand name, symbols, logos, packaging, and labelling. The design and the descriptive aspects of the product can be compared with the benefits that this product is expected to offer to the consumer. The product program will need to be synthesized with the market program to determine if there is in fact sufficient demand for this product. Also, the product program will need to be blended with the other marketing mix programs to develop the most efficient and effective marketing plan for the product.

The next step is to develop promotional plans for the product. You must have objectives and strategies for advertising, personal sales, publicity, and public relations. Also, you must determine how much of the promotional budget to allocate to each of these elements of promotion. The promotion campaign must be co-ordinated not only within promotion but with the other parts of the marketing mix (distribution and pricing) and with nonmarketing areas (e.g., production). Then within each element policy decisions must be made; for example, in examining advertising you must decide on what media to use, schedule media placement, and create advertisements. The idea is to constantly monitor and co-ordinate policy decisions with those related to product-market and other decisions within the marketing mix.

Determine which distribution channels are most appropriate for the product, then analyze and evaluate the various levels of distribution intensity and the structure of the distribution network. Decisions will have to be made as to what retailers, wholesalers, and agent intermediaries will be most appropriate for the product, and as to which territories will be the easiest to access. If trade discounts are offered to intermediaries, the pricing area of the mix will be affected.

The pricing objectives and strategies must be properly co-ordinated with the other areas of the marketing mix. Through market research, estimated demand for the product in the marketplace can be determined. Then a profitability and break-even analysis can be performed to determine if it is worth the time, effort, and money to market the product. If the results are positive, a specific factory price will be determined for the product, and trade discounts as determined through the distribution system will be applied to give a retail selling price for the product.

As an aid to preparing this product-analysis report, the following outline has been provided. Keep in mind that there may be topics that you or your instructor will want to cover that are not included in the outline.

Outline for a Product-Analysis Report

Title Page
Letter of Transmittal
Table of Contents

I. Introduction
   A. Purpose of report
   B. Product ideas and screening process
   C. Decision on product

II. Product (chapters 9 and 10)
   A. Description of product (design, features, and benefits to be derived by consumer)
   B. Sketch of product (or mock model)
   C. Brand name, symbols, and distinctive packaging
   D. Product strategies to be employed
   (Note: If the student so desires, this project can be based on a service instead of on a product.)

III. The Market (chapters 3 and 4)
   A. Market targets for the product
   B. Market segmentation strategies and other product market strategies to be employed
   C. Location of potential customers

IV. Distribution Strategy (chapters 14, 15, and 16)
   A. Distribution objectives
   B. Channel(s) of distribution for the product
   C. Intensity of the distribution
   D. Functions to be performed by intermediaries
   E. Types of wholesaling and retailing intermediaries to be used
   F. Trade discounts to be offered to intermediaries
   G. Mode of physical distribution
   H. Territory to be covered

V. Promotional Strategy (chapters 17 and 18)
   A. General promotional objectives
   B. Amount of funds to be allocated to advertising, personal selling, and sales promotion
   C. Advertising, personal selling, and sales promotion objectives
   D. Details of promotional campaign (including creation of advertisements, sales promotional plans, and personal selling activities)
   E. Territory to be covered by promotional campaign
   F. Distribution tie-ins with promotional activities
   G. Number of sales personnel to be employed to effectively sell the product, and the relevant costs
   H. Summary of marketing mix elements and their relationship to the target market

VI. Pricing Strategy (chapters 12 and 13)
   A. Summary of pricing objectives
   B. Specific price of product (calculated by means of a detailed break-even and profitability analysis)
      1. Total fixed cost per annum
      2. Variable cost per unit
      3. Various factory selling prices for the product
      4. Break-even points at various factory selling prices

5. Estimated demand for the product at various price levels calculated through hypothetically determined research
6. Profitability analysis at various factory selling prices (total revenue, minus fixed and variable costs, at each price level)
7. Specific factory price of the product (based on the break-even and profitability analysis)
8. Markup to be offered to intermediaries and suggested retail price of the product

C. Pricing policies for the product (e.g., discounts and allowances, geographical considerations, new product pricing, etc.)

VII. Conclusion

CHECKLIST FOR THE PRODUCT-ANALYSIS REPORT

This checklist makes it possible for you to keep track of your progress as you proceed through the product analysis. When this report is completed at the end of the course, you will have covered the topics listed below. The specific date for completion of your report should be set, and if you or your group are to make an oral presentation of your report, definite time schedules, preferably during the final week or two of the course, should be arranged.

The Report. The minimum length of your report will be established by the person in charge of this course. Also, a formal or informal report form should be specified. The normal length of a report is from twenty-five to thirty typed pages.

The Presentation. An oral presentation, if required, will be allotted a minimum and/or maximum time frame. Those oral presentations that include the use of transparencies, mock models of products, and other visual aids are usually the most effective.

What has to be completed? Check the items from the checklist provided below when they are completed. This checklist is not intended to be inclusive. It is provided strictly as a guide to mark your progress.

		Completed	Not Completed
	Title Page		
	Letter of Transmittal		
	Table of Contents		
I	*Introduction*		
II	*Product*		
	Description of Product		
	Sketch of Product		
	Brand Name, Symbols, and Packaging		
	Product Strategies		
III	*The Market*		
	Market Targets		
	Market Strategies		
IV	*Distribution Strategy (points A to H)*		
V	*Promotional Strategy (points A to H)*		
VI	*Pricing Strategy*		
	Pricing Objectives		
	Specific Price of the Product (points 1 to 8)		
	Pricing Policy		
VII	*Conclusion*		

PART TWO

Foundations of the Marketing Plan

- CHAPTER 3 — MARKET SEGMENTATION: FINDING A BASE TO START
- CHAPTER 4 — THE MARKET SEGMENTATION PROCESS
- CHAPTER 5 — OBTAINING DATA FOR MARKETING DECISIONS
- CHAPTER 6 — MARKETING STRATEGY AND THE MARKETING PLAN

Case 2 — Rowen Plastics and Manufacturing Company
Case 3 — Nova Scotia
Case 4 — Mountain Gallery of Art

CHAPTER 3

Market Segmentation: Finding a Base to Start

CHAPTER OBJECTIVES

1. Define, explain, or describe the key terms listed under "Vocabulary and Key Terms."
2. Explain the concept of market planning.
3. Describe a "market" and the characteristics of markets.
4. Explain the concept of market segmentation.
5. Identify and describe the following bases for market segmentation: demographic, geographic, psychographic, benefit. Apply this principle to the consumer and industrial markets.
6. Identify the major recent population shifts and the age groups that will grow faster during the 1990s.
7. Explain the use of the family life cycle as a means of analyzing markets.
8. Discuss the importance of considering income and expenditure patterns when analyzing markets.
9. Apply your knowledge of Chapter 3 to the activities provided in this chapter of the study guide.

VOCABULARY AND KEY TERMS

From the lettered terms listed below, select the one that best matches the meaning of each of the numbered statements that follows. Write the letter of that choice in the space provided.

a) market
b) consumer goods
c) industrial goods
d) market segmentation
e) family life cycle
f) Engel's Laws
g) SSWD
h) lifestyle
i) psychographics
j) AIO statements

1. _____ The process of taking the total market and dividing it into several homogeneous groups
2. _____ The way that one decides to live one's life
3. _____ The single-person household
4. _____ Psychological profiles of different consumers developed from quantitative research
5. _____ Those products purchased to be used, either directly or indirectly, in the production of other goods for resale

6. _____ Activity, interest, and opinion statements that help to create a psychological profile of consumers
7. _____ Those products and services purchased by an ultimate consumer for personal use
8. _____ A process that allows a marketing planner to combine the family characteristics of age, marital status, presence or absence of children, and ages of children in developing a marketing strategy
9. _____ Results of a study prepared more than 100 years ago to determine how expenditure patterns vary with increased income
10. _____ People with a willingness to buy, purchasing power, and the authority to buy

PRACTICE TEST

True-False: In the space to the right of each statement, check the appropriate line to indicate whether the statement is true or false.

	True	False
1. Some products, such as cleaning items, may be classified as consumer and industrial goods.	_____	_____
2. Market research is required in the planning process.	_____	_____
3. Picking a target market is the most critical decision made by the marketer in the planning process.	_____	_____
4. The first task of the marketer is to develop and implement a marketing program designed to satisfy a target market.	_____	_____
5. Consumer goods are products purchased to be used directly or indirectly in the production of other goods or for resale.	_____	_____
6. Products such as toothpaste, bread, and milk can be marketed to the general market, as there is no need for segmentation.	_____	_____
7. The women's market is general and not diverse.	_____	_____
8. The term "demographic" relates to the population characteristics of the market.	_____	_____
9. Determining the benefits to be derived from a product's use is an example of demographic segmentation.	_____	_____
10. Psychographic segmentation utilizes behavioural profiles in identifying market segments.	_____	_____
11. The western provinces contain the greatest percentage of foreign-born Canadians who are "old timers" (i.e., who immigrated to Canada prior to 1946).	_____	_____
12. The third-largest province based on territorial population is Alberta, with 9 percent of the Canadian population.	_____	_____
13. The number of emigrants from Canada has decreased in recent years.	_____	_____
14. Toronto has a population of in excess of 5 million people.	_____	_____
15. Climate can be considered a part of geographic segmentation.	_____	_____
16. One of the major problems with demographic segmentation is the difficulty of identifying and measuring markets.	_____	_____

17. Age, households, family life cycle, and income and expenditure patterns are important means for measuring markets on the basis of demographics.

18. Fifty-five percent of disposable income is in the hands of Canadians 50 years of age and over.

19. It is more effective to segment markets by age group than by family life cycle.

20. The buying patterns of a 25-year-old bachelor are similar to those of a father of the same age.

21. According to Engel's Laws, the percentage spent on clothing will increase as family income increases.

22. Psychographics make use of AIO statements to develop consumer profiles that can be used in segmentation.

23. Marketers now consider benefit segmentation to be one of the most useful methods for segmenting markets.

24. Because markets are diverse and customers are located in many geographic locations across the country, geographic segmentation is useful in segmenting industrial markets.

25. Product segmentation is not a basis for segmenting markets in the industrial market.

Multiple Choice: Choose the expression that best answers the question or best completes the sentence.

26. Canada's three largest metropolitan areas in 1990 were Toronto, Montreal, and
   a. Ottawa-Hull
   b. Vancouver
   c. Edmonton
   d. Calgary
   e. Hamilton

27. Which stage of the family life cycle is likely to be influenced by the need to purchase new, more tasteful furniture but is hard to influence with advertising?
   a. young married with children
   b. older married
   c. middle-aged married with children
   d. middle-aged married without children at home

28. Kmart, a discount house, is planning on locating one of its stores in a new suburban shopping centre in a low-income area of Calgary. The mall manager will not only attempt to find tenants that will blend in with Kmart, but will also evaluate
   a. the income and expenditure patterns of the primary trade area to the centre
   b. the demographics of the market in the primary trade area of the centre
   c. the potential sales that can be generated by Kmart and the other new tenants
   d. all of the above

29. Psychographic segmentation consists of
   a. lifestyle analysis
   b. age groupings
   c. income segments
   d. a and b
   e. none of the above

30. Which of the following statements about Canada's population is not true?
a. Emigration continues to decline.
b. Its mobility is one of the highest in the world.
c. It is still mostly rural and agricultural.
d. Its rural population is younger than its urban population.

31. Michel and Marie Langlois have just bought a new playpen and stroller for their second grandchild and are shopping for a set of dinnerware for their youngest daughter, who has recently moved into her first apartment. To marketers using family life-cycle analysis, the Langloises would be classified as
a. retired persons
b. middle-aged married without children at home
c. motivated buyers
d. middle-aged married with children

32. Which of the following would not be considered a part of situation analysis in the marketing planning process?
a. historical background
b. consumer analysis
c. product strategies
d. competitive analysis

33. A market may be defined as
a. people
b. people with the willingness to buy
c. people with the authority to buy
d. people with purchasing power
e. all of the above

34. Products purchased by ultimate consumers for their own personal use or consumption are called
a. industrial goods
b. convenience goods
c. impulse goods
d. consumer goods
e. shopping goods

35. A typewriter purchased by Sears for use by its secretaries may be classified as
a. a consumer good
b. an office good
c. an industrial good
d. component parts
e. installations

36. Marketers segment markets
a. because segmentation simplifies decision making
b. because they need some means of simplifying the task of finding buyers for their products
c. because the world is too large and filled with too many diverse people and firms for any one marketing program to satisfy everyone
d. so that when production lines go into operation, they will be able to manufacture the millions of items necessary to secure economies of scale
e. so that the competition will find it difficult to predict what is going to happen next

37. The following are all demographic bases for segmenting markets, except
a. sex
b. age

c. family life cycle
d. lifestyles

38. Under which of the following conditions would it be unwise to consider a market segmentation strategy?
a. The market's purchasing power and size can both be measured.
b. It appears feasible to promote to the market segment.
c. The various segments of the market seem to be large enough to be adequately profitable.
d. There are no apparent problems in providing the segments of the market with adequate service.
e. The number of segments in the market is greater than the capacity of the firm to serve them.

39. The bulk of the country's sales potential is in two provinces, Ontario and Quebec. It is estimated that these two provinces contain
a. 50 percent of the population
b. 25 percent of the population
c. 62 percent of the population
d. 76 percent of the population
e. none of the above

40. According to marketing experts, it is difficult to sell to older Canadians because they
a. perceive themselves as being younger
b. are very stubborn
c. already have everything
d. feel their life is almost over
e. have needs, wants, and desires that are difficult to satisfy

41. The family life cycle
a. is not useful for segmentation purposes
b. does not accurately reflect the SSWD market
c. refers to the formation, development, and dissolution of the family
d. is another name for age segmentation
e. is a reliable index for marketers who also do psychographic segmentation

42. Five years ago, Tobias spent 30 percent of his $20 000 yearly income on his bachelor apartment. Today Tobias is earning $35 000 annually. According to Engel's Laws, the percentage of money he will spend on an apartment will be
a. $6000 per year
b. much less than the original 30 percent
c. about 30 percent of his current income
d. about 52.5 percent (Because he had a 75 percent increase in pay, his household expense will also increase 75 percent, from 30 percent to 52.5 percent.)
e. much greater because he can afford to spend more

43. There are several reasons for the trend toward smaller households. Which of the following is not one of those reasons?
a. the ease and frequency of divorce
b. the tendency of young people to postpone marriage
c. higher fertility rates
d. the desire for more independence
e. the increasing number of older people in the population

44. Which of the following is a good example of benefit segmentation?
a. Coca-Cola's "Can't Beat the Feeling!" theme
b. Macleans selling their toothpaste with a brightness-of-teeth theme

c. McDonald's selling Big Macs by saying "We do it all for you at McDonalds."

d. CCM selling Tack skates with the theme, "No other skate can turn on the power like these."

45. The Timex Company became one of the largest watch companies in the world by focusing its market strategy on
a. demographic segmentation
b. benefit segmentation
c. geographic segmentation
d. psychographic segmentation
e. end-use segmentation

46. The market researcher using psychographic segmentation will make use of AIO statements to develop psychological profiles. AIO stands for:
a. aims, interest, and objectives
b. articles, inserts, and organizers
c. activities, interests, and opinions
d. attributes, interest, and options

47. According to Engel's Laws, as family income increases
a. a smaller percentage of expenditures goes for food, with the percentage spent on housing and household operations and clothing increasing
b. a larger percentage of expenditures goes for food, with the percentage spent on housing and household operations and clothing decreasing
c. the percentage of expenditures for food remains constant, with the percentage spent on housing and household operations and clothing increasing
d. a smaller percentage of expenditure goes for food, with the percentage spent on housing and household operations and clothing remaining constant
e. the percentage of expenditures for food remains constant, with the percentage spent on housing and household operations and clothing decreasing

48. Household expenditures can be divided into which of the following categories?
a. basic purchases of essential household needs
b. other purchases that can be made at the discretion of the household member before the necessities have been purchased
c. other purchases that can be made at the discretion of the household member once the necessities have been purchased
d. a and c
e. all of the above

49. Which of the following statements is not true about geographic segments of the market?
a. Regional variations in taste often exist.
b. Geographic segmentation is often the only segmentation necessary for a marketer.
c. Climate is an important factor.
d. Residence location within a geographic area is an important geographic variable.
e. Geography was one of the earliest bases for segmentation.

50. Which of the following statements is not true of the senior adult market?
a. At present, one out of ten people is sixty-five or older.
b. It does not present the marketing manager with a potentially profitable market segment.
c. The average life expectancy of a sixty-five-year-old retiree is at least another eleven years.
d. The growth in this market segment means an increased demand for medical care, apartments, and retirement homes.

ANSWER KEY: CHAPTER THREE

Vocabulary and Key Terms	True-False	Multiple Choice
1. d	1. T	26. b
2. h	2. T	27. d
3. g	3. T	28. d
4. i	4. F	29. a
5. c	5. F	30. d
6. j	6. F	31. b
7. b	7. F	32. c
8. e	8. T	33. e
9. f	9. F	34. d
10. a	10. T	35. c
	11. T	36. c
	12. F	37. d
	13. T	38. e
	14. F	39. c
	15. T	40. a
	16. F	41. c
	17. T	42. c
	18. T	43. c
	19. F	44. b
	20. F	45. b
	21. F	46. c
	22. T	47. d
	23. T	48. d
	24. F	49. b
	25. F	50. b

EXERCISE 3.1: THE AGING BABY BOOMERS

To segment or not to segment markets: that is the question. It is commonly known that a small percentage of a product's users account for the bulk of its sales. In fact, according to the 80/20 principle, 20 percent of customers account for 80 percent of sales; therefore, whether or not a marketer should segment is almost academic. As discussed in Chapter 3, there are many possible ways to segment the market, such as by demographics, geographic factors, or psychographics. This exercise focuses on segmentation centred around baby boomers and the aged.

Baby boomers — the generation born between 1946 and 1964 — account for nearly half the adult population. While the number of births per household has been declining, the population has increased because there are so many baby boomers having children. By the year 1995, the number of Canadians between the ages of 35 and 55 will have risen in a decade by better than a third. The median age of the Canadian population is now 32 (up from 26 in 1961). This trend toward an older population will force marketers to make changes in their marketing mix to account for age.

The April 23, 1990, issue of *Newsweek* points out that "63 million Americans over 50 control half the nation's discretionary income and 77% of its financial assets." The baby boomers will begin to turn 50 in 1996. What effect will this have on advertisers? For one thing, an aging segment doesn't want to be reminded that it is getting any older. Advertising is going to have to change to show the 50-plus market in a more favourable light. According to *Newsweek*, one consumer study "indicates that one third of people over 55 have deliberately not bought products because they didn't like the way age was stereotyped in ads."

The *Newsweek* article lists eight points for selling to the over-50 market:

1. Don't Separate Them: H.J. Heinz bombed with baby-food-like purees called Senior Foods in the 1950s.
2. Show the Solution, not the Problem: An Efferdent ad also recently passed muster; it features a blueberry pie, not stained dentures in a glass.
3. Subtract 15 Years: Studies repeatedly show that older people think of themselves as 15 years younger than they are.
4. Don't Mention Age: Some products that appeal to the elderly can be marketed effectively with no age reference at all.
5. Span Generations: Thus the best ads show mature people looking independent, yet related to everyone else.
6. Watch the Punch Line: Don't make jokes at the expense of your audience.
7. Laugh with Them, Not at Them: Much the same as number six. Good ads with effective humour can be developed that don't offend anyone.
8. Don't Generalize: Advertisers should never forget that the over-50 population is extremely diverse.

Questions

1. How would the buying patterns of the 65-plus age group differ from those of the 50–65 age group? Can you relate these two age groups to family life cycle? Discuss.
2. If you were the advertiser for Geritol or Preparation H, what type of ad would you develop? Take into consideration the eight points listed in the *Newsweek* article.
3. What businesses will have the greatest success with an aging population?
4. What other changes should a marketer evaluate in a society with an aging population?
5. Why are baby boomers having fewer children than their parents or grandparents? What effect does that have on the marketer?
6. Two reports from Statistics Canada suggest that the government of Canada will have to prepare for a huge wave of retiring baby boomers in the twenty-first century. What effects will the increasing baby-boomer retirement market have on the government, and what can it do to prepare for these changes?

Source: Melinda Beck, "Going for the Gold," *Newsweek*, 23 April 1990.

EXERCISE 3.2: A SPECIALTY SHOPPING CENTRE

The Yellow Canary, a restaurant and fashion-oriented specialty shopping centre, is an imaginative and thriving centre. Located just off a heavily travelled arterial street in a rapidly growing, high-income suburb of a major city, the Yellow Canary is built around a central pool, waterfall, and floral gardens, providing a very pleasing atmosphere for shoppers. Included in the tenant mix are two high-quality men's and six exclusive women's clothing stores, top-brand shoe stores, several expensive boutiques, and one moderately expensive and two expensive restaurants. The centre is unique in that it does not contain the usual retail stores found in malls (e.g., food and drug stores). Prices for merchandise are high relative to the typical centre.

The population of the centre's primary trade area (approximately a three-kilometre radius) is 150 000 and is projected to increase to 200 000 in the next ten years. The area's population is relatively young and affluent; only 5 percent are over sixty-five, and average household income is 60 percent higher than the average for the city.

Questions

1. Of what significance might Engel's Laws and income and expenditure patterns have been in the initial research for the development of this shopping centre?

2. Based on the limited amount of information available in this case, was this specialty shopping centre's location a good one? Why or why not?
3. Would the market factors of age and family life cycle be important in determining the target market for this shopping centre?
4. What other market factors were likely included in the original feasibility study for this centre?

CHAPTER 4

The Market Segmentation Process

CHAPTER OBJECTIVES

1. Define, explain, or describe the key terms listed under "Vocabulary and Key Terms."
2. Identify and explain each of the alternative product-market matching strategies.
3. Explain how market target decision analysis can be used in market segmentation.
4. Explain and demonstrate how market target decision analysis can be used to assess a product mix.
5. Outline the steps in the market segmentation process.
6. Apply your knowledge of Chapter 4 to the various activities provided in this chapter of the study guide.

VOCABULARY AND KEY TERMS

From the lettered terms listed below, select the one that best matches the meaning of each of the numbered statements that follows. Write the letter of that choice in the space provided.
a) market segmentation
b) undifferentiated marketing
c) differentiated marketing
d) concentrated marketing
e) market target decision analysis
f) positioning

1. _____ Firms that produce only one product and market it to all customers with a single marketing mix
2. _____ The evaluation of potential market segments by dividing the overall market into homogeneous groupings
3. _____ The process of taking the total heterogeneous market and dividing it into several submarkets, each with similar characteristics
4. _____ An extreme form of differentiated marketing, where a firm selects one segment of the total market and devotes all of its marketing resources to satisfying this single segment
5. _____ Shaping the product and developing it in such a way that the product is perceived to be different from the competitor's product
6. _____ The practice of firms developing different marketing programs for each segment of the total market

PRACTICE TEST

True-False: In the space to the right of each statement, check the appropriate line to indicate whether the statement is true or false.

	True	False

1. Attempting to satisfy everyone will always doom a marketer to failure.

2. Residence location within a geographic area is irrelevant in market segmentation.

3. Undifferentiated marketing refers to firms that produce numerous products to satisfy smaller market segments.

4. Firms that produce only one product and market it to all segments with one mix are practising undifferentiated marketing.

5. Efficiency resulting from longer production runs is one benefit of concentrated marketing.

6. Undifferentiated marketing strategies tend to maximize inventory costs.

7. Henry Ford, when he agreed to paint the car any colour "as long as it's black," was using a concentrated marketing strategy.

8. The first stage in the market segmentation process is to select market segmentation bases.

9. The last stage in the market segmentation process is to forecast probable market shares.

10. The market target decision analysis was the brainchild of author J.D. Salinger.

11. The success of the MuchMusic and TSN television networks illustrates how market segmentation can be used to develop a successful enterprise.

12. Market segmentation may take several forms, ranging from treating the entire market as a single entity to subdividing it into several segments.

13. There is no single way to segment a market.

14. A multi-offer strategy is an attempt to satisfy a large or a small market with one product and a single marketing program.

15. A company offering one product and one marketing program is practising differentiated marketing.

16. The "Beetle" that was popular in the 1950s and 1960s was the only product offered by Volkswagen; this is an example of a concentrated market strategy.

17. In selling only the Model T, Henry Ford was also using a concentrated market strategy.

18. In the 1990s the Ford Motor Company's market-matching strategy is a single-offer strategy.

19. There are five stages in the market segmentation process. _____ _____

20. Demand forecasts and cost projections are generally developed during Stage V (selecting specific market segments). _____ _____

21. The cross-classification process shows that the matrix in target decision analysis can be further subdivided to gather more specific data. _____ _____

22. Product mix refers to the assortment of product lines and individual offerings available to a marketer. _____ _____

23. Product positioning and market segmentation are identical in meaning to the marketer. _____ _____

24. Avis's theme in its advertising, "We are only number two, so why go with us? Because we try harder," is an example of a positioning strategy. _____ _____

25. Positioning is related strictly to promotion of the product and is therefore a promotion strategy. _____ _____

Multiple Choice: Choose the expression that best answers the question or best completes the sentence.

26. Stage I of the market segmentation decision process consists of
   a. forecasting market potentials
   b. selecting market segmentation bases
   c. forecasting probable market share
   d. developing relevant profiles for each segment
   e. selecting the specific market segment

27. Stage III of the market segmentation decision process consists of
   a. forecasting market potentials
   b. selecting market segmentation bases
   c. forecasting probable market share
   d. developing relevant profiles for each segment
   e. selecting the specific market segment

28. Stage V of the market segmentation decision process consists of
   a. forecasting market potentials
   b. selecting market segmentation bases
   c. forecasting probable market share
   d. developing relevant profiles for each segment
   e. selecting the specific market segment

29. One regional retail chain surveyed female customers and identified the following profile: age 25-55; 147-160 cm tall; 38-55 kg; career oriented, and having a $20 000 plus household income. This information was obtained as a result of
   a. forecasting market potentials
   b. selecting a specific market segment
   c. selecting a market segmentation base
   d. developing a relevant market segment profile
   e. determining the market share for a product

30. A toothpaste manufacturer indicated that if consumers could be convinced to replace their toothbrushes when they should, market opportunities would be great. This sort of analysis relating to market potential would be conducted during which stage of the market segmentation decision process?
   a. Stage I

b.   Stage II
c.   Stage III
d.   Stage IV
e.   Stage V

31. A travel agency has made a decision to direct its marketing effort at the 50 year and over market. This decision was made during which stage of the market segmentation decision process?
a.   Stage I
b.   Stage II
c.   Stage III
d.   Stage IV
e.   Stage V

32. Target market decision analysis
a.   is useful only after market segments have been identified
b.   is restricted to geographic segmentation
c.   is a tool used to develop market segments with distinguishing characteristics
d.   can be used for consumer markets but is too expensive to be used for industrial markets
e.   is generally done with just one population characteristic, such as age

33. A small firm with limited resources that analyzes the market potential for a proposed line of typewriters would first
a.   choose a geographic area and market the typewriters to the ultimate consumer
b.   select the demographic segment and advertise the line of typewriters
c.   price the typewriters and co-ordinate the marketing effort
d.   distribute the typewriters to the appropriate wholesalers
e.   decide on a market and the end-use benefits

34. Which of the following would be considered a positioning strategy?
a.   Johnson and Johnson promoting its baby shampoo as one to be used by adults who need a gentle shampoo
b.   7-Up advertising its product as the "Uncola"
c.   Procter & Gamble advertising Crest toothpaste during family TV shows as "the cavity fighter"
d.   Hyundai advertising its low price
e.   all of the above

35. A positioning strategy is
a.   a single-offer strategy
b.   a multi-offer strategy
c.   employed during Stage III of the market segmentation decision process
d.   the way in which the product is perceived by consumers as being different from a competitor's product
e.   the process of dividing the market into several segments, each with characteristics that are peculiar to that segment

36. Which of the following is the best example of differentiated marketing?
a.   Hewlett Packard's marketing effort is directed at the high-priced calculator market.
b.   Volkswagen during the 1950s and 1960s was successful in marketing the "Beetle."
c.   Procter & Gamble gets a higher market share by emphasizing many different brands of laundry soap to meet the specific needs of consumers.
d.   A small tire manufacturer does little advertising and the product is directed at consumers in general.
e.   none of the above

37. The main advantage of undifferentiated marketing is that it
a. produces more sales
b. provides for cost economies
c. allows for a lower advertising budget
d. allows for a company to concentrate on a specific market segment
e. offers many different products to meet the different needs of consumers

38. The main disadvantage of differentiated marketing is that it
a. cuts down on the product offerings to consumers
b. does not permit effective use of market segmentation
c. increases production and marketing costs
d. does not keep in tune with customer wants and needs
e. involves greater risks than concentrated marketing

39. Which one of the following is a multi-offer strategy?
a. undifferentiated marketing
b. differentiated marketing
c. concentrated marketing
d. product positioning
e. none of the above

40. The key steps in target marketing are
a. selecting your customers, developing an advertising program, and distributing your product to resellers
b. market segmentation, market targeting, and market positioning
c. developing segmentation bases, promotion, pricing, and distribution
d. none of the above

41. The following statements about marketing segments are all true except one:
a. Functional products, such as toothpaste, do not need to be aimed at a specific segment.
b. It is difficult for any one marketing mix to satisfy everyone.
c. A marketing segment is a homogeneous subset of customers.
d. Some products and services, such as an unbranded detergent, are aimed at the mass market.
e. An enormous number of variables are involved in aiming a product at a market target.

42. Which product would be the best candidate for an undifferentiated product-market strategy?
a. automobiles
b. salt
c. toothpaste
d. apples
e. Cabbage Patch dolls

43. Procter & Gamble produces an extensive line of soap products (e.g., Ivory Snow, Cheer, Tide). The company obviously follows a strategy of
a. differentiated marketing
b. undifferentiated marketing
c. concentrated marketing
d. concentric diversification
e. retention

44. The manufacturer of the Rolls-Royce luxury car is following a product market strategy of
a. undifferentiated marketing
b. market segmentation
c. diversification

d. concentrated marketing
e. differentiated marketing

45. Of the following, which is not one of the available product-market matching strategies?
a. concentrated marketing
b. differentiated marketing
c. undifferentiated marketing
d. diffused marketing

46. In undifferentiated marketing, firms
a. produce only one product and market it to all customers with a single marketing mix
b. produce numerous products with different marketing mixes that satisfy smaller market segments
c. concentrate all marketing resources on a small segment of the total market
d. produce numerous products and market them with a single marketing mix
e. produce a limited number of products and market them all with a single marketing mix

47. Which of the following is not a result of using undifferentiated marketing?
a. efficiency resulting from longer production runs
b. minimal inventories
c. problems with foreign markets
d. increased threat of competition
e. maximized inventories

48. Which of the following is not true about concentrated marketing?
a. A firm chooses to focus its entire effort on satisfying a small market target.
b. Concentration often allows a firm to maintain a profitable operation.
c. A change in the size of the segment may result in severe financial problems.
d. A change in customers' buying patterns results in severe financial problems.
e. none of the above

49. Which of the following is not a basic determinant of a product-market strategy?
a. company resources
b. product homogeneity
c. stage in product life cycle
d. competitive strategies
e. state of the economy

50. Which of the following is not one of the five stages in the decision process framework for use in market segmentation?
a. Identify the dimensions for segmenting markets.
b. Identify what stage the product is in its life cycle.
c. Forecast the total market potential for each segment.
d. Decide on selection of target market segments.
e. Forecast the costs and benefits for each segment.

ANSWER KEY: CHAPTER FOUR

Vocabulary and Key Terms	True-False	Multiple Choice
1. b	1. F	26. b
2. e	2. F	27. a
3. a	3. F	28. e
4. d	4. T	29. d
5. f	5. F	30. c
6. c	6. F	31. e
	7. F	32. c
	8. T	33. a
	9. F	34. e
	10. F	35. d
	11. T	36. c
	12. T	37. b
	13. T	38. c
	14. F	39. b
	15. F	40. c
	16. T	41. a
	17. F	42. b
	18. F	43. a
	19. T	44. d
	20. T	45. d
	21. T	46. a
	22. T	47. e
	23. F	48. e
	24. T	49. e
	25. F	50. b

EXERCISE 4.1: NOSY PEABODY'S NEW JOB

Nosy Peabody, a former insurance salesperson, has just been hired as a special consultant by the Kitchener Rangers of the Ontario Junior Hockey League to identify the typical hockey fan at Ranger games and to find ways of expanding the team's audience.

Sporting events, such as hockey, are service businesses. As a service, the event is short-lived. Vacant seats at a hockey game can never be recovered. Discussing his new job with an old friend, Buey Maegard, Nosy said, "Junior hockey is good value for the money. It will cost a customer anywhere from a third to half the price of an NHL game to see a junior hockey game. Once a customer attends a few games and gets to know the players, he or she usually becomes hooked on our game; the problem is to get these individuals to the arena. My job is to identify the typical patron at these games and to explore ways of drawing hockey fans who are not currently attending Ranger games."

Nosy visited an old acquaintance at the University of Waterloo, Dr. Sleuth McSwain. Nosy said, "As a professor of marketing, can you tell me how to identify the heavy users of our service and how to reach potential users?"

Questions

1. What basis for segmentation would be the most appropriate for this study? Thoroughly examine demographic, geographic, and psychographic segmentation.
2. Sleuth suggested to Nosy that the five steps of the market-segmentation process could be applied to this problem. How would you apply these steps?
3. Could Nosy make effective use of market target decision analysis? Illustrate and discuss.

EXERCISE 4.2: A NEW ELECTRIC CAR

The text indicates that there are three principal types of product-market strategies: undifferentiated marketing, differentiated marketing, and concentrated marketing. Raymond Whibbs has created a three-wheel electric car with a battery that requires recharging after every 3000 kilometres of driving. The price of the car has been tentatively set at $18 000, and that of the recharging device at $2000. Ray feels that he has overcome most of the problems associated with previous electric car models and that people will be clamouring for his vehicle. He anticipates that his main problem will be inadequate production facilities and capital to meet the demand for the Spitfire, as he calls his new car. He plans to use an undifferentiated market strategy, because he is convinced that the market for his product is general rather than segmented; that is, housekeepers will enjoy the car for shopping and visiting friends; students, for getting to class; workers, for commuting to and from work; and so on.

Ray feels a patent application is unnecessary, as this car will be difficult to duplicate. Also, a trademark search is not needed, as everyone knows there is not another Spitfire on the market.

Questions

1. Are there any weaknesses in Ray's marketing plans for this electric car?
2. What product-market strategy should be considered by Ray for the Spitfire?
3. Who would represent the primary market target for the Spitfire?
4. What additional research should be conducted?

CHAPTER 5

Obtaining Data for Marketing Decisions

CHAPTER OBJECTIVES

1. Define, explain, or describe the key terms listed under "Vocabulary and Key Terms."
2. Describe the development and current status of the marketing research function.
3. Outline and describe the steps in the marketing research procedure.
4. Discuss the types of primary and secondary data.
5. Identify the methods of collecting survey data.
6. Describe the concept of a marketing information system and the procedure for constructing an MIS.
7. Distinguish between marketing research and marketing information systems.
8. Outline and discuss the benefits possible with an MIS.
9. Apply your knowledge of Chapter 5 to a case analysis.

VOCABULARY AND KEY TERMS

From the lettered terms listed below, select the one that best matches the meaning of each of the numbered statements that follows. Write the letter of that choice in the space provided.

a) market research
b) exploratory research
c) hypothesis
d) research design
e) secondary data
f) primary data
g) observation method
h) survey method
i) experimental method
j) marketing information system (MIS)
k) focus group interview
l) sample
m) test marketing

1. _____ A tentative explanation about some specific event
2. _____ Data collected for the first time during a marketing research study
3. _____ The representative group selected by a researcher for the project at hand
4. _____ Previously published data that is useful for a research project
5. _____ Discussing the problem area of a proposed research study with people within and outside the firm, and examining secondary sources of information before embarking on formal research

6. _____ Collecting marketing information through the use of controlled experiments
7. _____ A series of advance decisions that make up a master plan or model for the conduct of the investigation
8. _____ A designed set of procedures and methods for generating an orderly flow of pertinent information for use in making decisions
9. _____ Personal interviews conducted on a group basis as a means of gathering research information
10. _____ Introducing a new, untried product into an area, and observing its degree of success
11. _____ An interviewing method used to collect information
12. _____ Collecting data by actually viewing the overt action of the respondent
13. _____ The systematic gathering, recording, and analyzing of data about problems relating to the marketing of goods or services

PRACTICE TEST

True-False: In the space to the right of each statement, check the appropriate line to indicate whether the statement is true or false.

	True	False
1. Exploratory research to uncover problems is required only when a detailed marketing survey is anticipated.	_____	_____
2. Both secondary and primary data may be used in a formal research project.	_____	_____
3. A major step in research design is to determine what data are needed in testing the hypothesis.	_____	_____
4. The most common types of marketing research studies are centred on the pricing function of a marketer's program.	_____	_____
5. There are three basic types of marketing research organizations that a firm may utilize.	_____	_____
6. A syndicated service is an organization that offers to provide a standardized set of data on a regular basis to all who wish to buy it.	_____	_____
7. Marketing research involves ten specific steps, the first of which is formulating a hypothesis.	_____	_____
8. Discussing a research problem with informed sources of information and examining already published information on the problem would be examples of exploratory research.	_____	_____
9. Exploratory research refers to a series of advance decisions that, taken together, make up a master plan or model for the conduct of the investigation.	_____	_____
10. Primary data are less expensive to collect than secondary data.	_____	_____
11. Primary data are previously published matter.	_____	_____
12. Data collection is a major part of the marketing research project.	_____	_____
13. The federal government provides the country's most important sources of marketing data.	_____	_____
14. The most frequently used government source of information is the census.	_____	_____

15. A.C. Nielsen Company is a government-owned company that distributes to companies and individuals secondary data supplied by government departments.

16. Less time is involved in locating and using primary data.

17. The observation method is conducted by actually viewing the overt action of the respondents.

18. Garbology is a technique that requires the researcher to monitor consumption behaviour by rummaging through select garbage.

19. Mail questionnaires are inexpensive and fast for obtaining limited quantities of relatively impersonal information.

20. Personal interviews account for the majority of all primary marketing research.

21. Mail surveys allow the marketing researcher to conduct national studies at a reasonable cost.

22. The total group that the researcher wants to study is called the population or universe.

23. Probability samples are arbitrary, and standard statistical tests cannot be applied.

24. A quota sample is an example of a nonprobability sample.

25. A probability sample that takes every Nth item on a list, after a random start, is called a systematic sample.

Multiple Choice: Choose the expression that best answers the question or best completes the sentence.

26. Exploratory research consists of
   a. discussing the problem with informed sources within the firm
   b. discussing the problem with wholesalers, retailers, customers, and others outside the firm
   c. examining secondary sources of information
   d. all of the above

27. The use of secondary data might be limited when
   a. the data may be obsolete
   b. classifications of the data may not be usable in the study
   c. data must be rearranged to be usable in the study
   d. all of the above
   e. a and b

28. Which of the following is not an example of internal secondary data?
   a. records of sales
   b. census data
   c. product-performance reports
   d. sales-force activities
   e. marketing costs

29. Which of the following is not one of the six steps in the marketing research process?
   a. defining the problem
   b. determination of objectives
   c. exploratory research
   d. formulating the hypothesis
   e. research design

30. In searching for the cause of a problem the researcher will learn about the problem area and begin to focus on specific areas for study. This is known as
   a. the research design
   b. formulating a hypothesis
   c. exploratory research
   d. procedure for collecting the data
   e. definition of the problem

31. A researcher is considering sources of secondary information for her project. Which of the following information would be most valuable for her project?
   a. Census of Canada
   b. Canada Year Book or Market Research Handbook
   c. The Financial Post Research Services
   d. Primary research will be of more value than secondary research for this particular project.
   e. The type of data that will be collected depends on the needs of the particular project.

32. The advantage of secondary data over primary data is that
   a. the assembly of previously collected data is almost always less expensive than the collection of primary data
   b. this type of data is always more valuable because it has already been collected and is less subject to interviewer bias
   c. less time is involved in locating and using secondary data
   d. none of the above
   e. a and c

33. Which of the following is a limitation of the observation method?
   a. Observer subjectivity creates problems and errors in interpretation are common.
   b. It is less accurate than questioning techniques like surveys.
   c. It is not a very effective method of getting first-hand information.
   d. It is a costly method for collecting information.
   e. Too much time is wasted in developing questionnaires.

34. Restaurant managers have gone through the garbage for years to monitor customer satisfaction. This research technique is known as
   a. garbageology
   b. garbology
   c. sanitation research
   d. refuseology
   e. none of the above

35. The most commonly used approach for collecting primary data is the
   a. experimental
   b. observation
   c. survey
   d. all of the above
   e. none of the above

36. The main limitation of personal interview technique is that
   a. the interviewer is limited by the length of the survey and lacks the flexibility to get fuller information on the questions asked
   b. interviewer bias may affect the validity of the survey
   c. everyone in the population of the survey must be interviewed
   d. personal interviews are slow and the most expensive method of collecting data
   e. none of the above

37. Which of the following is an example of probability sampling?
a. convenience sample
b. quota sample
c. judgment sample
d. simple random
e. All of the above are examples of nonprobability sampling.

38. The major problem of a controlled experiment is
a. over-control of all variables in the test situation
b. inability to identify all variables in the test situation
c. inability to control all the variables in a real-life situation
d. b and c
e. none of the above

39. Some marketing executives feel they do not need a marketing information system. Which of the following is not one of the reasons normally given for this belief?
a. The cost is too great for smaller companies.
b. The marketing research department already provides the same information as an MIS.
c. The size of the company does not warrant such a thorough system.
d. Marketing research normally focuses on a specific problem or project.

40. Marketing information systems (MIS)
a. provide a continual flow of information
b. are needed by companies that have marketing research departments
c. require the full support of top management for success
d. must be matched to the level of sophistication of the organization
e. all of the above

41. IBM presented a large firm with a proposal to purchase a sophisticated computer system. The executives of the firm agreed unanimously to buy the computer. However, the CEO felt that, rather than purchase a computer, the company should implement an entire marketing information system (MIS). The CEO then requested that each executive list the three most pertinent features that the MIS should have. The best list to present would be
a. market information, expansion capability of technology, and methods and procedures for decision makers to utilize the information
b. fastest technology available, provide the most current information, and have collection capacity large enough for competitive information
c. set procedures and methods for collecting information, generate sufficient information for all decision makers, and establish an information flow that would enable quick and accurate access
d. order the flow of pertinent, current, and forecastable market information, and generate a profile of market responses to company and competitor actions
e. current and forecastable market information, trends in competition, economic conditions, production quality control, and employee skills that enable efficient decision making

42. The key difference between marketing research and a marketing information system is that
a. marketing research is wider in scope
b. marketing research involves the continuous collection and analysis of marketing information
c. marketing research focuses on a specific problem or project
d. marketing research uses more types of data
e. marketing information systems are restricted to providing information about competitors

43. Which of the following characteristics is most closely identified with the experimental method of collecting primary data?
a. The most common use of this technique is in the area of test marketing.

b. This method is almost exclusively used in the laboratory in order to control the largest number of variables.

c. This method is unlike the focus group technique, which uses control groups to compare results.

d. This is the most widely used method of collecting information on consumer responses to new products.

e. Results of this technique cannot be considered reliable or valid.

44. If you are able to conduct a focus group interview, which of the following procedures would you follow?

a. Invite eight to twelve people to meet at one location for an open forum or discussion, which would allow each respondent an unrestrained opportunity to focus on his or her particular area of interest.

b. Invite eight to twelve individuals to a single location for candid dialogue about a product, firm, or service.

c. Invite ten people (plus or minus two) to a designated location at their convenience to discuss in depth a subject of interest.

d. Bring together eight to twelve people in a single location to complete a detailed form reflecting their opinions and attitudes about a subject of interest.

e. all of the above

45. Research is likely to be contracted to outside groups when which of the following requirements is met?

a. Problem areas can be defined in terms of specific research projects.

b. There is a need for specialized know-how or equipment.

c. Intellectual detachment is necessary.

d. all of the above

e. None of the above applies: the only consideration is cost.

46. Which of the following statements is not true regarding mail surveys?

a. They allow the marketing researcher to conduct national studies at reasonable cost.

b. Returned questionnaires for such studies usually average 80–90 percent.

c. The results of mail interviews are likely to be biased because of differences in characteristics of respondents and nonrespondents.

d. Follow-up questionnaires and/or telephone interviews are used to gather additional information from nonrespondents.

47. Where population lists are unavailable, a method of obtaining a random sample that utilizes blocks instead of individuals is known as

a. taking a census

b. simple random

c. area sampling

d. surveying

e. none of the above

48. Which of the following statements is false with regard to telephone interviews?

a. Telephone interviews account for 55–60 percent of all primary marketing research.

b. They are limited to simple, clearly worded questions.

c. Telephone interviews have no major drawbacks in terms of responses elicited.

d. With a telephone interview, it may be extremely difficult to obtain information on respondents' personal characteristics.

e. The survey may be prejudiced by the omission of households without phones and with unlisted numbers.

49. Which of the following questions to managers would probably not be helpful in developing a marketing information system?
   a. What meetings are you responsible for calling and leading?
   b. What data analysis programs would help you in making decisions?
   c. What types of information would you like to receive on a regular basis?
   d. What kinds of decisions are you called upon to make?

50. Personal interviews
   a. are typically the best means of obtaining detailed information
   b. can be conducted quickly and efficiently, and are the least expensive method of collecting survey data
   c. allow the interviewer to establish rapport with each respondent and explain confusing questions
   d. all of the above
   e. a and c

ANSWER KEY: CHAPTER 5

Vocabulary and Key Terms	True-False	Multiple Choice
1. c	1. F	26. d
2. f	2. T	27. e
3. l	3. T	28. b
4. e	4. F	29. b
5. b	5. F	30. c
6. i	6. T	31. e
7. d	7. F	32. e
8. j	8. T	33. a
9. k	9. F	34. b
10. m	10. F	35. c
11. h	11. F	36. d
12. g	12. T	37. d
13. a	13. T	38. c
	14. T	39. d
	15. F	40. e
	16. F	41. c
	17. T	42. c
	18. T	43. a
	19. F	44. b
	20. F	45. d
	21. T	46. b
	22. T	47. c
	23. F	48. c
	24. T	49. a
	25. T	50. e

EXERCISE 5.1: THE RESEARCH METHOD OF A SHOPPING CENTRE

The Garden of Eden Shopping Mall in Lethbridge, Alberta, is a suburban shopping centre with 50 stores, including Eaton's, Canadian Tire, Super Value supermarket, and two theatres. The manager of the mall has noted that the sales volume per square foot in 1990 was down from that of the previous year for many of the stores in the mall. The Super Value and other grocery retailers in the city have always suffered from Safeway's dominance of the market (approximately 70 percent of all grocery sales), and 1990 was no exception. However, the decline in sales for many of the other tenants was puzzling. The mall manager suspects that the mix of stores in the mall is not ideal for the type of customers shopping there. She feels that if she could determine the primary and secondary trading areas of the city, the type of customers the mall caters to, and the type of store that would fulfil the needs of these customers, then changes could be made to improve sales in the future.

She is now considering using the services of a marketing research firm in Calgary to study this situation. She wonders what types of information should be collected.

Questions

1. What would be the purpose of this research study?
2. What information should be collected to fulfil this purpose?
3. Should the observation, experimental, or survey method be used to collect the needed data? Why? If you suggest the survey method, which of three questionnaire techniques should be used? Why?
4. To collect all the information needed, is more than one type of study required to fulfil the overall purpose? How will this be accomplished?

EXERCISE 5.2: PROJECTING DEMAND

Nadine Chaney, a recent graduate from the business administration program at Acadia University, has been hired by a computer software company; one of her first tasks is to conduct a research study on a new spreadsheet software package. The purpose of the research is to identify the market potential for the product, to identify what features the product should possess, and to determine the possible pricing/advertising/channel strategies for the product.

Nadine has taken a couple of courses in marketing research at Acadia and has been involved in a class research project. She is in charge of this study and has to take the initiative in getting the project started. The first step in a research project is to define the problem; in this case, it has been clearly stated. Usually, the next step is to do exploratory research. At first, Nadine wondered whether she could find another company that had researched this problem; if so, she could cut down on the amount of information that needed to be collected.

Nadine now suspects that the bulk of the research will involve collecting primary data, and that the survey method should be used for collecting this data. However, she has yet to decide on the most useful method for getting the information, as well as how much help from the staff she will need to do the job. (Without competent personnel to carry out the research, the validity of the study might be questioned.) If she decides to go with the personal interview method, the next step will be to determine who to interview. This is a critical decision that will determine the value of the study; yet Nadine has still not determined her universe or a method for sampling that universe. Also, Tommy Pigeon, the marketing manager, has made it clear to her that the company anticipates using the findings from this study to develop the company marketing program for the new spreadsheet package.

Nadine has phoned Lana Varner, her marketing research professor at Acadia, with some questions on how to attack these problems.

Questions

1. Has the first step in the research process (i.e., defining the problem) been dealt with?
2. Would exploratory research be of value to this research study? If so, how should Nadine proceed?
3. Is taking a survey the most appropriate method for collecting data for this study? What kind of survey method would be most effective for this study? What are the advantages and disadvantages of each method?
4. What would be the limitations of secondary data in this project?
5. What sampling technique would most likely be useful for this study? Why?
6. What marketing research procedure would likely be recommended by Nadine's marketing instructor?

CHAPTER 6

Marketing Strategy and the Marketing Plan

CHAPTER OBJECTIVES

1. Show that a strategic orientation is important in marketing.
2. Indicate how marketing strategy is related to the overall strategy that has been developed for the organization.
3. Relate the marketing plan to marketing strategy.
4. Show that the marketing plan should be developed in relation to the character of the marketing environment.
5. Identify the steps in the marketing planning process.
6. Describe the marketing mix and show its importance in the development of the marketing plan.
7. Explain that the elements of the marketing mix can be combined in such a way as to produce synergistic effects.
8. Apply your knowledge of Chapter 6 to the various activities provided in this chapter of the study guide.

VOCABULARY AND KEY TERMS

From the lettered terms listed below, select the one that best matches the meaning of each of the numbered statements that follows. Write the letter of that choice in the space provided.
a. corporate strategy
b. marketing plan
c. marketing mix
d. mission statement
e. marketing strategy
f. marketing planning process

1. _____ A plan that focuses on developing a unique long-term competitive position in the market by assessing consumer needs and the firm's potential for gaining competitive advantage
2. _____ A program of activities that lead to the accomplishment of the marketing strategy
3. _____ The overall purpose and direction of the organization that is established in light of the challenges and opportunities found in the environment, as well as available organizational resources
4. _____ A statement that expresses the strategy of the enterprise
5. _____ The blending of the four elements of marketing to satisfy chosen consumer segments
6. _____ A plan put into place within a business organization to achieve the corporate strategy

PRACTICE TEST

True-False: In the space to the right of each statement, check the appropriate line to indicate whether the statement is true or false.

	True	False

1. Markets are homogeneous.

2. According to the marketing concept, marketing strategy must start with segmentation.

3. It was Theodore Levitt who said that the purpose of the enterprise is to create and keep a customer.

4. The development of a corporate strategy follows the development of marketing strategy in the marketing planning process.

5. The process of developing a corporate strategy starts with an analysis of market and environmental opportunities and threats facing the company as a whole.

6. The development of corporate strategy is the responsibility of the marketing manager.

7. A mission statement is simply the expression of the corporate strategy.

8. Segmenting by positioning analysis is the last step in the marketing-oriented approach to strategy formulation.

9. According to contingency theory, organizational processes will be effective to the degree that they fit the environment in which they operate.

10. Software firms playing a role in the production of industrial robots is an example of intertype competition.

11. In marketing planning the best approach is to avoid having a comprehensive marketing plan.

12. Social consciousness, such as concern for health and safety, cannot initially be included in a marketing plan.

13. A contingency approach enables a firm to be more relevant in its planning.

14. A situation analysis in the marketing planning process will include sales objectives, profit objectives, and competitive analysis.

15. The 4 Ps of marketing are production, pricing, promotion, and place.

16. Communication decisions are centred around the mix of personal selling, advertising, and sales promotional activities.

17. Distribution decisions involve the selection and management of marketing channels and the physical distribution of goods.

18. The marketing variables will be used by all companies in exactly the same way.

19.   When each element in the marketing mix is used to its best
       advantage and the results are greater than the sum of the parts,
       there is, in effect, synergy.   _____   _____

20.   Seldom is the marketing manager capable of developing a mar-
       keting plan that will satisfy the external factors in the
       environment.   _____   _____

Multiple Choice: Choose the expression that best answers or completes the sentence.

21.   Which of the following is not one of Theodore Levitt's four simple requisites for the success
          of a business?
   a.   The purpose of an enterprise is to create a customer.
   b.   You have to produce and deliver goods to customers at realistic prices.
   c.   Your company must be production oriented.
   d.   Purpose, strategy, and plans must be clearly stated and frequently reviewed.
   e.   An appropriate system of rewards, audits, and controls must be in place.

22.   In formulating strategy for a company, analyzing business strengths and weaknesses
   a.   normally follows a company's objective and strategy generation
   b.   precedes a company's determining objectives and formulating strategy
   c.   is a part of analyzing market and environmental opportunities and threats
   d.   is not a part of this process
   e.   is overlooked by many marketers although it is the most important element in strategy formulation

23.   A mission statement is expressed from a company's
   a.   corporate strategy
   b.   marketing strategy
   c.   objectives
   d.   overall plans
   e.   evaluation process

24.   The most important element in a company's marketing strategy is to
   a.   achieve maximum profits by producing quality products
   b.   understand the competition better in order to produce better products that will assist the com-
          pany's profit goals
   c.   develop short-term goals to satisfy customer wants
   d.   understand the long-term competitive position of the market by assessing consumer needs and
          being aware of the strengths and weaknesses of the competition
   e.   make sure employees are happy and well paid

25.   Which of the following is a good example of positioning?
   a.   Apple is positioned as the most user-friendly and versatile quality printer.
   b.   Apple clones are positioned on the basis of price.
   c.   Crest is positioned as a decay preventative.
   d.   NyQuil is positioned as a night medicine.
   e.   all of the above

26.   A company will usually have a mix of products, some producing a strong cash flow while others
          produce very little, if any, profit. This mix of products constitutes a company's
   a.   synergy
   b.   portfolio analysis
   c.   opportunity-strengths analysis
   d.   segment-by-positioning analysis
   e.   marketing strategy

27. A program of activities that lead to the accomplishment of marketing strategy is
    a. the marketing plan
    b. the corporate strategy
    c. the company audit
    d. synergy
    e. none of the above

28. Which of the following should be included in a company's marketing plan?
    a. an analysis of the competitive structure of the environment
    b. an assessment of the economic environment
    c. the implications of changes in the socio-cultural environment
    d. technological changes that may affect how the company will do business
    e. all of the above

29. An example of marketing planning would be
    a. establishing new product facilities
    b. outlining alternatives for product engineering
    c. making conceptual decisions on production scheduling
    d. selecting avenues for product movement and handling
    e. establishing stock prices for a firm going public

30. Which of the following is not a part of the situation analysis in the marketing planning process?
    a. historical background
    b. consumer analysis
    c. sales objectives
    d. competitive analysis

31. What question is asked in the situation analysis of the marketing planning process?
    a. Where are we now?
    b. Where do we want to go?
    c. What should we do with each of the marketing mix elements?
    d. Where have we been in the past?
    e. Whose idea was this anyway?

32. What question is asked in the marketing objective stage of the marketing planning process?
    a. Where are we now?
    b. Where do we want to go?
    c. What should we do with each of the marketing mix elements?
    d. Where have we been in the past?
    e. Whose idea was this anyway?

33. Which of the following is not one of the elements of the marketing mix?
    a. product
    b. production
    c. price
    d. distribution
    e. communication

34. The mix of personal selling, advertising, and sales promotional activities is referred to as a company's
    a. correspondence with the consumer
    b. networking
    c. communication
    d. services
    e. messages

35. Market plans are implemented through a company's marketing mix. Which element of the mix is involved with decisions on warehousing and transportation of the goods?
   a. product
   b. price
   c. distribution
   d. communication

36. Which element of the mix is involved with branding and packaging?
   a. product
   b. price
   c. distribution
   d. communication

37. Schweppes ginger ale, once advertised as the jet-set mixer, is now cleverly promoted as "affordable by everyone." This marketing approach focuses on
   a. pricing strategy
   b. undefined submarkets
   c. creating a new image
   d. comparative advertising

38. Marketing decision making can be classified into four strategies:
   a. product, pricing, distribution, and communication
   b. product, pricing, manufacturing, and communication
   c. communication, product, pricing, and selling
   d. distribution, product, pricing, and selling
   e. none of the above

39. The term marketing mix refers to
   a. the total assortment of products a given firm has on the market
   b. the blending of the four strategy elements of marketing decision making to satisfy chosen consumer segments
   c. the total assortment of advertisements used for any given period
   d. the group of people at whom a promotional campaign is aimed
   e. none of the above

40. The marketing planner will need to make many careful decisions about many subcategories of the marketing mix. Which of the following is not one of the sub-elements under advertising in Borden's marketing mix?
   a. amount to be spent on advertising
   b. copy platform to adopt
   c. mix of advertising
   d. burden to place on special selling plans or devices directed at or through the trade

ANSWER KEY: CHAPTER 6

Vocabulary and Key Terms	True-False	Multiple Choice
1. e	1. F	21. c
2. b	2. T	22. b
3. a	3. T	23. a
4. d	4. F	24. d
5. c	5. T	25. e
6. f	6. F	26. b
	7. T	27. a
	8. F	28. e
	9. T	29. d
	10. T	30. c
	11. F	31. a
	12. F	32. b
	13. T	33. b
	14. F	34. c
	15. F	35. c
	16. T	36. a
	17. T	37. c
	18. F	38. a
	19. T	39. b
	20. F	40. d

EXERCISE 6.1: POSITIONING ANALYSIS

As discussed in Chapter 4 of the text, *positioning* refers to shaping a product and developing a market mix in such a way that the product is perceived to be (and actually is) different from competitors' products. In Chapter 6, positioning is related to strategy formulation and evaluation. A company will position its product to the market and develop a marketing mix that will make this positioning strategy possible.

In the book *Marketing*, Kotler identifies several ways in which marketers can apply positioning strategy to their products. One of these is to position a product on the basis of its attributes. As the author points out, "Hyundai is positioned on its low price; Saab promotes performance." Product benefits can be a useful positioning strategy; for example, Crest is positioned as a decay preventative, and Macleans, as a whitener. According to Kotler, "To plan a position for a current or new product a company must first do a competitive analysis to identify the existing positions of its own and competing products (p. 202)." At this point, the company will be in a position to develop its marketing mix.

A company's success depends on developing an effective niche in the market for its products. According to Harvey Mackay,

> Turtle Wax has held a dependable — and sizable — share of the car-wax market for years — a market that is synonymous with something people hate to do. They did it with a product that has a reputation for being more difficult than others to apply, by exploiting a niche out there of people who literally "love" their cars. What better way to show love than the sacrifice, by lavishing care and devotion on the object of one's affection? (p. 162)

Fred Banks manufactures a line of three different fire-safe products — a fire-safe security chest that can substitute for a safety deposit box at a bank; a fire-proof security file that serves as an organizer for important papers and documents; and a fire-proof safe that provides protection for home valuables. The company's chief competition for the home market comes from Sentry. Although Fred's company is new to the market, Fred knows that his only real competitor is Sentry; thus, he wants to know whether there is a way in which niche marketing (positioning analysis) can be applied to fire-proof safes. He has discussed the issue with two graduate marketing students, who have volunteered, on a contract basis, to develop a marketing plan and to examine positioning analysis as part of that plan.

Questions

1. Identify bases for positioning other than those already listed in the above exercise.
2. If you were one of the graduate students working on the marketing plan for Fred Banks, what positioning strategy would you recommend for his fire-proof safes?
3. Using the marketing-process format described in this chapter, develop a marketing plan for the fire-proof safes.

Sources: Philip Kotler, Gordon McDougall, Gary Armstrong, *Marketing, Canadian Edition* (Toronto: Prentice-Hall, 1988), pp. 200–2. Reprinted by permission.
Harvey Mackay, *Beware the Naked Man Who Offers You His Shirt* (New York: Ivy Books, 1990), p. 162. Reprinted by permission.

EXERCISE 6.2: STRATEGIC-WINDOW SITUATIONS

Writing in *Business Horizons*, David Cravens defines a strategic window as "an optimal match of market requirements with the particular competencies of the firm that is serving the market." Cravens further states: "Taking action when the window is open (a good match exists) can gain marketing advantage" (p. 51).

In his article, Cravens discusses the success of Honda's venture into the luxury automobile market. Although it had previously sold only lower-price automobiles, Honda intended to sell its Acura Legend in the same market in which the Mercedes 190 was sold. The company therefore decided to sell this car through a new dealer network that did not carry Honda's lower-priced lines. The Acura was positioned as an expensive and prestigious automobile. The strategy worked; the Acura is one of the biggest sellers in the luxury import market.

Craven further notes that the microwave boom of the 1970s and 1980s created a need for quality microwave cookware, and that although Corning Glass Works is a dominant producer of cookware, it failed to take advantage of this window of opportunity. Competitors entered the market to meet consumer needs and gained market share from Corning.

On the other hand, a strategic move made by Coca-Cola's top management in 1985 had a positive, and significant, impact on the company's market share. The company decided to introduce New Coke to replace old Coke. Blind taste tests indicated to the company that consumers preferred the taste of New Coke over that of old Coke and Pepsi. A vocal minority considered Coca-Cola's move to be a betrayal, and began to hoard bottles of old Coke; the ensuing publicity began to hurt the company. In response, Coca-Cola devised an imaginative strategy: The company ordered all its departments to prepare for the reintroduction of old Coke. While New Coke would still be the standard, old Coke would be retained for die-hard fans of the original formula. Old Coke was renamed Coke Classic. The strategy paid off; Coke gained market share over its competitors.

Some may consider the move to New Coke to be a strategy mistake in the long run; while Coca-Cola is still the market leader, the company's success is currently tied to Coke Classic and Diet Coke. New Coke is again in trouble and may experience a name change or an overhaul sometime in the 1990s.

Questions

1. Explain the concept of strategic window in your own words. Give an example not included in this exercise.
2. Why do you think Corning Glass Works allowed competitors to beat them to the market with microwave cookware?
3. Japanese auto producers have gradually moved into the luxury car market. The Acura was their first entry; the Lexus is the latest. Examine an ad for Acura or Lexus and write a strategy statement.

4. Do you think Coca-Cola's strategy in 1985 was to introduce New Coke, discard old Coke, and reintroduce old Coke as soon as die-hard old Coke fans began to react unfavourably to the move? Is it realistic to think that Coca-Cola planned the whole strategy?

Source: David Craven, "Gaining Strategic Marketing Advantage," *Business Horizons* (September/October 1988), pp. 44–54.

Case 2

ROWEN PLASTICS AND MANUFACTURING COMPANY

Rowen Plastics is a wholly owned subsidiary of a large, international chemical company. Located in a small British Columbia city, Rowen Plastics specializes in producing small plastic articles, such as eyeglass frames and other assorted items. Since it is a small firm, its market is limited geographically to the western provinces.

The plastic eyeglass frames have proven to be the most profitable item in its line of products, but recently sales of these frames have declined markedly. The company manufactures many different styles of plastic frames but concentrates primarily on men's styles; they are the most profitable because of their basic style and fairly uniform size and weight. The frames are priced competitively and shipped to wholesalers, who handle the final distribution of the products. The other plastic products are manufactured mainly to round out production, since demand for these products is limited.

Feeling the financial effects of decreased sales, the company decided to try to find out why sales had declined. In a survey of all of its wholesalers, it found that the agents canvassed their assigned territories extremely well. These agents generally had accounts such as large department stores as well as many small, independent opticians. The consensus of the agents was that they were unable to maintain previous order levels. In some cases they found that they were unable to sell plastic eyeglass frames at any price because of the revival and increasing popularity of metal frames. This was particularly true in the larger, cosmopolitan areas.

In order to increase their understanding of the extent to which people were switching from the plastic to the metal frames, the management conducted market surveys in Vancouver, Victoria, Edmonton, Calgary, Regina, and Winnipeg. The surveys were given to men wearing plastic-framed glasses, picked at random in large shopping areas in these cities. The interview was a brief one, asking: (1) How long have you worn glasses? (2) How long have you had your present frames? (3) How long did you have your previous frames? and, if applicable, (4) Were the previous frames also plastic? and (5) If you are considering buying new glasses, what type of frames would you select? If the answer to the last question was metal frames, that was all that was requested. However, if the responder replied that he would continue to buy plastic frames, he was shown a selection of a dozen of Rowen's most popular styles and asked to pick out which style he preferred. The results indicated that more than one of every three men surveyed said they would purchase metal frames, and those who chose plastic frames did not indicate a strong consensus for any particular style.

With production costs rising because of the sales decline, Rowen was unable to maintain its competitive prices, and the wholesalers were being forced to take a correspondingly smaller percentage of profits. Consequently, some wholesalers were considering dropping the line altogether, and Rowen found it necessary to reduce the work force in the frame production department by 50 percent. Rowen's income statement also indicated that the company would incur a substantial loss this year if the trend continued.

The management has ruled out the possibility of producing the metal frames because of the expense involved in changing over the present machinery and investing in new machinery to form and produce the metal frames.

Relying on the hope that the metal frame demand will be short-term, Rowen is considering increasing its inventory of plastic frames. This will allow the company to meet the increase in plastic frame demand that will occur again after the fad for metal frames dies out. However, the statistics show that the demand for metal frames is not tapering off but instead is showing continuous growth.

Rowen is not in a sufficiently strong financial situation to absorb any long-term losses; therefore, the idea of shutting down the present facilities is also being considered by the management.

Questions

1. Evaluate the actions that Rowen Plastics and Manufacturing Company has taken in defining and analyzing its target market.
2. Describe the steps that Rowen should take in order to define and analyze its target market for eyeglass frames more effectively.
3. Considering the approximate resources of the company, how can Rowen change its operations to meet the continuously changing needs of its target market?

Source: James Sood, *Situations in Marketing* (Homewood, Ill.: Business Corporations Inc., 1976). Reprinted by permission of Business Publications, Inc.

Case 3

NOVA SCOTIA

The U.S. Market for Canadian Travel Services

The more than 12 million Americans who travel to Canada annually constitute 42 percent of all departures from the United States. The U.S. market is of crucial importance to the Canadian tourism industry because 95 percent of all tourists are Americans, who spend approximately $2.7 billion a year on these trips.

The 1980s have witnessed a major escalation in campaigns that try to lure tourists to a particular state or foreign country. Tourism areas spent over $100 million in U.S. media in 1985, and the level is expected to grow considerably. Tourism Canada, the government tourist organization, in 1986 launched a campaign with the theme "Come to the world next door" as an umbrella campaign for Canada as a whole. The provinces will conduct their own independent campaigns to segments they deem most attractive and profitable. For example, ads for Manitoba are mostly written for the outdoor vacationer.

FIGURE C3-1 BENEFIT MATCHING MODEL

Markets	Benefits Sought	Benefit Match	Benefits Provided	Destinations
A	A_S, B_S	S	A_P, B_P	X
B	B_S, C_S	M	C_P, D_P	Y
C	C_S, D_S	N	E_P, F_P	Z

S = Supermatch
M = Match
N = Mismatch

Source: Arch G. Woodside, "Positioning a Province Using Travel Research," *Journal of Travel Research* 20 (Winter 1982): 3.

The Canadian Government Office of Tourism (CGOT) sponsored a large-scale benefit-segmentation study of the American market for pleasure travel to Canada, the results of which are summarized in Table C3-1. Segmenting the market by benefits provides many advantages over other methods. Segmenting by attitude toward Canada or by geographic area would be feasible if substantial variation occurred. This is not the case, however. Segmenting by benefits reveals what consumers were and are seeking in their vacations. Knowing this is central to planning effective marketing programs.

A Benefit-Matching Model

Figure C3-1 summarizes a strategic view for understanding tourism behaviour and developing a market campaign. The model emphasizes the dominant need to define markets by benefits sought and the fact that separate markets seek unique benefits or activity packages. Membership in the segments will fluctuate from year to year; the same individuals may seek rest and relaxation one year and foreign adventure the next.

Identifying benefits is not enough, however. Competitors (that is, other countries or areas) may present the same type of benefits to the consumers. Because travellers seriously consider only a few destinations, a sharp focus is needed for promoting a destination. This also means that a destination should avoid trying to be "everything to everybody" by promoting too many benefits.

Combining all of these concerns calls for positioning; that is, generating a unique, differentiated image in the mind of the consumer.

FIGURE C3-2 NOVA SCOTIA AND ITS MAIN MARKETS

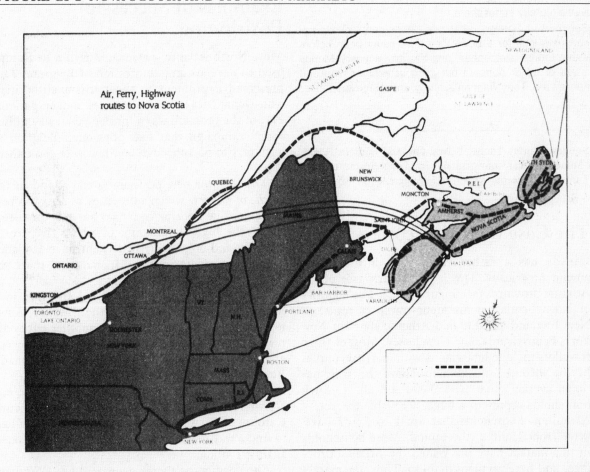

Source: "Nova Scotia", *The Travel Agent*, February 27, 1986, 14.

TABLE C3-1 BENEFIT SEGMENTS OF U.S. TRAVELLERS TO CANADA

Segment I: Friends and relatives — nonactive visitor (29 percent). These vacationers seek familiar surroundings where they can visit friends and relatives. They are not very inclined to participate in any activity.

Segment II: Friends and relatives — active city visitor (12 percent). These vacationers also seek familiar surroundings where they can visit friends and relatives, but they are more inclined to participate in activities — especially sightseeing, shopping, and cultural and other entertainment.

Segment III: Family sightseers (6 percent). These vacationers are looking for a new vacation place that would be a treat for the children and an enriching experience.

Segment IV: Outdoor vacationer (19 percent). These vacationers seek clean air, rest and quiet, and beautiful scenery. Many are campers and availability of recreation facilities is important. Children are also an important factor.

Segment V: Resort vacationer (19 percent). These vacationers are most interested in water sports (for example, swimming) and good weather. They prefer a popular place with a big-city atmosphere.

Segment VI: Foreign vacationer (26 percent). These vacationers look for a place they have never been before with a foreign atmosphere and beautiful scenery. Money is not of major concern but good accommodation and service are. They want an exciting, enriching experience.

Source: Shirley Young, Leland Ott, and Barbara Feigin, "Some Practical Considerations in Market Segmentation," *Journal of Marketing Research* 15 (August 1978): 405–12.

The Case of Nova Scotia

Canada has a rather vague and diffuse image among Americans. This is particularly true of the Atlantic provinces (see Figure C3-2). The majority of Nova Scotia's nonresident travellers reside in New England and the mid-Atlantic states of New York, Pennsylvania, and New Jersey. Most of these travellers include households with married couples having incomes substantially above the U.S. national average; that is, $50 000 and above. Such households represent a huge, accessible market — 10 million households that are 1 to 2 1/2 days' drive from Halifax, the capital. Most households in this market have not visited the Atlantic provinces and have no plans to do so. Thus, the market exhibits three of the four requirements necessary to be a very profitable customer base for the province: size, accessibility, and purchasing power. The market lacks the intention to visit for most of the households described. Nova Scotia is not one of the destinations considered when the next vacation or pleasure trip is being planned. Worse still, Nova Scotia does not exist in the minds of its largest potential market.

In the past, Nova Scotia had a number of diverse marketing themes, such as "Good times are here," "International gathering of the clans," "The 375th anniversary of Acadia," "Seaside spectacular," and the most recent, "There's so much to sea" (see Figure C3-3). These almost annual changes in marketing strategy contributed to the present situation both by confusing the consumer as to what Nova Scotia is all about and by failing to create a focused image based on the relative strengths of the province. Some critics argue that Nova Scotia is not being promoted on its unique features but benefits that other locations can provide as well or better.

Examples of Successful Positioning

Most North Atlantic passengers flying to Europe used to have a vague impression of Belgium. This presented a problem to the tourism authorities, who wanted travellers to stay for longer periods. Part of the problem was a former "Gateway to Europe" campaign that had positioned Belgium as a country to pass through on the way to somewhere else.

The idea for new positioning was found in the *Michelin Guides*, which rate cities as they do restaurants. The Benelux countries have six three-star cities (the highest ranking), of which five are in Belgium and only one (Amsterdam) is in Holland. The theme generated was, "In Belgium, there are five Amsterdams." This strategy was correct in three different ways: (1) it related Belgium to a destination that was known to the traveller, Amsterdam; (2) the *Michelin Guides*, another entity already known to the traveller, gave the concept credibility; and (3) the "five cities to visit" made Belgium a *bona fide* destination.[1]

The state of Florida attracts far more eastern North American beach seekers than does South Carolina. Tourism officials in South Carolina had to find a way in which the state could be positioned against Florida.

The positioning theme generated was, "You get two more days in the sun by coming to Myrtle

Beach, South Carolina, instead of Florida." Florida's major beaches are a one-day drive beyond the Grand Strand of South Carolina — and one additional day back. Most travellers to Florida go in the May-to-October season when the weather is similar to that in South Carolina. Thus, more beach time and less driving became the central benefit by the state.

Positioning Nova Scotia

The benefits of Nova Scotia as a Canadian travel destination cover segments III to VI of U.S. travellers (see Table C3-1). Those providing input to the planning process point out water activities, seaside activities, camping, or scenic activities. The segment interested in foreign adventure could be lured by festivals and other related activities.

FIGURE C3-3 EXAMPLE OF "THERE'S SO MUCH TO SEA" CAMPAIGN

Source: "Nova Scotia Insert," *Travel Weekly*, April 15, 1986.

The argument among planners centres not so much on which benefits to promote, but which should be emphasized if differentiation is desired. The decision is important because of (1) the importance of the industry to the province and (2) the overall rise in competition for the travellers in Nova Scotia's market, especially by U.S. states.

Questions

1. How would you position Nova Scotia to potential American travellers? Use the benefit-matching model to achieve your supermatch.
2. Constructively criticize past positioning attempts, such as "There's so much to sea."

3. What other variables, apart from positioning, will determine whether Americans will choose Nova Scotia as a destination?

Source: This case was written by Arch G. Woodside and Ilkka A. Ronkainen for discussion purposes and not to exemplify correct or incorrect decision making. The case is largely based on Arch G. Woodside, "Positioning a Province Using Travel Research," *Journal of Travel Research* 20 (Winter 1982): 2–6. Reprinted by permission.

Note
1. Al Ries and Jack Trout, *Positioning: The Battle for Your Mind* (New York: McGraw-Hill, 1980), pp. 171–8.

Case 4

MOUNTAIN GALLERY OF ART

Mountain Gallery of Art (MGA) is the only "fine arts" gallery in a certain resort town in the Canadian Rockies. The town has a year-round population of around 10 000, but during the peak tourist season, the population may rise to as much as 30 000. MGA is owned and operated by Jim Dalton and his wife, Susan Dalton. The gallery was formally opened in the fall of 1982 as an independent art gallery. During the first two years of operation, the gallery was never able to make a profit, although the Daltons hoped that eventually it could be made a profit-generating organization. Gross sales for the gallery reached nearly $60 000 by the end of 1985.

MGA began to see a definite increase in sales after 1985. Jim Dalton believes that the finances began to show an improvement because of the quality of the art shown at MGA. The gallery had developed a working relationship with more than 100 artists in the professional field. The work of each of these artists has been carefully screened and analyzed by the directors of the gallery to ensure it is suitable for display at MGA. The Daltons have very high standards, and insist that the gallery carry only works of art of the "highest quality." Susan Dalton points to sales of over $100 000 as evidence of the success of this program.

The retail price of all art work displayed at MGA is set by the artists. Prices are usually in the $500 to $3000 range. The gallery does not attempt to bargain over prices with an individual customer.

The Daltons believe it is the right of the artist to determine the worth of an individual piece of art. They do attempt to advise an artist if they believe that the price set is out of line with similar art work shown at MGA.

MGA receives 40 percent of the retail price of all art sold at the gallery. All work is placed in the gallery on a consignment basis and is fully insured against theft and damage. MGA also provides a framing service for its customers. Sales from the framing department have risen to a point where they account for about 50 percent of the sales of MGA

The gradual increase in sales that started with the opening of the gallery met with a sudden reversal following a local slump in 1988. The decline was rapid and continual, and by the end of 1990, sales for MGA were down to less than $40 000. The Daltons knew something had to be changed in the operation of MGA, but they were not sure exactly what the proper direction should be. Susan felt that if they could encourage more traffic through the gallery, sales might increase. In an attempt to do this, they began exhibiting art work by students of a local college. In addition, the gallery now exhibits on a regular basis reproductions, prints, and posters. These works sell for less than the traditional works the gallery displays, and now Susan Dalton is afraid that this might lessen the quality image of MGA, and decrease sales instead of increasing them.

MGA has also moved into corporate sales by attempting to sell paintings and other works of art to local businesses for their offices. This operation has been moderately successful, but only a few firms have purchased from the gallery. Jim Dalton feels that in corporate selling he might be able to move a few paintings, but he does not feel that this is a way to increase sales by any "substantial amount."

In spite of all their efforts, the Daltons have not been able to put MGA on a profitable basis. In an effort to see if maybe some physical problem exists with the gallery itself, Jim Dalton contacted several artists whom he was friendly with to see if they had any suggestions. All the artists he talked with seemed to think that physically MGA is an excellent place to display art. Many felt that the lighting and space at MGA are comparable to some of the better galleries in Vancouver. None of the artists could make any major suggestions concerning the physical space.

One of the artists did tell Dalton that although the gallery is excellent physically, it is somewhat lacking in the method in which it is managed. He felt a definite lack of creativity in MGA and suggested the gallery is not innovative enough. He even told Dalton that he lacks the correct attitude and energy to sell paintings and other works of art. He seemed to suggest that the Daltons were not "hustlers," and that they should attempt to "push" the art a little more.

This criticism was a surprise to Dalton, because he always felt that they had done well in the past. The Daltons know from experience that "good art sells itself." High-pressure selling would probably drive the customers away. Jim and Susan have always made it a policy that any promotion done for MGA must be of the highest quality, and must not give the gallery a department store image.

In the past, advertising at MGA has been minimal. Occasionally, they place an advertisement in the local paper; and the gallery has always been listed in the yellow pages of the local phone book. The Daltons have always felt that the major form of promotion for MGA should be in direct mailings prior to openings of exhibits. These mailings invite customers to attend the opening, and give some information about the type of art to be displayed. MGA usually has around twelve openings a year. The gallery has a mailing list of approximately 200 previous purchasers or people who have visited the gallery. Everyone on the mailing list always receives an invitation prior to each opening.

One area where Jim and Susan Dalton can see some problems is with the local community. Susan took an informal survey, and less than 50 percent of the local community was even aware that there is a fine-arts gallery in the area. Most of MGA's sales are to people who visit the gallery while on vacation in the area. Even the Daltons' attempts at gaining support from a local college community have not brought much additional revenue to the gallery. They have always hoped that since the gallery was located in the town's major shopping area, the local people would eventually provide the major source of customers.

The Daltons believe they have done everything possible to increase business, and are afraid they will never again be able to make MGA successful. They feel that local advertising has been unsuccessful and are, therefore, considering eliminating it altogether. "No use sending good money after bad!"

Jim and Susan Dalton must soon make a decision on what to do about MGA. They know there must be a market for high-quality professional art, but they are at a loss to locate it. Their sales have always been well received, and the customers who buy are always getting quality for their money. The Daltons know that if they cannot increase the business at the gallery in the very near future, they will have to close it. Neither Jim nor Susan wants to do this, but without more paying customers the end of MGA as a business enterprise will come soon.

Question

1. Prepare a marketing program for MGA by (a) identifying the most appropriate market target(s) and (b) by identifying any required changes in the firm's present marketing mix.

Source: This case was prepared by Professor Eric R. Pratt of New Mexico State University and Professor W. Daniel Rountree of Midwestern State University. This case is designed to be used as a basis for class discussion rather than to illustrate either effective or ineffective handling of an administration situation. Copyright © 1977 by Eric R. Pratt and W. Daniel Rountree. Presented at a Case Workshop and distributed by the Intercollegiate Case Clearing House, Soldiers Field, Boston, Mass., 02163. All rights reserved to the contributors.

PART THREE

Consumer Behaviour

- CHAPTER 7 — CONSUMER BEHAVIOUR
- CHAPTER 8 — INDUSTRIAL BUYER BEHAVIOUR

Case 5 — Aqua-Craft Corporation
Case 6 — Leduc Manufacturing Company

CHAPTER 7

Consumer Behaviour

CHAPTER OBJECTIVES

1. Identify personal and interpersonal influences on consumer behaviour.
2. Distinguish between needs and motives.
3. Explain perception.
4. Describe how attitudes influence behaviour.
5. Demonstrate how learning theory can be applied to marketing strategy.
6. Explain the role of culture in consumer behaviour.
7. Consider the effect of reference groups on consumer behaviour.
8. Understand and explain the consumer decision process.
9. Understand and complete the various activities provided in Chapter 7 of the study guide.

VOCABULARY AND KEY TERMS

From the lettered terms listed below, select the one that best matches the meaning of each of the numbered statements that follows. Write the letter of that choice in the space provided.

a) need
b) motive
c) perception
d) learning
e) drive
f) cue
g) response
h) Weber's law
i) subliminal perception
j) attitudes
k) cognitive dissonance
l) reference groups
m) opinion leaders
n) self-concept
o) culture
p) subculture
q) social class
r) consumer behaviour
s) reinforcement

1. _____ A person's knowledge, enduring favourable or unfavourable evaluations, emotional feelings, and pro and con action tendencies toward some object or idea
2. _____ Any changes in behaviour, immediate or delayed, that occur as a result of experience

3. _____ The groups with which an individual identifies and which set his or her standards and determine behaviour patterns

4. _____ The inner state that directs a person to satisfy a felt need

5. _____ Subgroups with distinguishing modes of behaviour based on factors such as race, age, religion, and location

6. _____ The acts of individuals in obtaining and using goods and services, including the decision processes that precede and determine those acts

7. _____ The individual in a group who is a trend-setter (i.e., who is more likely to purchase new products and serve as an information source for others in the group)

8. _____ Any strong stimulus that impels action during the learning process

9. _____ The complex of values, ideas, attitudes, and other symbols that shape human behaviour and are transmitted from one generation to the next

10. _____ A method of communicating with people without their being aware of the communication process

11. _____ Pre- or postdecision anxiety experienced by a purchaser of goods or services

12. _____ As people perceive by exception, a change in stimulus that is sufficiently great to gain an individual's attention

13. _____ The divisions in a society into which individuals are categorized, based on prestige and community status

14. _____ Any environmental object that represents the nature of one's response to a drive

15. _____ The theory that one's actions, including purchase decisions, are dependent upon one's mental conception of self

16. _____ An individual's reaction to cues and drives

17. _____ The lack of something useful, or the starting point in the purchase-decision process

18. _____ The meaning that each individual attributes to stimuli received through the five senses

19. _____ The reduction in drive that results from a proper response

PRACTICE TEST

True-False: In the space to the right of each statement, check the appropriate line to indicate whether the statement is true or false.

	True	False
1. Consumer behaviour is strictly a function of personal influences.	_____	_____
2. A need must be sufficiently aroused before it can serve as a motive.	_____	_____
3. According to Maslow's hierarchy of needs, an individual will not proceed to a higher-order need until most of his or her lower-order needs have been satisfied.	_____	_____
4. Subliminal advertising can induce individuals to purchase a product even if they did not consciously see it advertised.	_____	_____
5. It is generally easier to change a product to match consumer attitudes than to make the attitudes of consumers consonant with the product.	_____	_____
6. Needs are inner states that direct us toward the goal of satisfying a felt motive.	_____	_____
7. A person can satisfy safety needs only after physiological needs have been completely satisfied.	_____	_____

8. The Michelin Tire ad with the baby sitting on the rim of the tire exploits the desire to satisfy a safety need. _____ _____

9. With esteem needs the individual desires not only acceptance but also recognition and respect. _____ _____

10. Empirical research supports the existence of a universal ordering of needs in specific individuals. _____ _____

11. Our perception of an object or event is the result of the interaction of two types of factors: stimulus factors and individual factors. _____ _____

12. In this chapter, psychophysics is tied to Weber's law. _____ _____

13. A subconscious level of awareness relates to the concept of selective perception. _____ _____

14. Subliminal perception is aimed at the subconscious level of awareness so as to avoid the perceptual screens or viewers. _____ _____

15. The affective component of attitudes is the information and knowledge one has about an object. _____ _____

16. Culture is the broadest environmental determinant of consumer behaviour. _____ _____

17. Once a marketing program has been proven successful in Canada, it can be applied directly to a foreign country. _____ _____

18. Canada has many subcultures but only one founding culture — English. _____ _____

19. The influence that groups and group norms can exert on individual behaviour has been called the Asch phenomenon. _____ _____

20. In order for a group to influence an individual, that individual must be a member of the group. _____ _____

21. Selected reference groups have little influence on whether or not people smoke cigars or on what brand they choose. _____ _____

22. Income is a main determinant of social class. _____ _____

23. Syncratic decisions are those that are made independently by one partner or the other. _____ _____

24. The search process is the second stage in the decision process. _____ _____

25. The number of brands that a consumer actually considers in making a purchase decision is known as the evoked set. _____ _____

Multiple Choice: Choose the expression that best answers the question or best completes the sentence.

26. Personal influences on consumer behaviour include all of the following, except
   a. individual needs and motives
   b. individual perceptions
   c. reference groups
   d. attitudes

27. Interpersonal influences on consumer behaviour include
   a. reference groups
   b. culture
   c. social class
   d. the family
   e. all of the above

28. The lack of something useful is called a(n)
a. motive
b. need
c. cue
d. drive
e. attitude

29. If the Bennetts have been satisfied Buick owners for 30 years, they will probably not be affected by automobile advertisements because selective perception
a. ignores information not in keeping with experience
b. has no effect on them
c. stores information about the rejected alternatives in the mind
d. keeps them informed

30. The slogan that most closely appeals to the safety needs of a consumer is
a. "Canon personal copiers, nothing but the originals."
b. "Mazda, it just feels right."
c. "American Express — don't leave home without it."
d. "Can't beat the feeling! Coca-Cola Classic."
e. "Canadian, Our world revolves around you."

31. Kurt Henry ate dinner at the Bon Ton Cafe because he wanted to use the 20-percent discount coupon that he clipped from the newspaper advertisement. He was so impressed with the food and service that he plans to return tomorrow night. This is an example of the learning process that is called a
a. response — clip coupon
b. cue — restaurant service
c. reinforcement — cheap price
d. cue — newspaper coupon
e. drive — desire for money

32. In the purchase decision process, the "evoked set" includes
a. all brands and types of products that may be capable of doing the intended job
b. only those brands and types of products suitable for the job with which the consumer may have had previous experience
c. those brands and types of products that the consumer is aware of and that have not been excluded because they are too costly, because they have been unsatisfactory in prior use, or because they have a negative image due to advertising or word-of-mouth communications
d. only one product — the one that is ultimately chosen
e. the various problems that the consumer seeks to solve with some scheme to prioritize them

33. In the study of social class it was found that
a. income is the main determinant of social class behaviour
b. an individual's activities, interests, opinions, and buying behaviour were significantly affected by social class
c. reference groups were more a factor affecting consumer behaviour
d. it is more meaningful to think of differences among individuals in terms of variations in lifestyles
e. b and d

34. In a study that assessed the extent of reference-group influence on product and brand choices, this influence was found to be weak for product and brand for
a. automobiles
b. colour television
c. golf clubs

d. cigarettes
e. furniture

35. In the study that assessed the extent of reference-group influence on product and brand choices, reference-group influence was found to be weak for product but strong for brand for
a. automobiles
b. colour television
c. golf clubs
d. cigarettes
e. furniture

36. Cognitive dissonance
a. is buyer confusion generated by the number of brands available in marketplace
b. is predecision anxiety related to the purchase of a product
c. increases as the dollar value of the purchase increases and when the rejected alternatives have desirable features not present in the chosen alternative
d. is dissatisfaction with the brand or type of good that is presently being used
e. is the step in the decision process that follows search

37. Which of the following statements about status and role is untrue?
a. Status is one's relative position within a group.
b. A role consists of the expectations that group members have of an individual of a certain status in the group.
c. Within family groups, there are no status and role distinctions.
d. Group membership is a prerequisite for acquiring status and role.

38. Which of the following is not a subculture?
a. Italian Canadians
b. Mormons
c. doctors
d. West Coast residents

39. Marketing research studies are useful in determining the following concerning the buying habits of consumers:
a. whether or not a given product does what it is supposed to do
b. who the consumers are and when and where they buy
c. what and how consumers buy
d. b and c
e. none of the above

40. Which of the following is not a basic determinant of consumer behaviour?
a. aspirations
b. motives
c. attitudes
d. perceptions
e. needs

41. The most basic need in Maslow's hierarchy is
a. safety need
b. social need
c. physiological need
d. the need to excel
e. all of the above

42. Maslow's need hierarchy is based upon certain important assumptions. Which of the following is not one of these assumptions?
   a. Our needs are arranged in a hierarchy of importance.
   b. Our primary motivation is economic.
   c. As soon as one need is at least partially satisfied, another emerges and demands satisfaction.
   d. Only the needs that have not been satisfied can influence behaviour.
   e. We are wanting animals, whose needs depend upon what we already possess.

43. Which of the following slogans most appeals to safety needs?
   a. "Fly the friendly skies of United."
   b. "Kawasaki lets the good times roll."
   c. "You're in good hands with Allstate."
   d. "First-class all the way with Samsonite."

44. Which of the following statements is not one of the reasons subliminal advertising cannot induce purchasing?
   a. Strong stimulus factors are required just to gain perception.
   b. Stimulus must be consciously understood to induce purchasing.
   c. Only a very short message can be transmitted.
   d. Individuals vary greatly in their thresholds of consciousness.
   e. A subliminal message may not be perceived the same way by different individuals.

45. From where do the most important influences on consumer purchase actions come?
   a. social class
   b. family
   c. reference groups
   d. cultural environment
   e. all of the above

46. For the influence of a reference group to be great, which of the following factors must be present?
   a. The item must be one that can be seen and identified by others.
   b. The item must be conspicuous.
   c. The item must be a brand or product that not everyone owns.
   d. all of the above
   e. a and b

47. Opinion leaders
   a. tend to be generalized in scope of product influence
   b. are characterized by considerable knowledge and interest in a particular product or service
   c. are found within all segments of the population
   d. b and c
   e. none of the above

48. The consumer decision process involves the following stages, in order:
   a. problem recognition, evaluation of alternatives, purchase decision, postpurchase evaluation, search, purchase act
   b. problem recognition, search, purchase decision, evaluation of alternatives, purchase act, post-purchase evaluation
   c. evaluation of alternatives, problem recognition, search, purchase decision, purchase act, post-purchase evaluation
   d. problem recognition, search, evaluation of alternatives, purchase decision, purchase act, post-purchase evaluation

49. A phenomenon closely associated with postpurchase evaluation is
a. cognitive dissonance
b. cognitive anxiety
c. postpurchase inadequacy
d. a and b
e. none of the above

50. All of the following are examples of an internal search for information except
a. actual personal experiences
b. personal observations
c. store displays
d. memories of exposures to persuasive marketing efforts
e. information stored in memory dealing with similar products

ANSWER KEY: CHAPTER 7

Vocabulary and Key Terms	True-False	Multiple Choice
1. j	1. F	26. c
2. d	2. T	27. e
3. l	3. T	28. b
4. b	4. F	29. a
5. p	5. T	30. c
6. r	6. F	31. d
7. m	7. F	32. c
8. e	8. T	33. e
9. o	9. T	34. d
10. i	10. F	35. e
11. k	11. T	36. c
12. h	12. T	37. c
13. q	13. F	38. c
14. f	14. T	39. d
15. n	15. F	40. a
16. g	16. T	41. c
17. a	17. F	42. b
18. c	18. F	43. c
19. s	19. T	44. b
	20. F	45. e
	21. T	46. d
	22. F	47. d
	23. F	48. d
	24. T	49. a
	25. T	50. c

EXERCISE 7.1: SUBLIMINAL SEDUCTION — REAL OR UNREAL?

Is it possible to communicate with persons without their being aware of the communication? The process is referred to as subliminal perception. A message may be inserted into a film, one frame every five seconds for 1/300th of a second, or placed in a magazine ad aimed at the subconscious level of awareness of the viewer. This practice is condemned in Canada as being not only unethical but also illegal. Yet the onus of proof is on the accuser. The advertiser can simply declare that the accuser is imagining things that are not really there.

In his two books, *Subliminal Seduction* and *The Clam-Plate Orgy*, Wilson Bryan Key contends that some advertisers are making frequent use of subliminals. For example, an ad for Johnny Walker Scotch appeared in virtually every U.S. national magazine (e.g., *Playboy*, *Time*, *Newsweek*, and *The New Yorker*) over a three-year period. The ad pictured a drink glass with five ice cubes in the glass and one cube on the table outside the glass. The caption under the glass reads: "The road to success is paved with rocks. Let us smooth them for you." Key states that "an estimated $2 million was invested in magazine space in which to display this single ad, which must have been extremely successful in selling Scotch to have justified the prodigious investment.... At a $2 million investment level, this ad would have to sell $33 million in JW Scotch to break even." As Key says, nobody is in business to just break even, and this investment of $2 million would have to gross $50 million in order to pay for itself.

According to Key, the rocks (ice cubes) represent images that involve nightmares, hallucinations, self-destruction, and self-immolation. Why such images? It is Key's contention that this company is attempting to reach heavy alcohol consumers with this ad. He states that "it is impossible to spend much time around alcohol consumers, especially those who have not yet been formally classified as alcoholics, without becoming aware they are involved in some monstrous kind of self-destructive syndrome ... alcoholic consumption easily becomes addictive, leading the compulsive drinker into indescribable agonies undreamed of even by Dante." Recognize, too, that these images are perceived below one's threshold of conscious awareness.

Martin Steiner, a student at the University of Alberta working part-time for Kinsley Advertising Agency, a small firm in the business, has read both books by Key, with interest and with inner trepidation. He is suspicious that Joe Hardy, a member of the firm, is using subliminals in magazine ads placed for a certain brewery. Martin feels this practice is morally wrong but does not have absolute proof that Hardy is involved. Besides, even if he had proof, does it really matter, as "everyone," according to Key, appears to be involved with it? He would like to become permanently employed in advertising when he graduates from university, but he feels cynical about the industry because of the "subliminal" issue.

Questions

1. Do you believe advertisers are using subliminals in advertising or does Key have an overactive imagination? Discuss.
2. Should Martin Steiner ignore his suspicions of Joe Hardy's involvement with subliminals? What should he do?
3. What advice would you give Martin with respect to his apprehension about a career in advertising?

Source: Wilson Bryan Key, *The Clam-Plate Orgy* (New York: New American Library, 1981), pp. 29, 32–3. Reprinted by permission.

EXERCISE 7.2: TILLIE SMITH REFUTES THE SOCIAL-CLASS CONCEPT

Tillie Smith takes introductory marketing at a southern Ontario community college. Her professor, Blarney Twist, has just finished lecturing on social class; she is skeptical of this concept and decides to approach her professor after class. "Professor Twist," Tillie says, "you make social class sound like a caste system in which everyone is pigeonholed on the basis of class. Those in lower class seem to be relegated to that class because they happen to make less money than those in the classes above them.

"I don't believe people can be so easily categorized. For instance, my mother's brother, Sam Smedley, is a moderately successful businessman who acquired wealth a few years ago when an unknown relative in London, England, left him an unexpected inheritance of approximately nine million dollars. According to what I've heard this morning on social class, I'm guessing he would now be placed in the upper social class; yet he has continued to operate his business since the windfall. He has renovated his home but the family still lives at the same address, and his friends have not changed. The Smedleys still belong to the same bridge club and bowl every Thursday. The inheritance has made it possible for them to send their daughter to York University; but has their class really changed?"

Without giving Blarney Twist a chance to respond, Tillie continues: "It seems to me that reference groups have more of an affect than social class on consumer behaviour. Sam and Sarah Smedley still associate with the same crowd and belong to most of the same clubs. In the way they dress, the cars they drive, the restaurants and the stores they visit, and the events they attend, they are quite similar to their friends.

"Therefore, Professor Twist," says Tillie, "would you not agree that reference groups have a greater influence on consumer behaviour than social class? Furthermore, doesn't my example of Sam Smedley show that social class is really an invalid concept?"

Questions

1. What are the determinants of social class? Relate these determinants to the Sam Smedley example. On the basis of your knowledge of social class, how would you explain Sam's behaviour?
2. Why is it false to say that a rich person is simply a poor person with more money? Does this statement apply to Sam Smedley?
3. How would you respond to the closing statement made by Tillie to Professor Twist? Is social-class theory in conflict with reference-group theory? Discuss.

CHAPTER 8

Industrial Buyer Behaviour

CHAPTER OBJECTIVES

1. Define, explain, or describe the key terms listed under "Vocabulary and Key Terms."
2. Relate buying behaviour in individual and government markets to the variable of the marketing mix.
3. Differentiate among the three types of industrial markets.
4. Identify the three distinctive features of industrial markets.
5. Identify the major characteristics of industrial market demand.
6. Outline the basic categories of industrial products.
7. Discuss the nature of the industrial purchase.
8. Distinguish between a straight rebuy, a modified rebuy, and new task buying.
9. Explain the buying centre concept.
10. Explain the steps in the industrial purchasing process.
11. Compare government markets to other industrial markets.
12. Apply your knowledge of Chapter 8 in a case analysis.

VOCABULARY AND KEY TERMS

From the lettered terms listed below, select the one that best matches the meaning of each of the numbered statements that follows. Write the letter of that choice in the space provided.

a) bid
b) capital item
c) consumer market
d) derived demand
e) expense item
f) buying centre
g) industrial market
h) joint demand
i) modified rebuy
j) new task buying
k) producers
l) reciprocity
m) Standard Industrial Classification
n) straight rebuy

1. _____ The demand for an industrial good to be used jointly with another industrial good
2. _____ The demand for an industrial product that is linked to demand for a consumer good
3. _____ A marketplace made up of customers who purchase goods and services for use in producing other products for resale

4. _____ Long-lived business assets that must be depreciated over time

5. _____ Industrial customers who purchase goods and services for the production of other goods and services

6. _____ In the industrial market, the highly controversial practice of extending purchasing preference to suppliers who are also customers

7. _____ Those individuals who buy goods and services for personal use

8. _____ In the industrial market, a written sales proposal from a vendor to an organization or firm that wants to purchase a good or service

9. _____ A classification system developed for use in collecting detailed information about the various industries that make up the industrial market

10. _____ Everyone who participates in some way in an industrial buying action

11. _____ Products and services used within a short time

12. _____ A recurring purchase decision, where an item that has performed satisfactorily is purchased again by a customer

13. _____ Purchasers willing to reevaluate their available options

14. _____ First-time or unique purchase situations requiring considerable effort by decision makers

PRACTICE TEST

True-False: In the space to the right of each statement, check the appropriate line to indicate whether a statement is true or false.

		True	False
1.	The buying centre is a wholesale exchange system in which industrial buyers parlay their wares.	_____	_____
2.	Reverse reciprocity is the extension of purchasing preference to suppliers who are also customers.	_____	_____
3.	When two products have a joint demand relationship, the reduction in quantity demand for product X has a direct effect on the quantity demand of product Y.	_____	_____
4.	Buyer behaviour varies significantly depending on how the purchaser is treated from an accounting viewpoint.	_____	_____
5.	Capital items are long-lived business assets that must be depreciated over time.	_____	_____
6.	Industrial goods must be products provided for direct use in consumer goods and service.	_____	_____
7.	A recent trend in government purchasing is increased emphasis on special order contracts rather than on off-the-shelf products.	_____	_____
8.	The addition of a rare stamp to a stamp collector's collection is an example of an industrial purchase.	_____	_____
9.	Relatively uniform buying patterns for industrial goods result in the development of a classification system based upon product uses.	_____	_____
10.	Trade industries are organizations, such as retailers and wholesalers, that purchase for resale to others.	_____	_____
11.	The government is very small in comparison to other industrial markets.	_____	_____

12. There are over 38 000 manufacturers in Canada and the total value added by production in 1986 was $107 billion.

13. The value added by manufacturing is the increase in value of input material when transformed into semi-finished or finished goods.

14. The market for industrial goods in Canada is much less concentrated geographically than that for consumer goods.

15. The industrial market is widely scattered and characterized by a large number of small buyers.

16. Wholesalers are less frequently used in the industrial market, and the marketing channel for industrial goods is typically much shorter than that for consumer goods.

17. The SIC code is made up of eighteen individual divisions, and under each division is a list of major groups into which all types of business are divided.

18. Derived demand as a concept is not affected by the economic state of the economy at any particular time.

19. The relative impact that changes in consumer demand have upon industrial market demand is called the accelerator principle.

20. Expense items tend to be used over a longer period of time than capital items.

21. The purchasing agent normally is the key person in the organization responsible for decisions relating to all purchases, whether it be minor expense items or major installations.

22. The purchase of component parts is an example of a straight rebuy purchase situation in which purchasers are willing to reevaluate their available options.

23. The law specifies that most government purchases must be made on the basis of bids, that is, quotes from interested potential customers.

24. Personal selling is the main element in the promotional mix of most industrial firms.

25. Government expenditures account for more than half of Canada's gross domestic product.

Multiple Choice: Choose the expression that best answers the question or best completes the sentence.

26. A modified rebuy occurs
  a. when suppliers re-evaluate their available options
  b. when industrial purchasers use established purchasing guidelines to look at alternative product offerings
  c. because of a change in perceived quality and cost difference
  d. a and b
  e. all of the above

27. Reciprocity is most likely to occur in which of the following instances?
  a. Products of competing suppliers are relatively homogeneous.
  b. Derived demand is characteristic of the industry.

   c.   The prices of competing products are similar.
   d.   Customer firms produce products needed by supplier firms.
   e.   a, c, and d

28.   Trade industries consist of
   a.   the government
   b.   wholesalers
   c.   retailers
   d.   producers
   e.   b and c

29.   Producers consist of
   a.   manufacturing firms
   b.   farmers
   c.   service providers to industrial firms such as banks
   d.   wholesalers and retailers
   e.   a, b, and c

30.   Which of the following is not one of the three distinctive features of the industrial market?
   a.   geographic market concentration
   b.   the buying centre concept
   c.   a relatively small number of buyers
   d.   systematic buying procedures

31.   If the economy is strong, the consumer will be more likely to buy automobiles, refrigerators, and other products made of steel; this will further stimulate sales of steel to manufacturers who make those products. This is a good example of
   a.   joint demand
   b.   demand variability
   c.   inventory adjustment
   d.   derived demand
   e.   elastic demand

32.   Organizational purchases tend to be more complex than consumer purchases because
   a.   they are more geographically spread out
   b.   the cost per item is much lower
   c.   they require the approval of more people
   d.   the item(s) being purchased is/are more complex
   e.   there is an abundance of sales representation

33.   The disproportionate impact that changes in consumer demand have upon industrial markets is called the
   a.   accelerator principle
   b.   demand variability factor
   c.   concept of derived demand
   d.   reverse reciprocity factor
   e.   principle of joint demand

34.   Major installations such as a new plant or assembly line equipment are examples of
   a.   expense items
   b.   capital items
   c.   component parts
   d.   convenience goods
   e.   manufacturing items

35. Which of the following is not one of the reasons for the increased complexity of industrial purchase behaviour?
   a. Many persons may exert influence in industrial purchases, and considerable time may be spent in obtaining the input and approval of various organizational members.
   b. Many organizations attempt to utilize several sources of supply as a type of insurance against shortages.
   c. The purchasing agent is the key player and the final decision will rest with this office even though considerable consultation will be carried out within the organization.
   d. Organizational purchasing may be handled by committees with greater time requirements for majority or unanimous approval.

36. Marketers who service accounts that are in the straight rebuy category should
   a. maintain a good relationship with the account by providing adequate service and delivery
   b. try to assess the factors that would make the account want to reconsider its decision
   c. provide the account with enough substantive information about the product that direct comparisons with competing products can be more easily made
   d. sell other accounts; these straight rebuys accounts are "in the bag" and really don't need any service
   e. try to lower the price in order to increase the quantity of purchase

37. In which of these rebuying situations is it critical for the industrial marketer to work very closely with the purchaser?
   a. straight rebuy
   b. modified rebuy
   c. new task buying
   d. none of the above
   e. a, b, and c

38. The person who controls the information to be reviewed by other members of the buying centre is the
   a. decider
   b. user
   c. influencer
   d. gatekeeper
   e. buyer

39. The buying situation in which purchasers are willing to re-evaluate their available options is called a
   a. straight rebuy
   b. modified rebuy
   c. new-task situation
   d. negotiable rebuy
   e. complex rebuy

40. Reverse reciprocity mainly emerges
   a. during periods of prosperity
   b. in times of production surpluses
   c. in times of shortages
   d. only during periods of high inflation
   e. as part of a rebate program of the manufacturer

41. At what stage in the industrial buying process model does word-of-mouth on the product mainly occur?
   a. need recognition
   b. information search

c. delineation of suppliers
d. review of internal proposals
e. final decision

42. Government expenditures represent
a. approximately 20 percent of Canada's gross domestic product
b. 52 percent of Canada's gross domestic product
c. 35 percent of Canada's gross domestic product
d. an insignificant percentage of gross domestic product
e. a high percentage of gross domestic product, with the actual percentage being unknown because the federal government does not permit publication of these figures

43. The Canada–U.S. Free Trade Agreement requires that both countries
a. recognize that sales to each other's government are not permitted
b. open their tendering to suppliers from the other country
c. permit sales between governments on a nonbid basis
d. operate their tendering method in line with the practice used in the United States
e. b and d

44. The demand for steel can be derived from the demand for automobiles. If the demand for automobiles declines, auto manufacturers may delay further purchase of steel. This is an example of which form of demand?
a. inelastic
b. joint demand
c. inventory adjustments
d. demand variability
e. none of the above

45. Research by Agarwal, Burger, and Venkatesh suggested the process model of industrial buyer behaviour, listing the steps in the following order:
a. information search, need recognition, delineation of suppliers, sales demonstration/proposal, word-of-mouth, final decision
b. need recognition, delineation of suppliers, information search, sales demonstration/proposal, word-of-mouth, final decision
c. need recognition, delineation of suppliers, sales demonstration/proposal, final decision, word-of-mouth
d. need recognition, information search, delineation of suppliers, sales demonstration/proposal, word-of-mouth, final decision

46. The industrial market consists of
a. producers, trade industries, and consumers
b. producers, government, and suppliers
c. producers, trade industries, and government
d. trade industries, government, and foreign nations

47. Which of the following statements is not correct regarding the government market?
a. There is less paperwork than in private industry.
b. Tax exemptions are available.
c. There is timely payment for purchases.
d. There is enhanced opportunity for future sales to government once the first sale is made.
e. It is a relatively stable market.

48. When the demand for some industrial goods is related to the demand for other industrial goods, it is called
a. derived demand

b.   joint demand
c.   inventory adjustment
d.   demand variability
e.   none of the above

49. The demand for cash registers is affected considerably by demand at the retail level. This is an example of
a.   derived demand
b.   joint demand
c.   inventory adjustment
d.   demand elasticity
e.   none of the above

50. A raw materials supplier is bombarded with new orders, following rumours of a major price increase. This is an example of
a.   derived demand
b.   joint demand
c.   inventory adjustment
d.   demand variability
e.   none of the above

ANSWER KEY: CHAPTER 8

Vocabulary and Key Terms	True-False	Multiple Choice
1. h	1. F	26. e
2. d	2. F	27. e
3. g	3. T	28. e
4. b	4. F	29. e
5. k	5. T	30. b
6. l	6. F	31. d
7. c	7. F	32. c
8. a	8. F	33. a
9. m	9. T	34. b
10. f	10. T	35. c
11. e	11. F	36. a
12. n	12. T	37. c
13. i	13. T	38. d
14. j	14. F	39. b
	15. F	40. c
	16. T	41. d
	17. T	42. b
	18. F	43. e
	19. T	44. d
	20. F	45. d
	21. F	46. c
	22. F	47. a
	23. T	48. b
	24. T	49. a
	25. T	50. c

EXERCISE 8-1: INDUSTRIAL BUYING BEHAVIOUR

Huron Electric produces light bulbs in a wide array of wattages for retailers to sell to ultimate consumers. They also produce light bulbs and lamps to the individual specifications of equipment manufacturers in the automobile and other industries. As well, the company manufactures photographic light bulbs and bulbs for street lamps.

Sales for 1990 were down 10 percent from those of the previous year. At a general meeting of Huron Electric, Joe Wroclawski, the marketing manager, wonders aloud how the light bulb company can improve its market share. Joe says, "We are a small player in this industry when compared with Canadian General Electric and others, so we must find ways of letting industrial buyers know about our products. We have some good salespeople, and they have been well trained; but I wonder if they are getting our message to the right people in these organizations."

Monique Lebeau, the advertising manager, responds: "It is obviously critical to get our message to the decision maker in each buyer's organization. Maybe we should make more effective use of advertising in order to make it easier for the salesperson to get in to see that decision maker. We have to think of ways of co-ordinating our advertising and sales effort to maximize our goals in a way that in the end will translate to greater market share."

"The downturn in the economy has affected our sales," says Marty Rubachuk, the production manager. "And the demand for light bulbs is derived from sales of consumer goods. If the market continues to slide, then I don't expect us to rebound. Not only is our market tied closely to the consumer market, it is also affected by the demand for other industrial products. Derived demand in the light-bulb industry is related to, and often creates, immense variability in industrial demand. I'm sure we recognize how vulnerable we are to the economy and to decisions made by others that affect our industry."

Joe calls the meeting to a close after further discussion. All parties agree to meet the next morning to decide on a concrete approach to being more aggressive in the marketplace.

Questions

1. Who constitutes the market for light bulbs?
2. How can the principle of derived market demand be applied to the sale of light bulbs and lamps to the industrial market?
3. Is the decision to buy Huron bulbs and lamps made only by the purchasing agent of a company or are other people involved? Is it important for Huron to identify which people will be involved in a purchase decision? Why or why not?
4. Describe situations involving the purchase of light bulbs and lamps that would be defined as (a) a straight rebuy, (b) a modified rebuy, and (c) a new-task situation.
5. What type of promotion would be the most effective in reaching the decision maker within an organization? Discuss.

EXERCISE 8-2: THE INDUSTRIAL BUYING PROCESS

In the past ten years, the Dilly Company has relied on Easy Business Datatron to maintain Dilly's information-system network. Most of the company's internal records (including sales records and cost data) are also kept by Easy Business Datatron.

Dilly is in the business of producing plastic pipes and tubes for use in the production operations of various businesses. Some customers need plastic pipes and tubes soon after placing their orders. Unfortunately, Dilly has recently experienced delays in retrieving information, from Easy Business Datatron's system, that was vital in making bids on specific customer contracts. In some cases the company lost contracts because bids weren't submitted on time. Dilly wants a cost-efficient and effective method for processing information, and is considering discontinuing its relationship with Easy Datatron and converting to a company-owned microcomputer system.

If Dilly proceeds with this conversion, many activities not performed by Easy Business Datatron, such as inventory control and physical distribution planning, could be tied into the system. The company has enlisted Beatrice Wolfchild to research whether or not the system should be installed, and if so, how. Beatrice is using the model of the industrial buying process (Figure 8-5, *Foundations of Marketing*) to clarify her own thinking and to arrive at a recommendation for the company. Put yourself in the position of Beatrice and complete the following.

Questions

1. What event triggered the need?
2. What information search should be conducted?
3. What procedure should be followed in the next two steps (i.e., delineation of suppliers and sales demonstration/proposals)?
4. Before you make a final decision, what should be done during stage two? Present your ideas.

Case 5

AQUA-CRAFT CORPORATION

Aqua-Craft manufactures a broad line of boats designed for the mass market. The fifty models in the line include cruisers, runabouts, canoes, sailboats, and utility and fishing boats. The company follows a competitive pricing policy, with specific prices ranging from $149 for a nine-foot flat bottom to $4495 for an inboard or outboard cruiser. The boats are distributed by the company's own sales force and by the salespersons of five independent distributors to more than 150 dealers located throughout Canada.

The company has enjoyed a remarkable rate of growth. Sales increased from $520 000 in 1950 to $1.3 million in 1960. Despite a levelling-off trend in industry sales in the 1960s, Aqua-Craft continued to grow, and by 1979 sales reached an all-time high of $3 million.

By the summer of 1983, however, management was becoming increasingly concerned about the ability of the company to sustain its past rate of growth. Management felt that its past differential advantages were likely to become less effective in the future.

The company has pioneered numerous technological innovations in boat construction and was generally regarded by dealers and boat owners as a quality builder. However, it was becoming apparent, particularly in recent years, that competitors could match the company's manufacturing expertise. As a consequence, management wondered how long it could rely on its quality image to stimulate increased sales.

The company's other major differential advantage — a strong dealer organization — also showed signs of decaying. In recent years many of the company's independent distributors began carrying two or three other lines of boats. Because there were minimal differences in the profitability of these lines, many distributors were not pushing the Aqua-Craft line to the degree that they had in the past. Although the company was finding it more and more difficult to exert the desired degree of control over distributors, it had decided, at least for the time being, that it would have to accept the system, because the investment required to establish company-owned distribution was considered prohibitive.

The growing number of competitors, particularly large firms like Chrysler, was also a source of concern. If a large competitor decided to get into the boat business in a major way, management feared that the company's sales and market share would decline precipitously.

Current Use of Consumer Behaviour Information

In the past, the company made only minimal use of information on consumer attitudes and behaviour. Product strategies were formulated largely on the basis of the availability and price of materials, on metals technology, and on production-run considerations. The company always depended on executive insights and hunches about what consumers want in boats. In the company's early years, this seemed to be a workable strategy, because the company manufactured only fishing boats and because many executives — particularly Hull and Claude Whipple, the company's founders — were, as sporting enthusiasts, intimately familiar with the desirable attributes of this type of boat.

Several developments in recent years convinced many of Aqua-Craft's executives that executive intuition about consumer attitudes was a risky approach to product strategy considerations. The company had expanded into other lines of boats, and company executives knew less about what consumers were looking for. Moreover, most competitors were producing boats with nearly identical functional features. As a result, competitors were shifting other dimensions: styling, colour, trim configurations, and so on. It was becoming increasingly difficult to estimate which of these dimensions would be most effective in establishing brand preference. And the cost of estimating incorrectly was rising because of the dramatic increase in inventory investment resulting from product-line proliferation.

Pricing decisions also were made almost completely independent of consumer considerations. The company balanced cost and competitive price considerations in setting prices. All models were priced to provide the maximum contribution to overhead and profit and to still be reasonably close to competitor's prices. In the past, the models not making any contribution to overhead and profit were dropped from the line. The company had done little experimenting with price variations, and executives admitted that they did not really know how important price was when consumers were deciding between different brands.

The company had relied mainly on the judgement of the independent distributors in selecting dealers to handle Aqua-Craft boats. In the past, distributors had been fairly successful in achieving broad distribution for the line. In the past few years, however, problems have arisen. The growing number of boat manufacturers caused many distributors to become brand-indifferent, and many dealers reduced the number of brands carried in order to minimize their investment in inventory. Management was wondering whether or not the importance of various types of dealers was changing, whether the company had distribution with the right types of dealers, and how intense distribution should be.

The amount to be spent on advertising was determined by applying a fixed percentage of forecast sales (1.5 percent). Readership studies of boat owners conducted by boating magazines were used to select advertising media and vehicles.

Sources of Consumer Behaviour Information

Aqua-Craft learned about the behaviour of boat owners from several sources. Distributor invoices were used to tabulate boat sales by model, price, colour, style, and geographic location. This information was used along with comparable data for the entire industry to product sales and schedule production inventory requirements.

The company collected similar information from its warranty program. The company guarantees its boats against defects in workmanship and in materials, providing certain conditions are met. The information from the warranty card is used by management to analyze the movement of boats by model, colour, price, and geographic location.

Occasionally, the company's advertising agency conducted studies dealing with various dimensions of consumer behaviour. The agency has determined how sales vary by occupation and the reasons people buy boats.

First, it was found that sales to various occupational groups followed the pattern of their segment of the industry. Skilled workers accounted for 23.6 percent of sales, followed by semiskilled workers with 19.3 percent, and professionals with 16.9 percent. In addition, the following were the reasons stated as to why people buy boats (total exceeds 100 percent because of multiple mention):

	%
Cruising	53
Fishing	41
Hunting	8
Water-skiing	62
All other	6

These were the only internal sources of information about consumer behaviour available to management. Information from external sources was limited to publicly circulated industry reports. Typically, these dealt with industry sales patterns by manufacturer and model with the reasons people buy boats.

Current Problems

By spring, management was growing increasingly concerned about the lack of information pertaining to the market they were attempting to penetrate. This came to a head when the media schedule was being finalized. The advertising agency proposed that the company follow the same schedule with the same publications as used in the past, including *Field and Stream*, *Yachting*, *Popular Science*, *Popular Mechanics*, and *Motor Boating*. Past advertisements had shown boating as a quiet, restful sport (fishing and cruising) or as a social activity involving water-skiing and attractive young people.

Management's greatest concerns were caused by the increasing role of teenagers in the decision to purchase a boat. It was felt that the homemaker has a significant say as well, especially in view of the major expenditure required. Therefore, the advertising agency was directed to undertake a study to show the relative influence of various members of the family in the purchase of a boat.

Questions

1. Has management focused on the most important research question? Are there other types of information about the decision process that should be a higher priority?
2. Outline the way in which the agency should proceed in determining the roles of family

members in the purchase of a boat. What types of questions should be asked? Who should be interviewed?
3. Indicate the specific ways that the results of the family decision-making study could be used in designing marketing strategy.

Source: Roger Blackwell, James Engel, and David Kollat, *Cases in Consumer Behaviour*, Copyright 1969 by Holt, Rinehart and Winston, Inc. Reprinted by permission of the Dryden Press. Some materials are disguised.

Case 6

LEDUC MANUFACTURING COMPANY

On October 3, 1984, William R. Nelson, division manager of Leduc Manufacturing Company and vice-president of its multimillion-dollar conglomerate parent company, has called a meeting of the division's top echelon to expedite the launch of a new line of pipes and tubing. He is chagrined that, according to production manager Ian McMichaels, the scheduled commercialization date of July 1, 1985, cannot be met.

This impatience is shared by Dale N. Schroder, Ph.D. (chemical engineering), director of research and development, who personally contributed much to the new line. Also attending is controller Frank B. Abt, RIA, an enthusiastic advocate of formal planning. The final participant is J. Robertson (Bob) Hellas, sales manager. All of these executives, now in their 50s, have been with the division a long time.

Sales Department

A major producer of plastic pipes and tubes, Leduc Manufacturing Company has a functional organization. (See Figure C6-1.) In the sales department, executives reporting to Bob Hellas include four regional industrial sales managers (corresponding to Leduc's four factories), an advertising manager, and a consumer-goods product manager. The regional sales managers supervise 35 salespersons. The sales force obtains leads and exhortations from headquarters and from regional sales managers, but, by and large, they make up their own sched-

ules. In addition to prospecting for orders, following up customers, and so on, an important part of their job is verifying that distributors are well stocked with Leduc's wares.

Compensation of the sales force is salary plus 10 percent commission on total dollar sales above individual quota. On the average, salespersons' earnings derive 50 percent from salary and 50 percent from commission. Leduc also reimburses each salesperson for travel and entertainment expenses in accordance with the company's policy manual.

Leduc confines its industrial advertising to reminder-type messages in specialized industry periodicals serving the division's markets. An advertising manager, Peter Munn, was hired in 1984. A former public relations officer, he deals with Leduc's industrial sales promotion campaigns; designs collateral materials such as catalogues, brochures, point-of-purchase displays, and booklets; reserves space at trade shows; releases publicity; and relieves the sales manager of other nonselling promotional tasks.

Consumer goods, mainly garden hose and sprinklers, are under the jurisdiction of Tony Pasco. Determination of consumer goods' brand names, prices, advertisements and sales promotions, and distribution channels is separate from the industrial unit. Hellas is very satisfied with the profit and progress of this subdivision and lets product manager Pasco run it almost autonomously on a modest budget. According to the controller, this business could and should be tripled, even at the risk of losing some component business, i.e., sales of plastic piping and tubing to lawn equipment manufacturers.

FIGURE C6-1 ORGANIZATION OF LEDUC MANUFACTURING COMPANY

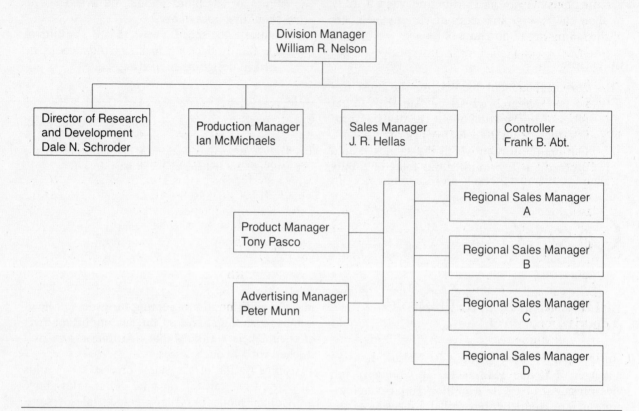

Product Lines

In 1983, sales of Leduc plastic tubes and pipes amounted to $53 million — about the same as in 1982 and 1981. The burgeoning department of consumer goods registered a new high of $340 000 in 1983.

On tubes and pipes up to 30 cm in diameter, plastic resins are in many uses more flexible, more durable, and more economical than conventional materials. The main resins are polyvinyl chloride and styrene. Lately, supply of these resins has occasionally been interrupted or threatened because of shortages of raw materials and dangers to the health of suppliers' employees. The general consensus is that over the next 10 years these supply problems will become worse.

Over the past two years, the research and development department of Leduc Manufacturing Company has developed a patented energy-efficient formulation. Proved workable in the laboratory, this new formulation substitutes readily available synthetics for petroleum-based inputs. Leduc pins its hopes for the future on this forthcoming line to recapture leadership among its established customers and to penetrate hitherto closed markets.

End Uses

All industrial distributors and most end users of plastic pipe and tubing divide their purchases among several competing vendors. Leduc's market share has slipped from number one to number two.

A major end use of polyvinyl chloride pipes and components is irrigation for farms and turfs. Plastics are superior to metal and open-ditch water transportation systems. Due to consolidations and industrialization, much of agriculture buys on a rational basis. The faster-growing turf irrigation market is comprised of municipal park districts and manufacturers of lawn watering installations.

Another important end use is residential and commercial construction. Sales to large buyers, such as electrical and mechanical contractors and mobile home manufacturers, are direct, often on a bid basis; so are most sales of electrical conduits for the protection and insulation of electric power lines and telephone lines to public utilities and large construction companies. Smaller users buy from various distributors.

Over the past 10 years, acceptance of plastic pipe has been more rapid in public than in private systems. Many local building codes specify copper, aluminum, steel, or iron, thus excluding plastic pipe from home systems. This exclusion has been strongly advocated by plumbing unions, which point to the traditional materials' superior strength and resistance to thermal expansion, melting, and crushing. Where plastic pipe has been allowed, it has proved to generate substantial labour saving because both installation and maintenance are much simpler.

Plastic pipe and tubing are also used in the production operations of various industries. Sales potential seems to be smaller than in the aforementioned uses, but business can be much more profitable.

Technical and commercial services must satisfy the particular needs of these industries. Hi-tech industries, for example, insist on the highest quality and are willing to trade off cost for highest performance. The medical equipment industry is similarly disposed. Leduc Manufacturing Company is still number one in medical equipment. With its effective reliability and quality assurance procedures, Leduc is in a superior position to serve these customers.

Electronics manufacturers and mines, on the other hand, are price conscious. In between these extremes are food processors and paper companies. These last two industries are especially concerned about contamination of their raw materials from migrating plastic ingredients.

A recent study ranked growth prospects in the 1980s as follows, from highest to lowest: electronics, medical equipment, hi-tech, mining, food processing, paper manufacture. Leduc Manufacturing Company is very strong with medical equipment, paper mills, and food processors, but relatively weak in the other fields.

Besides price and quality, an important consideration for most buyers is delivery. Except for some specialities, plastic tubes and pipes from different manufacturers are interchangeable. Buyers often switch from one source to another based on earliest availability.

List prices FOB factory on competing plastic pipes and tubes are the same. Even slight price cutting leads to immediate retaliation. Leduc's four geographically dispersed plants have low freight rates and speedy transit to all buyers. This capability is an important competitive advantage.

Altogether, Leduc's success rests largely on the momentum from early aggressive entry into this field, large size, high quality, and excellent physical distribution.

Physical Status of the New Line

When the top-echelon meeting on the stalled innovation convenes, the discussion turns quickly to the production department. "The new formulation works perfectly in the lab," the R&D director noted. "I see no reason why we don't proceed with full-scale production now."

Ian McMichaels, the production manager, is still irate over the loss of production and the cost of extruder repairs that was charged to his department when R&D personnel experimented with the new formulation on the production floor last month. The new formulation works only within very narrow tolerances. Slight deviations in the mix proportions can clog the dies and cause the electrical system to overheat, and apparently this is what occurred. Nothing like this has ever happened before.

McMichaels explains calmly that factory operations are not controllable to the same extent as laboratory trials. Small batches in the lab are not necessarily indicative of long runs in the plant. Jobs will have to be redesigned and machine surveillance tightened. Quality control has advised him that standard grades of raw materials vary more widely than R&D specifications for the new formulation allow. As of now, the new formulation is not producible. Another difficulty is post extrusion bath.

The controller interrupts, "What does the union say about job redesign?"

"That's a good question," replies McMichaels. "As I was saying, the present single bath . . . "

"Hold it!" This time it is Nelson, the division manager, who breaks in. "Rather than go over technical details that we can figure out for ourselves, you may be better served by a systematic approach. I suggest that you and Dale [R&D director] get together this week and work out a practical method for speedy and smooth transition from R&D to production.

"Could the three of us meet on Monday in my office at 10:00 a.m. to discuss your plan? Let's go over all feasible options and your reasons for recommending one particular approach." The two executives nod, signifying acquiescence.

Marketing Status

"This brings us to the second point," resumes William Nelson, "our entry marketing strategy." Nelson looks at Hellas. The sales manager concedes that he lacks detailed knowledge about the new line. "I guess I've been too busy producing profitable business. No apologies needed for that, eh?"

Somewhat defensively, Hellas explains that the new line does not pose any new marketing problems. When the new formulation has been debugged, Leduc will simply ship it instead of the old. Customers will, of course, receive notice. None is likely to object. No price increase will be necessary, according to the accounting department. And the last he has heard, the R&D department has proved performance of the new is identical with the old.

Schroder, the R&D director, confirms this reasoning. Total discontinuation of the old formulation will be necessary. Changeovers between old and new are too expensive and time consuming. The sensitivity of the new formulation requires perfect purification of the machines before a run starts. This entails first producing scrap from the residues of the old then running an industrial cleanser until all vestiges are removed. Extra tests are needed to assure that the new formulation is properly balanced. All of this applies only to changes from old to new formulation. There is no difficulty other than minor setup for adjustments *within* either formulation. Product mix changes per se are simple.

In the opinion of Abt, the controller, the unfurling challenges call for formal planning. There are things to be done between now and the time when shipments begin, but this suggestion does not sit well with the other functional managers.

At this point, an urgent telephone call for Nelson from the corporate president requires him to adjourn the meeting. The managers decide to break for lunch and resume the meeting at 2 p.m.

Question

1. What recommendations would you make to the division manager?

Source: This case was prepared by Harold W. Fox, George A. Ball Distinguished Professor in Marketing at Ball State University. Names and data of the co-operating firms have been altered to preserve anonymity. Reprinted by permission.

PART FOUR

Products

- CHAPTER 9 — PRODUCT STRATEGY
- CHAPTER 10 — PRODUCT MANAGEMENT
- CHAPTER 11 — SERVICES

Case 7 — Robitussin
Case 8 — Tootsizer Canada

CHAPTER 9

Product Strategy

CHAPTER OBJECTIVES

1. Define, explain, or describe the key terms listed under "Vocabulary and Key Terms."
2. Relate product-strategy concepts to the other variables of the marketing mix.
3. Define the term "product" and be able to differentiate the components of a product.
4. Outline and describe the four stages of the product life cycle as well as its uses and limitations.
5. Outline and discuss the four marketing strategies that have given an extended life to the product.
6. Describe the consumer adoption process and outline the five categories of purchasers based on relative time of adoption.
7. Explain the five determinants that govern the rate of adoption of an innovation.
8. Define consumer and industrial goods and identify and discuss the classification system for both.
9. Outline and discuss the characteristics of consumer and industrial goods.
10. Apply your knowledge of Chapter 9 to the various activities in the study guide.

VOCABULARY AND KEY TERMS

From the lettered terms listed below, select the one that best matches the meaning of each of the numbered statements that follows. Write the letter of that choice in the space provided.

a) product
b) warranty
c) product life cycle
d) adoption process
e) consumer innovator
f) diffusion process
g) consumer goods
h) industrial goods
i) convenience products
j) preference products
k) shopping products
l) specialty products
m) installations
n) accessory equipment
o) fabricated parts and material
p) raw materials
q) supplies

1. _____ In the industrial market, such specialty goods as factories, heavy machinery, or other major capital assets
2. _____ The path of a product from introduction to deletion; the stages in the life of a product — introduction, growth, maturity, and decline

3. _____ A bundle of physical service, and symbolic characteristics designed to produce consumer want satisfaction

4. _____ Products used to operate a business; not part of the finished good

5. _____ The various decisions a consumer makes about a new product

6. _____ Products that possess unique characteristics to encourage a consumer to make a special effort to purchase a specific brand

7. _____ Finished industrial goods that actually become part of a final product

8. _____ Products destined for use by an ultimate consumer and not intended for resale or further use in producing other goods

9. _____ The first purchasers of new products and services

10. _____ A guarantee to a buyer that a manufacturer or retailer will replace a defective product or refund its purchase price during a specified period of time

11. _____ Products that are slightly higher on the effort dimension and much higher on risk than convenience products

12. _____ Products used directly or indirectly in producing other goods for resale

13. _____ The way in which new products are adopted by customers in a particular community or social system

14. _____ Capital assets that are less expensive and shorter-lived than installations

15. _____ Products purchased by a consumer only after he or she has compared competing goods on the basis of price, quality, style, and colour

16. _____ Natural components of a final product

PRACTICE TEST

True-False: In the space to the right of each statement, check the appropriate line to indicate whether the statement is true or false.

	True	False
1. During its growth stage, a company will often engage in comparative advertising, emphasizing subtle differences between its product and the products of competitors.	_____	_____
2. The life of the branded product Nylon was extended through marketing strategies designed to find new uses for the product.	_____	_____
3. Late-majority adopters are younger, have a higher social status, are better educated, and are more cosmopolitan than other categories of adopters.	_____	_____
4. Consumers usually make purchases only after visiting several stores and comparing prices, brands, and the quality of products.	_____	_____
5. Brands are often less important for convenience products than for shopping products.	_____	_____
6. Pricing, marketing channels, and marketing communications are all based on the nature of the product.	_____	_____
7. A warranty is a marketing communications strategy.	_____	_____
8. Videotape machines are now in the maturity stage of the product life cycle.	_____	_____
9. CD players are in the introduction stage of the life cycle.		

10. Profits as a percentage of sales will be higher in the growth stage than in any other stage of the life cycle.

11. Promotion during the introduction stage is designed to stimulate selective demand responses from the consumer (i.e., "Buy my brand, it's better.").

12. Losses are common during the introduction stage because of heavy promotion and high production costs.

13. Price cutting is most likely to occur during the maturity stage of the life cycle.

14. The pyramided cycle is the stage at which a product is adopted through new technology or a revised marketing strategy.

15. Fads are currently popular products that tend to follow recurring life cycles.

16. Most fads experience short-lived popularity and then fade quickly.

17. If a farmer were to try a new hybrid seed much earlier than other farmers nearby, he or she would be placed in the early-adopter category of the diffusion process.

18. Divisibility is the degree to which the results of the product may be observable or communicated to others.

19. Convenience products are lowest in terms of both effort and risks.

20. The most prominent examples of preference products are in the appliance industry (e.g., refrigerators and stoves).

21. The major distinction between shopping and specialty products may be made on the basis of effort, not risks.

22. Convenience goods are purchased only after the consumer has made a comparison of competing products.

23. Price is almost never the deciding factor in the purchase of installations.

24. Long distribution channels are a general characteristic of industrial products.

25. Operating supplies are the convenience products of the industrial products market.

Multiple Choice: Choose the expression that best answers the question or best completes the sentence.

26. Which of the following is an example of a product in the growth stage of the product life cycle?
   a. a refrigerator
   b. the Buick Century Automobile
   c. a CD player
   d. a pocket calculator

27. The stage in the product life cycle that is characterized by word of mouth and mass advertising to induce hesitant buyers to try the product, as well as by an increase in profits and the entry of some competition in the marketplace, is the
   a. introduction stage
   b. growth stage

c. maturity stage
d. decline stage

28. Price cuts, diminishing differences among products, and heavy competition are all characteristics of what stage of the product life cycle?
a. introduction
b. growth
c. maturity
d. decline

29. Products that simply do not make it when placed on the market are referred to as
a. instant busts
b. fads
c. fashions
d. aborted introductions
e. specialty items

30. After some products are introduced, information derived from test markets indicates that changes must be made if the product launch is to be successful. Once the changes have been made and the product is relaunched, it is referred to as a(n)
a. instant bust
b. fashion
c. aborted introduction
d. pyramided cycle
e. specialty item

31. Faltering demand, fierce competition, shrinking numbers of competitors, and a battle to retain distribution are all characteristics of the
a. introduction stage
b. growth stage
c. early maturity stage
d. late maturity stage
e. decline stage

32. The original use of Kleenex was to take makeup off women's faces. Only later by accident was the product found to be an effective substitute for the cloth hanky. This is an example of extending the product life cycle by
a. increasing the frequency of use by present customers of the product
b. adding new users for the product
c. finding new uses for the product
d. none of the above

33. Apple developed the market for their computers by going after the home market. Today, Apple hasn't forgotten the home market, but they are also zeroing in on the business market. This is an example of extending the product life cycle by
a. increasing the frequency of use by present customers of the product
b. adding new users for the product
c. finding new uses for the product
d. none of the above

34. What is the correct order of the consumer decision process?
a. awareness, trial, evaluation, interest, adoption
b. interest, awareness, trial, evaluation, adoption
c. awareness, interest, evaluation, trial, adoption
d. interest, evaluation, trial, awareness, adoption

35. The acceptance of new products and services by members of a community or social system is known as the
   a. adoption process
   b. consumer innovation process
   c. divisibility factor
   d. diffusion process
   e. confusion process

36. The degree to which an innovation may be used on a limited basis is the statement that refers to the following characteristic of the innovation:
   a. relative advantage
   b. complexity
   c. compatibility
   d. divisibility
   e. communicability

37. Those products that are slightly higher on the effort dimension and much higher on risk than convenience products are categorized as
   a. impulse products
   b. specialty products
   c. shopping products
   d. preference products

38. What consumer products category is highest on both effort and risk?
   a. impulse products
   b. convenience products
   c. specialty products
   d. preference products
   e. shopping products

39. New aircraft for Air Canada, locomotives for Canadian National, or a new assembly line for Ford Motors are examples of
   a. specialty products
   b. assembly equipment
   c. accessory equipment
   d. installations
   e. component parts

40. Champion spark plugs and Goodyear tires may become parts of an assembled car. Orlon or Dacron may be purchased by Burlington Mills as material for sweaters and other clothing items. These are examples of industrial products that fall into the category of
   a. installations
   b. component parts and materials
   c. accessory equipment
   d. operating supplies
   e. raw materials

41. Which of the following is the best definition of a product?
   a. an object that is purchased for a specific purpose
   b. an object or service that is manufactured in the production process
   c. a bundle of physical, service, and symbolic attributes designed to produce consumer want satisfaction
   d. a and b
   e. none of the above

42. Which of the following characterizes the introductory stage of the product life cycle?
   a. stress on information about product features
   b. growing profits
   c. efforts made to induce intermediaries to carry the product
   d. a and b
   e. a and c

43. Which of the following is not characteristic of the growth stage?
   a. There is a rapid rise in sales volume.
   b. Losses are common.
   c. Mass advertising is used.
   d. Early customers make repeat purchases.

44. Which of the following is not true of early adopters?
   a. They are regarded by others as role models.
   b. They have the greatest opinion leadership.
   c. They are empathetic.
   d. They are tradition-oriented.
   e. They engage in social participation.

45. Extensive purchase-planning time, unimportance of convenient location, and short channel length are all characteristics of
   a. convenience goods
   b. specialty goods
   c. impulse goods
   d. industrial goods
   e. shopping goods

46. Which stage of the product life cycle is characterized by information directed toward intermediaries, extensive research and development, and lack of profits?
   a. maturity
   b. development
   c. growth
   d. decline
   e. introduction

47. Which is not characteristic of the maturity stage of the product life cycle?
   a. Sales reach a plateau.
   b. There are few competitors.
   c. Available products exceed industry demand.
   d. Differences between products diminish.
   e. Price cutting is common.

48. Which of the following is not true of laggards?
   a. They have some opinion leadership.
   b. They have fear of debt.
   c. They have the lowest income.
   d. They are tradition-oriented.
   e. They engage in little social participation.

49. Which of the following is not a characteristic of the installation classification of industrial products?
   a. The product's life span is long, with large unit value.
   b. Negotiations involve a minimum number of top managers, with the final decision often made by the firm's director of purchasing.

c. Higher technological expertise is often supplied by the seller.
d. Price plays a relatively minor role in the purchase decision.
e. Most installations utilize direct channels.

50. Which of the following is characteristic of accessory items?
a. They are less expensive than installations.
b. They have longer channels of distribution.
c. Less technical expertise is required of the seller.
d. Higher importance is placed on price in the decision process.
e. all of the above

ANSWER KEY: CHAPTER 9

Vocabulary and Key Terms	True-False	Multiple Choice
1. m	1. F	26. c
2. c	2. T	27. b
3. a	3. F	28. c
4. q	4. T	29. a
5. d	5. F	30. c
6. l	6. T	31. d
7. o	7. F	32. c
8. g	8. T	33. b
9. e	9. F	34. c
10. b	10. T	35. d
11. j	11. F	36. d
12. h	12. T	37. d
13. f	13. T	38. c
14. n	14. T	39. d
15. k	15. F	40. b
16. p	16. T	41. c
	17. F	42. e
	18. F	43. b
	19. T	44. d
	20. F	45. b
	21. T	46. e
	22. F	47. b
	23. T	48. a
	24. F	49. b
	25. T	50. e

EXERCISE 9.1: SMALL PRODUCTS FROM A HIGH-TECH WORLD

Monica Woo, the marketing manager of a small electronics wholesaler, has discovered that a number of manufacturers in the United States and elsewhere are producing hand-held electronic products. These smaller versions of well-known products will be new to the market, and she is convinced that the market will be receptive.

One of these products, a hand-held bible, is made by Franklin Electronics Publishers in the United States and sells for $400 retail; she speculates that its wholesale price would be around $240. This bible, approximately one-third the size of the printed King James and Revised Standard editions, has a keyboard and computer memory. If one can remember a passage from the Bible, such as, "Those who were not my people, I will call my people, and her who was not beloved, I will call my beloved," one need only input all or parts of the chapter and the electronic bible will identify where it came from (in this case, the 9th chapter of Romans). Monica figures the market for the bible would be not only the clergy, who could use this product as a quick reference source, but also the general congregation. Franklin also produces a sophisticated hand-held electronic encyclopedia, which, Monica believes, would find a good market among educators, students, and businesses, as well as the general public.

Monica read in *Newsweek* about an electronic road map, produced by the German firm Blaupunkt, that is displayed on a four-by-four-inch television screen. The *Newsweek* article states that the map "employs tiny sensing elements on your car's tires, plus an electronic compass, to determine position and speed. The maps are recorded on compact discs, with sufficient storage ability that all of Germany, down to alleys, can be held on a single CD." Monica would like to find out if Blaupunkt is interested in marketing this product to Canada and how long it would take to develop a map disc for Canada. The product, priced at $3500 in Germany, is definitely an expensive toy, so salespeople and business people would likely be the initial market for it, at least until its price came down.

Monica has also read, in *Business Week*, about Zelco Industries in New York, a firm with a reputation for producing innovative small products, such as the Itty-bitty Book Light, a shirt-pocket-size fluorescent lantern, and a left-handed calculator. The Itty-bitty Book Light has been the company's biggest success, finding a market among many bedroom readers.

Monica is now considering the next step. Should she approach companies such as Franklin Electronics and Zelco Industries in order to negotiate the rights to sell these hand-held products in Canada? Would there be a market for products of this nature in Canada?

Questions

1. At what stage of their life cycle are hand-held products? What sort of marketing effort would be required to sell products at this stage of the life cycle?
2. Monica will have to do some research to determine whether or not any other wholesaler or retailer has been granted the rights to distribute these products in Canada. If none has, should she negotiate? Do you think there would be a market for products of this nature? Who do you think would be interested?
3. In which retail outlets would a consumer expect to find these products?
4. Are these products just fads? Discuss.

Sources: "It's a Small World," *Newsweek*, 21 January 1991, pp. 46–7.
"For Noel Zeller, Good Design Is Just the Beginning," *Business Week*, 5 November 1990.

EXERCISE 9.2: HAIR COLOURING FOR THE MALE MARKET

During most of the twentieth century, it has been considered quite acceptable for women to colour their hair, whether to cover up grey, to see if blondes really have more fun, or for any other reason. Males, on the other hand, have not considered colouring their hair to be a viable option, because an unexplainable stigma has attached to the process. In the 1980s, Grecian Formula made some headway in the male market in Canada, with ads showing former sports heroes such as Maurice "The Rocket" Richard colouring their hair. Now Clairol has introduced the products Clairol Gradual and Clairol Instant with ads such as one that shows an illustration of three U.S. former Olympians (Frank Shorter, Mark Spitz, and Bob Seagren) below a headline that says

AFTER YOU'VE WON OLYMPIC GOLD, YOU DON'T SETTLE FOR SILVER

Under the picture of the three Olympians is the following ad copy:
One of these Gold Medalists is using Clairol Option to cover his gray hair. Can you tell who it is? These Olympians have never settled for silver — not in the way they compete or in their appearance. That's what got them to the Olympics then and keeps them competitive

in sports and business now. Whatever you do, you need confidence to be your best. And using Clairol Option can be part of that. Whether you cover all your gray or just a little, you'll have hair that looks and feels soft and natural.

A medium-sized firm that makes personal grooming products is considering entering the Ontario market with hair colouring products for both males and females. The marketing manager is speculating on what the company's chances of success will be in convincing older males with greying hair to try these products.

Questions

1. The text indicates that the adoption rate is influenced by the five characteristics of the innovation. How might the marketing manager manipulate these characteristics (listed below) to speed the rate of adoption?
   a. relative advantage
   b. compatibility
   c. complexity
   d. divisibility
   e. communicability
2. Why is it still less acceptable for men to colour their hair? Relate this topic to the chapters in the text on consumer behaviour.
3. What market is Clairol after with its ad? How do you think the target market will respond to this message? Explain.

Source: © 1990, Clairol, Inc. Reprinted by permission.

CHAPTER 10

Product Management

CHAPTER OBJECTIVES

1. Define, explain, or describe the key terms listed under "Vocabulary and Key Terms."
2. Relate product mix decisions and new product planning to the other variables of the marketing mix.
3. Explain the reasons most firms develop a line of related products rather than a single product.
4. Describe the four alternative organizational arrangements for new-product development — new-product committees, new-product departments, new-product managers, and venture teams.
5. Outline and describe each of the stages in the product development process.
6. Identify and discuss the different methods of product identification.
7. List and discuss the characteristics of a good brand name.
8. Outline and discuss the various branding strategies employed in marketing.
9. Identify the major functions performed by packaging and labelling.
10. Identify major government legislation related to packaging and labelling as well as product safety and state the principal provisions of the relevant legislation.
11. Apply your knowledge of Chapter 10 to the various activities provided in this chapter of the study guide.

VOCABULARY AND KEY TERMS

From the lettered terms listed below, select the one that best matches the meaning of each of the numbered statements that follows. Write the letter of that choice in the space provided.

a) product line
b) new-product committees
c) new-product departments
d) product manager
e) venture teams
f) concept testing
g) test marketing
h) brand
i) brand name
j) trademark
k) generic name
l) individual brand
m) family brand
n) national brand
o) private brand
p) brand recognition
q) brand preference

r)   brand insistence
s)   generic products

1.   _____ A line of merchandise offered by a wholesaler or retailer under its own label
2.   _____ A series of related products produced by a firm
3.   _____ The selection of a specific city or area considered typical of the total market, and the introduction of a new product to this area, complete with a total promotional campaign
4.   _____ A brand that has been given legal protection and has been granted solely to its owner
5.   _____ An organizational arrangement combining representatives from different departments who are responsible for the development of new products or services
6.   _____ A consumer's awareness and familiarity with a specific brand
7.   _____ An organizational arrangement usually composed of representatives of top management who function as a committee for new-product development
8.   _____ A product offered by a manufacturer under its brand name
9.   _____ An organizational arrangement that is involved with new-product development on a permanent, full-time basis
10. _____ A brand name that is used for several products made by a single firm
11. _____ The evaluation of product ideas prior to the actual development of physical products in the new-product development process
12. _____ Food and household staples characterized by plain labels, little or no advertising, and no brand names
13. _____ A name, term, sign, symbol, design, or some combination of these used to identify the products of one firm and to differentiate them from competitive offerings
14. _____ A commonly used word that is descriptive of a particular type of product
15. _____ That part of the brand consisting of words or letters that make up a name used to identify one firm's offering from those of competitors
16. _____ A management officer with complete responsibility for determining objectives and establishing marketing strategies for one product or product line
17. _____ A product given its own brand name rather than the name of the company producing it or an umbrella name covering similar items
18. _____ A consumer's preference for a specific brand, to the extent that the consumer will accept no alternative and will search extensively for the product
19. _____ A consumer's choice of one product over competing brands, based on previous experience with the product

PRACTICE TEST

True-False: In the space to the right of each statement, check the appropriate line to indicate whether the statement is true or false.

		True	False
1.	The range of products in a company is known as the product mix.	_____	_____
2.	The width of assortment in a product line refers to the number of products under each product line.	_____	_____
3.	Cannibalization occurs when one product's profits are eaten up by those of other products.	_____	_____
4.	Firms that market only one product are rare today.	_____	_____
5.	A study of the decay of new products concluded that 50 percent of all new products will become market successes.	_____	_____

106

6. A market development strategy concentrates on finding new markets for existing products. _____ _____

7. Product development strategy refers to the development of new products for new markets. _____ _____

8. A product improvement strategy refers to modifications made in existing products. _____ _____

9. Product managers are deeply involved with setting prices and developing advertising and sales promotional plans. _____ _____

10. Long-term durable products, such as television sets, VCRs, and dishwashers, are frequently test-marketed to determine market need. _____ _____

11. A firm will never carry an unprofitable product, as it affects a company's bottom line. _____ _____

12. A trademark is simply the brand name with legal protection. _____ _____

13. Tefelsadrout would be an example of a good brand name because it is not a dictionary name. _____ _____

14. It is to Kleenex's advantage that its product is a descriptively generic name for paper tissue. _____ _____

15. Bayer's aspirin is the only tablet permitted to carry that protected trademark in the United States and Canada. _____ _____

16. Formica, Xerox, and Zipper are no longer brand names of a specific company. _____ _____

17. The ultimate stage in brand loyalty is brand insistence (i.e., consumers will accept only one brand). _____ _____

18. Individual brand names should be used for dissimilar products. _____ _____

19. Manufacturer brands are also commonly known as private brands. _____ _____

20. Michelin Tires is an example of a private brand. _____ _____

21. Approximately $9 billion is spent annually on packaging in Canada. _____ _____

22. The original purpose of packaging was to provide an additional avenue for advertising. _____ _____

23. The Universal Product Code was introduced to cut expenses in the supermarket industry. _____ _____

24. The Packaging and Labelling Act is a piece of legislation dealing with product safety. _____ _____

25. A majority of Canadians now rate environmental issues as the country's primary problem. _____ _____

Multiple-Choice: Choose the expression that best answers the question or best completes the sentence.

26. A product that takes sales from another offering in a line is said to be
    a. an unwise addition to a product line
    b. cannibalizing the product line
    c. a line-extension strategy to proliferate the company's offerings
    d. a strategy of product diversification
    e. none of the above

27. An assortment of product lines and individual offerings available to a company is called the
   a. product mix
   b. product line
   c. cannibalization process
   d. product strategy
   e. product component

28. Church and Dwight's strategy of finding new uses and new markets for its baking soda is an example of a
   a. product improvement strategy
   b. market development strategy
   c. product development strategy
   d. product diversification strategy
   e. none of the above

29. Which one of the following is not one of the characteristics of a superior product?
   a. It meets customers' needs better than competing products.
   b. It offers features or attributes to the customer that competing products do not.
   c. It is highly innovative, and totally new to the market.
   d. It permits the customer to reduce costs.
   e. all of the above

30. The success of a new product is determined by the
   a. relative strengths of the new product and its marketplace launch
   b. nature and quality of the information available during the product development process
   c. relative proficiency of new-product development efforts
   d. characteristics of the marketplace at which the new product is aimed
   e. all of the above

31. Chrysler's Magic Wagon was a success because it provided customers with a spacious vehicle that was easy to drive and was as comfortable as a car. This is an example of a
   a. product improvement strategy
   b. market development strategy
   c. product development strategy
   d. product diversification
   e. product undertaking strategy

32. The most common organizational arrangement for new-product development is the
   a. venture team
   b. product manager system
   c. new-product committee
   d. new-product department
   e. individual initiative concept

33. In the new-product development process, concept testing of a product occurs during the
   a. idea stage
   b. screening stage
   c. business analysis stage
   d. product development stage
   e. commercialization stage

34. If a company utilized venture teams, they would most likely be composed of
   a. a random sampling of consumers with certain psychographic and demographic characteristics
   b. specialists from the areas of finance, marketing, and engineering

c.   strategic members of the board, financial investors, and stockbrokers
d.   top-level executives who make the final decisions
e.   a group of product managers

35. Which of the following is a drawback to the use of test marketing?
a.   If the test is carefully controlled, consumers will not be aware that it is taking place.
b.   After the test has been going on for a few months, the firm can estimate the product's likely performance in a full-scale introduction.
c.   Test marketing can cost between $250 000 and $1 million, depending on the size of the test market city and the cost of taking out ads.
d.   The results of the test marketing should represent the overall population in such characteristics as age, sex, and income.
e.   Test market locations are typically chosen so that they are of a managable size.

36. Which of these brand names was ruled to be descriptively generic?
a.   Coke
b.   aspirin in Canada
c.   Kleenex
d.   Nylon
e.   Jell-O

37. Which of the following connotes the benefits to be derived from the use of the product?
a.   Ban deodorant
b.   Campbell's soup
c.   Tide detergent
d.   Beautyrest mattress
e.   Ski-Doo snowmobile

38. Which company follows a policy of the same "family" brand on all of its products?
a.   Procter & Gamble
b.   Molson
c.   Black & Decker
d.   Campbell Soup
e.   c and d

39. Which of the following is not an advantage of using a family brand strategy?
a.   The general prestige of a brand can be spread to other items in the product line.
b.   It is best suited for products that are dissimilar in nature and satisfy different needs of consumers.
c.   It costs less to introduce a family brand than to introduce an individual brand.
d.   The consumer is already familiar with the brand name.
e.   none of the above

40. What is characteristic of a good brand name?
a.   It should suggest something about the product's use, or the benefits to be derived from the product.
b.   It should be easy to pronounce, spell, and recognize.
c.   It should be a common name that people understand.
d.   It should be similar to competitors' brand names.
e.   a and b

41. Which of the following is a potential source for new-product ideas?
a.   the markets that are served
b.   finding new uses for old products
c.   employees

   d.   similar products presently on the market
   e.   all of the above

42. Which of the following alternatives in successful medium- to large-sized companies is not normally used in locating organizational responsibility for new-product development?
   a.   product managers
   b.   new-product committees
   c.   engineering departments
   d.   venture teams
   e.   new-product departments

43. A group of high-level executives in charge of new-product development is typically a
   a.   new-product committee
   b.   new-product department
   c.   product manager
   d.   venture team
   e.   none of the above

44. Geographical test markets are highly recommended in new-product development unless
   a.   management wants to maintain secrecy
   b.   the relative advantage of the new product is great
   c.   the new product could be duplicated quickly and inexpensively
   d.   all of the above
   e.   none of the above

45. The venture team is an efficient method of developing new-product ideas for the following reason:
   a.   The team is closely integrated with the organization and linked directly to top management.
   b.   The team usually begins as a highly structured group with definite new-product goals.
   c.   The team must meet such criteria as return on investment, uniqueness of product, existence of a well-defined need, and patent protection.
   d.   Team members consist of top management from the major functional areas who meet and plan new-product strategy, but their prime job responsibilities are outside the team.
   e.   all of the above

46. Which of the following job responsibilities does not pertain to the product manager?
   a.   setting prices
   b.   controlling the sales force
   c.   developing advertising programs
   d.   setting objectives
   e.   none of the above

47. Which of the following functions does a brand not perform?
   a.   It allows for repeat purchases.
   b.   It acts as the linking factor in the consumer's mind for the image and quality of the product.
   c.   It acts as legal protection from competitors associating similar goods with the brand.
   d.   It allows the firm to escape some of the rigours of price competition.
   e.   all of the above

48. Which of the following is an argument for using individual brand names?
   a.   The brand name is usually related to the name of the company producing the product.
   b.   A brand name enables promotional outlays to benefit all the products in the line.
   c.   Products are dissimilar.

d. It facilitates the task of introducing product to consumers and retailers.
e. all of the above

49. Which of the following is a reason to have a broad product line?
a. increased market share
b. optimal use of company resources
c. exploitation of product life cycle
d. desire to grow
e. all of the above

50. Which of the following statements is correct?
a. National brands are often referred to as private brands.
b. National brands can be referred to as manufacturer's brands.
c. Sears' brands, such as Kenmore, are national brands.
d. National brands are sometimes labelled as generic products.
e. none of the above

ANSWER KEY: CHAPTER 10

Vocabulary and Key Terms	**True-False**	**Multiple Choice**
1. o	1. T	26. b
2. a	2. F	27. a
3. g	3. F	28. b
4. j	4. T	29. e
5. e	5. F	30. e
6. p	6. T	31. c
7. b	7. F	32. c
8. n	8. T	33. c
9. c	9. T	34. b
10. m	10. F	35. c
11. f	11. F	36. d
12. s	12. T	37. d
13. h	13. F	38. e
14. k	14. F	39. b
15. i	15. F	40. e
16. d	16. T	41. e
17. l	17. T	42. c
18. r	18. T	43. a
19. q	19. F	44. d
	20. F	45. c
	21. T	46. b
	22. F	47. c
	23. T	48. c
	24. F	49. e
	25. T	50. b

EXERCISE 10-1: PRODUCT SPINOFFS OR A MARKETER'S LINE/ BRAND EXTENSIONS

Brand names are an important part of product recognition; thus, one critical decision that companies must make is whether to introduce a new brand name (individual branding) or use the same brand name (family branding) for a new product. Sometimes a company must determine how closely related the new product is to the existing branded product, while keeping in mind that it takes more time and money to introduce a new brand name. In the 1990s, companies have leaned toward brand or line extension. As pointed out in the July 9, 1990, issue of *Newsweek*:

> In many cases, line extensions can make good sense. They offer companies a way to trade on their best asset — a good name. They also eliminate the need for extensive test marketing. And since they often aren't subject to the fees levied on new brands, they provide a cheap way to get a product on the shelves. Yet spinoffs can lead to pitfalls. When companies slap a famous brand name on every new product, they carry all their corporate eggs in one basket. If one product proves harmful or defective, sales of all brand items can suffer.

The family-brand strategy can give a new product a better-than-average chance of succeeding, so companies are emphasizing this strategy. Procter & Gamble, the creator of the individual branding concept, has recently experimented with family branding; its original soap product, Ivory, has been line extended to include Ivory dishwashing liquid and Ivory shampoo. P&G has also added Liquid Tide as an extension of Tide. Kraft General Foods is another company that has long heralded individual branding but has line extended strong-branded products such as Jell-O, which has been extended to Jell-O pudding pops, Jell-O Fruit and Cream dessert bars, and Jell-O cake mix.

One of the dangers of spinoffs is that the new brand may cannibalize the sales of the regular brand. For example, Liquid Tide is selling well but at the expense of sales of regular Tide. On the other hand, the more products a company has to offer consumers, the better its chance of gaining market share or being competitive. If P&G didn't have a liquid detergent, a competitor would likely introduce a similar product and gain market advantage. Using the family brand made it easier for P&G to persuade customers to try its product and to get shelf space in retail stores.

In the later 1980s and early 1990s, there has been a trend toward company takeovers. One reason for this trend is to add new brands to the company lines. For example, in the mid 1980s, P&G took over Richardson-Vicks, which has such successful brand names as Vicks' cough drops, NyQuil cough syrup, Oil of Olay lotion, and Vidal Sassoon shampoos. P&G had previously spent years unsuccessfully trying to gain market share with their Wondra skin lotion; by acquiring Richardson-Vicks, they moved to the top of the market with Oil of Olay. This example shows how difficult it can be for a company to move its products from brand recognition to brand insistence. As pointed out in the *Newsweek* article, "[Because] the cost of launching a new brand runs upwards of $50 million, companies are turning to low-budget, low-risk retreads. Last year two thirds of the 5,779 packaged goods introduced to the marketplace were improved formulations, new sizes or new packages for existing brands."

Questions

1. When should a company use a family brand strategy? When is an individual branding strategy more appropriate?
2. What are the advantages and disadvantages of line extension?
3. Provide some examples (other than Jell-O and Tide) from your product knowledge of line extension.
4. What is cannibalizing of sales? Can cannibalization be minimized? Why would a company introduce a new product with the same brand name as an old product if the sales from the new product are going to take sales away from the old product?
5. Why is it so important for a marketer to move a customer from brand recognition to brand preference to brand insistence?

Source: "Sequels for the Shelf," *Newsweek*, 9 July 1990, pp. 42–3.

EXERCISE 10-2: NEW PRODUCTS AND THEIR SUCCESS RATE

In an article in the *Journal of Consumer Marketing*, Herbert Blum points out that "new products are a humbling experience with the high failure rate and the fact that only 4 percent of all new products reach the $20 million sales level. If $100 million is the blockbuster success number, then only one-half of one percent succeed. That makes the odds 200 to 1 against a new product." With such a high failure rate, why would a company bother with a new product? As Blum emphasizes: "Of the brands that sell $1 million or more in grocery stores today, nearly 20 percent were not around in 1970. Beyond that . . . consumers want new products."

But why the high failure rate? In most cases, it is simply poor planning or timing. For example, the Edsel automobile was introduced in the 1950s, when demand for large cars was diminishing; again, the DeLorean sports car was introduced at a time when the market was in a downturn. Poor planning is due in part to inadequate market research. A company may inaccurately assess demand for the product in the marketplace, the price may be too high, distribution may be inadequate, or promotion may be directed at the wrong market target.

In many cases, companies have problems with facilities, supplies, or staffing; sometimes even profitable products are dropped for lack of proper production or marketing. For example, in the 1950s Monsanto decided not to compete in the detergent business, even though it had developed the first low-sudsing detergent, because of the expense of hiring a new sales force to handle the product. Instead, the company sold its product, *All*, to Lever Brothers.

Sometimes a company greatly underestimates its production costs, and ends up with a product that is priced too high for the intended market. Other times, the competition hears that a company has a product planned, and beats that company to the marketplace with a similar product; Kellogg rushed its Pop Tarts on to the market before the company that had created the prototype had taken it out of test marketing.

A company may be forced to recall a product because it is defective, because health problems have been associated with it, or simply because it is wrongly packaged and marketed. Gerber Products' food-in-a-jar, Singles, which was aimed at the singles market, failed both because consumers associated it with baby food and because single people didn't want to be reminded that they ate alone.

To give its new products a better chance of success, a company needs to zero in on specific target markets; one of the largest markets is baby boomers. As pointed out in the August 1990 issue of *Canadian Business*, "There are 8.2 million of them surfing the crest of a huge Canadian population wave that's been washing over the 20th century for the past 44 years. . . . One in three Canadians is a baby boomer — defined strictly as anyone born between 1946 and 1964 . . . and by the end of the century, boomers born prior to 1955 will preside over 40% of the North American spending power." What goods and services are of interest to this group? According to *Canadian Business*, "Home renovations, saunas, exercise rooms and ultrasophisticated home theatres — replete with compact disks, video cassette recorders, variously shaped televisions and surround sound — will become household staples." These products will sell because they fit the image that baby boomers have of themselves. "Distinction" and "quality" are key words in marketing to this group: "They want quality in products and are willing to pay for it." Marketing will become ever more competitive as companies attempt to address the specific needs and wants of groups such as baby boomers.

Questions

1. Why do new products fail? List the reasons given in this exercise for new-product failure and try to think of other reasons why products fail.
2. Given the high failure rate of new consumer goods as well as the high cost of developing new products and introducing them to the marketplace, why should a company bother with new products?
3. Think of new products that you have seen advertised on television or seen in a retail store. What, in your opinion, are the chances that these products will succeed?

4. If you were a manufacturer of videocassette recorders and you were trying to reach the older baby boomers, what type of product would you develop for them and what sort of message (communication via promotional media) would you present?

Sources: Herbert M. Blum, "New Products: I Can Feel When They're Right," *Journal of Consumer Marketing* 4, no. 4 (Fall 1987): 41–5.

John Lorinc, "The NEXT WAVE: New Products and Services for Baby Boomers," *Canadian Business*, August 1990, pp. 59–60.

CHAPTER 11

Services

CHAPTER OBJECTIVES

1. Define, explain, or describe the key terms listed under "Vocabulary and Key Terms."
2. Elaborate on the discussion of products by exploring the concept of the service product.
3. Discuss the similarities and differences between goods and services.
4. Explain the main characteristics of services.
5. Outline the major issues that have to be addressed by marketers for each of the characteristics of services.
6. Apply your knowledge of Chapter 11 to the various activities provided in this chapter of the study guide.

VOCABULARY AND KEY TERMS

From the lettered terms listed below, select the one that best matches the meaning of each of the numbered statements that follows. Write the letter of that choice in the space provided.

a) services
b) tangible
c) intangible
d) perishability
e) heterogeneity
f) inseparability

1. _____ The term that relates that production and consumption occur simultaneously
2. _____ A product without physical characteristics; a bundle of performance and symbolic attributes designed to produce consumer want satisfaction
3. _____ The term that points out that services cannot be seen, smelled, or touched before purchase
4. _____ The term that points out that services cannot be stored
5. _____ The term that recognizes that goods can be displayed, examined, and compared before purchase
6. _____ The term that recognizes that standardization and quality control are difficult to achieve, as service performance varies from person to person

PRACTICE TEST

True-False: In the space to the right of each statement, check the appropriate line to indicate whether the statement is true or false.

		True	**False**
1.	People have to trust the service well enough to buy it before they can try it.		
2.	In Canada, services account for less than 25 percent of consumer expenditures.		
3.	A service is a product with physical characteristics.		
4.	Goods businesses sell things and service businesses sell performances.		
5.	Products that can be physically examined and compared are low in search qualities.		
6.	Even after purchasing products with credence properties, the buyer has to trust that the supplier has performed the correct service.		
7.	In intangibles, credence (buying a promise) and experience qualities are dominant, while search qualities are central for tangible products.		
8.	A service is tangible, inseparable, and heterogeneous.		
9.	Services can be stored and used on another occasion.		
10.	Services are ineligible for a patent.		
11.	Marketing messages should use personal sources more than nonpersonal sources.		
12.	Service marketers have found that postpurchase communication is a useful strategy.		
13.	A strong accounting system is not as critical in service marketing as it is in goods marketing.		
14.	Services are first produced, then sold, then consumed.		
15.	Multi-site locations are a response to the fact that services cannot be sent from a warehouse to a retail outlet.		
16.	The main marketing problem arising from heterogeneity is that standardization and quality control are difficult to achieve.		
17.	No service can be produced before it is required, and stocked up to meet future demand.		
18.	Services are totally integrated with the environment.		
19.	Research confirms that there is not a direct relationship between the price and quality of a service.		
20.	The person who produces a service must also be able to market that service.		

Multiple Choice: Choose the expression that best answers or best completes the sentence.

21. In Canada, services account for
   a. 24 percent of consumer expenditures
   b. 47 percent of consumer expenditures
   c. 27 percent of consumer expenditures
   d. 54 percent of consumer expenditures
   e. 15.6 percent of consumer expenditures

22. A recent report published by GATT estimates that total trade in services between the 96 nations of that organization has reached
   a. $540 million
   b. $680 billion
   c. $560 billion
   d. $12 trillion
   e. $980 million

23. A product without physical characteristics is a
   a. good
   b. service
   c. bundle of performance and symbolic attributes designed to produce consumer-want satisfaction
   d. tangible item
   e. b and c

24. Fast-food shops and custom-fitted suits would be placed on Ruston and Carson's scale of elemental dominance as
   a. intangibles
   b. tangibles
   c. intangible elements dominant
   d. tangible elements dominant
   e. not on the scale

25. Advertising agencies and teaching would be placed on Ruston and Carson's scale of elemental dominance as
   a. intangibles
   b. tangibles
   c. intangible elements dominant
   d. tangible elements dominant
   e. not on the scale

26. Three types of product properties are attached to every good or service: search qualities, experience qualities, and
   a. buying a promise
   b. credence qualities
   c. intangible elements dominant
   d. tangible elements dominant
   e. attachment qualities

27. Search qualities are central for
   a. credence qualities
   b. attachment qualities
   c. tangible products
   d. intangible products
   e. experience qualities

28. A hockey arena provides seats for entertainment. Revenue from empty seats is lost forever. Which one of the marketing problems related to intangibility of service is represented here?

a. Services cannot be stored.
b. Services cannot be protected by patent.
c. A service is difficult to communicate or display.
d. A service is difficult to price.
e. none of the above

29. An advertisement used by a stock brokerage firm, showing a testimonial by a famous pro golfer, is an example of which promotional strategy?

a. making the service more tangible by personalizing it
b. creating a favourable image
c. showing the tangible benefits of purchasing an intangible service
d. none of the above
e. all of the above

30. Which of the following is a marketing problem associated with the unique service feature of intangibility?

a. Services cannot be stored.
b. Consumers are involved in production.
c. Standardization and quality control are difficult to achieve.
d. Services cannot be inventoried.
e. Centralized mass production of services is difficult.

31. Which of the following is a marketing problem associated with the unique service feature of inseparability?

a. Services cannot be stored.
b. Prices are difficult to set.
c. Consumers are involved in production.
d. Standardization and quality control are difficult to achieve.
e. Services cannot be inventoried.

32. Which of the following is a marketing problem associated with the unique service feature of heterogeneity?

a. Services cannot be stored.
b. Prices are difficult to set.
c. Consumers are involved in production.
d. Standardization and quality control are difficult to achieve.
e. Services cannot be inventoried.

33. Which of the following is a marketing problem associated with the unique service feature of perishability?

a. Services cannot be stored.
b. Prices are difficult to set.
c. Consumers are involved in production.
d. Standardization and quality control are difficult to achieve.
e. Services cannot be inventoried.

34. Which of the following is a marketing strategy used to solve the problem of intangibility?

a. Use strategies to cope with fluctuating demand.
b. Use multi-site locations.
c. Customize service.
d. Stress tangible cues.
e. Industrialize service.

35. Which of the following is a marketing strategy used to solve the problem of inseparability?
  a. Use strategies to cope with fluctuating demand.
  b. Use multi-site locations.
  c. Customize service.
  d. Stress tangible cues.
  e. Industrialize service.

36. Which of the following is a marketing strategy used to solve the problem of heterogeneity?
  a. Use strategies to cope with fluctuating demand.
  b. Stress tangible cues.
  c. Create strong organizational image.
  d. Customize service.
  e. Engage in postpurchase communications.

37. Which of the following is a marketing strategy used to solve the problem of perishability?
  a. Use strategies to cope with fluctuating demand.
  b. Stress tangible cues.
  c. Create strong organizational image.
  d. Customize service.
  e. Engage in postpurchase communications.

38. Restaurants, airlines, and other service businesses often give special discounts for use of their services in periods of low demand. This is a marketing strategy associated with the marketing problem of
  a. inseparability
  b. intangibility
  c. perishability
  d. heterogeneity
  e. tangibility

39. A customer may get a hair styling on the same date as two friends, but with quite different results. This is the service marketing problem associated with
  a. inseparability
  b. intangibility
  c. perishability
  d. heterogeneity
  e. tangibility

40. Which of the following is one of the ways that the evidence can be managed by service marketers?
  a. management of the environment
  b. appearance of service providers
  c. setting the right price for the service
  d. none of the above
  e. a, b, and c

ANSWER KEY: CHAPTER 11

Vocabulary and Key Terms	True-False	Multiple Choice
1. f	1. T	21. b
2. a	2. F	22. c
3. c	3. F	23. e
4. d	4. T	24. d
5. b	5. F	25. c
6. e	6. T	26. b
	7. T	27. c
	8. F	28. a
	9. F	29. a
	10. T	30. a
	11. T	31. c
	12. T	32. d
	13. F	33. e
	14. F	34. d
	15. T	35. b
	16. T	36. d
	17. T	37. a
	18. T	38. c
	19. F	39. d
	20. T	40. e

EXERCISE 11.1: MARKETING THE TORONTO BLUE JAYS

Success in professional sports depends on more than the quality of a team's talent. The Toronto Blue Jays are a winning ball club, but it is successful marketing that has made them a box-office draw and given the team a favourable image from coast to coast in Canada.

During their formative period, the Blue Jays conducted an effective publicity campaign through the media. In the years since, promotional spinoffs have earned approximately 20 percent of the club's revenues. For example, the organization claims, one out of every ten Canadians wears a Blue Jay cap. Blue Jay caps, shirts, jackets, cushions, helmets, handbags, playing cards, and specialty items such as pens and calendars are also sold across the country.

National television coverage has also helped to establish the team as Canada's own. This is doubly impressive in light of the fact that Toronto did not receive a baseball franchise until 1976, seven years after Montreal acquired the Expos.

Since the Jays moved to the SkyDome, attendance at games has soared, breaking a major league record in 1990. A major reason for this is that the SkyDome is not just a ball park, it is a tourist attraction and entertainment centre whose name is a familiar one to most Canadians.

Questions

1. Are the Blue Jays marketing a product or a service? Discuss.
2. What is the primary target market for the Blue Jays? Is there a secondary target market for the team? If so, define it. If not, explain why not.
3. Who competes with the Blue Jays?
4. How important is promotion to the success of the ball club? What advertising media would mainly be used?
5. Discuss the significance of the other elements of the marketing program (i.e., distribution and pricing).

EXERCISE 11.2: ADVERTISING A SERVICE

Read the magazine advertisement placed by the Certified General Accountants' Association of Canada.

Questions

1. What services are being promoted in this ad?
2. Who is the target market for these services?
3. Is this an effective ad? Why or why not?
4. There is more advertising today by professional organizations, particularly in the United States, than there has been in past years. Is there a reason for this trend? Do you think this type of advertising will spread to professions in Canada (e.g., legal and medical professions) that currently do little, if any, advertising? In a recent TV ad, a U.S. legal firm advises, "If you have an accident or injury claim, call our lawyer." Do you consider this to be responsible advertising? The Pharmaceutical Manufacturers Association of Canada is doing extensive advertising of brand-name prescription medicines. Is it acceptable for an association to promote its cause?

Case 7

ROBITUSSIN

The Company

A.H. Robins, Inc., has evolved from a small community pharmacy opened 1866 in Richmond, Virginia, by Albert Hartley Robins to a diversified multinational corporation operating in more than 100 countries. The research centre opened in 1963 with more than 325 scientists and technicians engaged in research in many product areas.

The A.H. Robins Company is engaged principally in the manufacture of finished-dosage forms of pharmaceutical products. Finished products are manufactured and packaged from raw materials purchased from suppliers of pharmaceutical-grade chemicals. The company's principal products are ethical prescription and over-the-counter drug products which are promoted by field representatives to physicians, dentists, and pharmacists.[1] Some of Robins' best-known brand names are Robitussin, a cough and cold syrup; Donnatal, an antispasmodic drug; and Robaxin, a skeletal muscle relaxant.

Robins' products are distributed to drug wholesalers which sell to retail drug stores and to hospitals. This distribution system has proven successful in the past. But, in the current market, drug-store chains turn over more than half the volume of the industry. If these large chains buy direct from a manufacturer (at a lower price), they give those brands in-store marketing support, such as end aisle displays, extra shelf facings, and co-op advertising.

While maintaining its major position as manufacturer and researcher of Pharmaceuticals, A.H. Robins has diversified into consumer products. In 1963, Robins acquired Morton Manufacturing, the producer of Chap Stick lip balm. In 1967, Robins acquired Polk Miller Products, producers of the Sergeant's line of pet care products. These two companies later formed Miller-Morton Company in an effort to consolidate consumer product activities. Robins enjoyed further success in the consumer goods area with the introduction of Lip Quencher, a lipstick utilizing the moisturizing qualities of Chap Stick. In 1967, it continued its entry into the consumer field with the acquisition

A BUSINESS THAT DOES NOT EMPLOY THE SERVICES OF A CGA IS DEFINITELY MISSING SOMETHING.

It seems obvious, doesn't it.

Then again, so many things in business seem that way at first. Before the real world slips in.

Professionals with the Certified General Accountant designation have a rock solid grasp of the real issues facing Canadian businesses.

You see, we attract the kind of individual who is remarkably action oriented.

Then we train them with a thorough-ness and degree of hands-on computer and business experience that is unparalleled in the field.

So while CGA s are at home in the theoretical world of accounting they have whole other levels of talent for problem solving and entrepreneurial insight.

We believe that is the foundation for success stories in operations across the country.

For more information call toll-free 1-800-663-1990.

CGA. BUSINESS SOLUTIONS FOR THE REAL WORLD.

of Parfums Caron, a leading producer of French fragrance products. Consumer products are advertising nationally and marketed through department stores, specialty shops, and drug outlets.

A.H. Robins entered the international market in the 1960s. Subsidiaries in Australia, Brazil, Canada, Colombia, France, Mexico, the Philippines, South Africa, the United Kingdom, Venezuela, and West Germany provided a base for the company's growing international operations. In recent years, 33 percent of net sales and 34 percent earning before tax, interest, and amortization expenses have come from international operations.

The Product

Robitussin, a cough and cold syrup, is marketed in five forms, one of which is a prescribed form; the other four are over-the-counter forms. The product to date has been marketed only through wholesalers and directly to nonproprietary hospitals. Demand is stimulated by detailers who call on members of the medical profession and "detail" the drug — describing its advantages and features so that physicians may either prescribe or recommend the product.

Promotion is complemented by sampling, trade deals, and trade medical profession journal advertising. However, demand for the product is now static as it has reached the mature state in its present market segment.

The cough syrup market has grown 5 percent in the past year. The largest growth has been in food stores, which now account for 24 percent of total sales and are increasing at a faster rate than sales in drug stores. Most drug-store sales are in the chains and large independents who want to purchase directly from the manufacturer rather than through wholesalers in order to gain greater margins for retail outlets.

While the ethical segment of the cough syrup market is still increasing slightly in dollar terms, the proprietary brands in food and drug outlets exhibit a healthy 10 percent increase compared with a 2 percent increase for the ethical segment.

In unit terms, the cough syrup market is not growing; but within the segments, food store sales are moving up in importance while drug store units are declining. One study has shown that the average homemaker visits the grocery store about three times a week and the drug store twice a month. In the drug stores the ethical brands are holding their share while proprietary brands are declining.

By way of comparison with other cold-remedy products, the cough syrup market is 12 percent larger than the cold-tablet market and more than three times larger than the nasal-spray market.

Cough syrup preparations differ from most categories of cold products since the heaviest users usually do not purchase their own product because half of them are under eighteen years of age. The prime prospects can be described as follows:

- Female head of household 25–49 years old
- Households with children 2–17 years old and with 5 or more persons
- Household annual income of $20 000 or lower
- Less educated

The breakdown of unit sales by brand is as follows: Robitussin has a 21.6 percent share of unit sales in drugstores compared to Vicks' 16 percent. In food and drugstores combined, Robitussin has an estimated 14 percent share to Vicks' 27 percent. Based on an earlier survey, the leading brands of cough syrup used were Formula 44, doctor's prescription, and NyQuil.

Toward the end of the financial year, as the planning stage for the following year is being finalized, George Mancini, Robitussin's product manager, has noted that over the past several years the line had only been growing in the 1 to 2 percent range in comparison with the 6 to 8 percent growth of the overall cough syrup market. Robitussin is becoming a mature product in its present segment of ethical over-the-counter drugs.

Questions

1. Relate this case to the product life cycle concept.
2. What action should A.H. Robins take with respect to Robitussin?

Source: Reprinted by permission of Ian Stewart, A.H. Robins, Inc., and Professors Thomas D. Giese and Thomas J. Cosse, University of Richmond.

Note
1. Drug industry practice is to classify products as either "ethical" or "proprietary" depending on the marketing method employed. Ethical products are marketed by promotion directly to the medical profession. The ethical classification is further subdivided into those drugs which require prescription and those which can be purchased without a prescription and are called "over-the-counter" (OTC) drugs. Proprietary products are promoted directly to the consumer.

Case 8

TOOTSIZER CANADA

Tootsizer is the only patented plant food in North America. It had never been marketed in Canada when Traff Green became interested in it in 1982. Green, a farm equipment dealer in Winnipeg, heard about Tootsizer from his brother Bruce, who had assisted its inventor while teaching university in Rolla, Missouri, and held the patent and marketing rights for Canada. The two brothers got together because Traff's present business had largely fall and winter sales and Tootsizer, with a spring and summer sales period, would balance the cash flow.

Tootsizer Canada, Ltd. seemed to be going well. Despite this, Traff Green, the president, realized that the roof could fall in if Tootsizer's venture into television advertising did not pay off. In 1984 he decided to reevaluate the total marketing strategy of the firm.

Green hired consultants to study buying behaviour and the effectiveness of advertising plant food and fertilizer in the Winnipeg market. He hoped that this information would help him to plan his strategy for the next year. The results of their survey, conducted soon after Tootsizer's 1984 ad campaign, are summarized in Figure C8-1.

Production

Originally, Bruce Green produced Tootsizer as a one-man operation from his basement, in very limited quantities. When Tootsizer Canada, Ltd. was formed in 1983, Traff Green set up a mass-production facility in the garage behind his farm equipment lot. With the welding equipment from his business, he custom-built some of the processing machinery and purchased the bottling line from the United States. These were capable of supplying well in excess of the projected Canadian demand.

In fact, during the first year of mass production, Tootsizer was almost a custom bottler: when it received a large order, it would make it up and restock the warehouse. More than 20 000 bottles, the equivalent of about six hours' factory production time, were sold per week.

The garage consisted of about 230 m² of usable production and storage space. It was leased from the city for $900 rent plus $625 in taxes, heating, and light per month.

The Product

Tootsizer is a concentrated liquid plant food fertilizer. The manufacturing process starts with the same basic raw materials (nitrogen, phosphates, and potash) that are used to make most fertilizers. Magnesium is added, then the mixture is put through a patented chemical process that duplicates the first stage of food processing that goes on within plants. Five elements go into the reaction, producing fifteen different chemicals.

Theoretically, this product enables plants to conserve energy. By not having to process their food at the first level, plants can apply the energy saved to manufacturing fibre within their bodies. As a result, they will grow faster and be more productive. There are indications that this could be true. Edgar van Wick in Roland, Manitoba, who grows world-record pumpkins (about 200 kg), uses Tootsizer for his garden. Green claims to have grown 2 m corn stalks at his cottage when none of his neighbours could raise plants more than 1 m high. The majority of people who try Tootsizer are convinced of its merits.

In tests of the product under controlled conditions at a company greenhouse and in independent studies conducted at the University of Manitoba, Tootsizer always outperformed competitive plant foods and fertilizer.

Despite these successful results, there were problems with the product. Tootsizer is a concentrate, and unless diluted properly will burn the roots of a plant and kill it. Tootsizer has to be mixed with water, in a ratio of 30 g to 4 L water, for optimum results. Adding a drop of Tootsizer to the soil and then watering does not work because the plant food is not spread evenly to all the roots and might burn some roots. On the bottle label, recommended dilution and instructions for use are given, but the dangerous short cut is not mentioned. There are also advantages to the purchaser of a concentrate such as Tootsizer. The product, while quite convenient to use, will treat a great deal of garden area.

FIGURE C8-1 SELECTED FINDINGS FROM MARKET RESEARCH STUDY

The following is a summary of the results of each question based on the number of responses to that particular question.

1. Do you have potted plants in your home?
   Yes 99.0%
   No   1.0%
2. Do you have a garden?
   Yes 80.8%
   No   19.2%
3. Do you use plant food?
   Yes 80.8%
   No   19.2%
4. Do you use a fertilizer?
   Yes 63.6%
   No   36.4%
5. What type of fertilizer(s) or plant food(s) do you use?
   Organic fertilizer   10.3%
   Liquid fertilizer   65.5%
   Powder fertilizer   50.6%
6. How often do you use your plant food?
   More than once a week   0.0%
   Once a week   6.9%
   Once a month   27.6%
   Once every two months   33.3%
   Once every six months   14.9%
   Less than once every six months 10.4%
7. Which of the following statements best describes the reason why you use your present fertilizer?
   Recommended by a family member   30.4%
   Recommended by a friend   17.7%
   Recommended by a gardener, florist or other knowledgeable person   45.6%
   Radio advertisement   1.3%
   Newspaper or magazine advertisement 3.7%
   Television advertisement   1.3%
8. When you purchased your present fertilizer (or plant food), did you know what brand you were going to purchase before you entered the store?
   Yes 46.6%
   No   53.4%
9. When you made your last fertilizer (or plant food) purchase, did you investigate and compare more than one brand?
   Yes 33.0%
   No   67.0%
10. If you answered yes to question number 8, did you purchase the brand you had intended to purchase?
    Yes 93.2%
    No   6.8%

11. How often do you purchase fertilizer (or plant food)?
    Less than once a year   53.9%
    Once a year   28.1%
    Twice a year   14.6%
    More than twice a year   3.4%
12. In which months of the year did you make your last fertilizer (or plant food) purchase?
    January-February   11.5%
    March-April   37.2%
    May-June   30.8%
    July-August   5.1%
    September-October   9.0%
    November-December   6.4%
13. Have you seen or heard of Tootsizer Plant Food?
    Yes 71.5%
    No   28.3%
14. If yes, which of the following statements best describes the medium through which you first saw or heard of Tootsizer?
    Saw it in a store   40.3%
    Saw it on a television advertisement   4.2%
    Saw it in a newspaper or magazine advertisement   11.1%
    Heard it on a radio advertisement   26.4%
    Heard about it through a conversation with some other person   18.0%
15. Through which of the following media have you seen or heard advertisements for Tootsizer? Check all applicable.
    Television   26.8%
    Radio   35.2%
    Newspaper   42.3%
    Magazine   35.2%
    In-store advertising   76.2%
16. Have you ever purchased Tootsizer?
    Yes 15.6%
    No   84.4%
17. If you have tried Tootsizer, how do you rate its performance as a fertilizer?
    Poor   13.4%
    Fair   0.0%
    Average   33.3%
    Good   33.3%
    Excellent   20.2%

Another problem with Tootsizer was that the solids used in the formulation quickly settled to the bottom of the container and it required some effort to get them into suspension again. This made the product less convenient to use and less attractive on the shelf for customers. In the spring of 1983, Green solved one problem with the aid of the Faculty of Pharmacy at the University of Manitoba. He substituted a different suspension fluid, which gave the product a more uniform appearance and required just one or two shakes of the container to put the solids into suspension. This improved product went into production in midsummer 1983, but was not put on the retail shelves until the old stock was sold.

Price Policy

Green sold Tootsizer at the same price to all customers. One supermarket chain store acknowledged that it was a good product but would not consider buying unless given a 5 percent discount. Even though the chain store might have opened up the large eastern market to Tootsizer, Green held to his price (and lost the sale that year).

The wholesale selling price was $22 per case of twelve 500 mL bottles, with 2 percent/10/net 30 terms. Suggested retail price was $3.29 per bottle, but one chain sold them at $2.79 per bottle. The total cost of packaging and product for one bottle was 41 cents. Another 46 cents per bottle was set aside for advertising.

Compared with other products on the store shelves, Tootsizer appears to offer good value. Each bottle holds 34 percent nutrient value and, when used as directed, should last for about nine months of heavy home use on houseplants.

Competitive plant foods sell for about $1.59 per 500 mL bottle of 3 percent nutrient mixture. However, they are not concentrates. Although concentrates are not common on the shelves of grocery stores, garden shops carry most forms of concentrated plant food. Typically, the concentrates cost in the range of $1.39 for 250 mL of concentrate with about 30 percent nutrient value and have dilution instructions similar to Tootsizer's.

Distribution Strategy

Bruce Green first sold Tootsizer in 1981. It was tough going and he literally sold the product in the streets to anyone he could convince to try it. He carried a case in the trunk of his car and was ready to bend anyone's ear on the virtues of Toot-

sizer. He managed only $1200 in sales that year, but the people who tried it returned for more.

After Tootsizer Canada was formed in 1983, Traff Green took over the marketing of the product. He decided to concentrate primarily on large-volume orders. As a single-product manufacturer with no track record, Green was asked to make numerous concessions to the large retailers before they would even consider his product, much less give it shelf space. "Yes, it sounds good, but what can you do for us?" was a typical response. They not only wanted guaranteed advertising expenditures, but also required that people ask for the product before they would order it.

Finally, with the aid of Midway Brokers (a food brokerage firm supplying grocery stores), Green got Tootsizer listed in the Safeway supermarket chain from Manitoba to Thunder Bay. Then the Loblaws chain followed, on the strength of Tootsizer's radio and newspaper advertising. In the meantime, Green personally sold to individual stores and garden florist shops in and around Winnipeg. This was difficult and slow. Most orders were for one case of twelve bottles. These outlets did not seem to be interested in the product.

By the end of 1983, sales (including those made through Safeway) were $40 000 for the Winnipeg area. There were reorders and Safeway kept the product listed for stocking in its Winnipeg warehouse. Green was pleased and wanted to expand his sales area. With the advice of a consultant and his advertising agency, Baker Lovick, he approached other major chain stores again. This time he made more concessions. First, he committed himself to a six-week television ad campaign from mid-May through June of 1984 with banner mentions of the firms that were carrying Tootsizer. Also, to retailers who preordered, he offered "guaranteed sales" (i.e., any goods not sold could be returned for cash).

On this basis, Tootsizer achieved distribution from Thunder Bay to Alberta. After Safeway, the biggest chain, signed up, other chains became interested; eventually Eaton's, The Bay, Simpsons, Gambles, Woolco, Dominion, and Federated Co-Op all ordered the product. Still, Winnipeg was the only centre where any small stores had been approached. Furthermore, it must be remembered that distribution and stocking for chain stores was controlled by the regional warehouses, not by Tootsizer.

By February 1984, Tootsizer had over $50 000 of sales prebooked. In 1983, first-half sales had been $21 000; Green was looking for over $100 000 in sales in 1984.

Supplying Tootsizer was no problem. In fact, all the booking orders were shipped before April to the central warehouses for the chain stores. Members of chains ordered from their company warehouses, which handled deliveries, while the stocking and shelf space decisions were made centrally by company executives. Any sales to individual stores were sent direct from the factory.

Advertising

In 1982 the advertising was strictly word-of-mouth and mostly by Bruce Green. When Traff Green took over in 1983, he needed advertising to be able to approach any major outlets and convince them that there was a demand for the product.

The advertising was all consumer-oriented and done mainly through Winnipeg radio stations and newspapers. All through the summer, Tootsizer had weekly ads in both Winnipeg dailies stressing its technical merits. The company also ran radio advertising on CJOB, a middle-of-the-road station, and on CKRC, a light rock station. The ads, aimed at a younger audience, were produced by the stations and were humorous in nature. In one, plants explained why Tootsizer was the only plant food for them. In another, the outdoor plants went on strike against a homeowner for more Tootsizer. Green liked the ads; they were fun and brought attention to the Tootsizer name.

At the point of purchase there was no special advertising. Tootsizer is in plain plastic bottles with small stick-on labels that give the product's name and instructions for use. The package is not particularly eye-catching.

One ploy that paid good dividends was a special promotion made to key people in the media. Cases of Tootsizer were sent to the hosts of radio and television garden shows and to the garden columnists for the daily papers, along with a note asking them to try the product and to give their opinions to Tootsizer. One result was that Mike Willis, a garden expert and Tootsizer employee, appeared on a 26-week garden show on CKND-TV and made guest appearances on CJOB radio's Problem Corner to answer plant questions.

In all, Tootsizer spent $15 000 on advertising in 1983, including $11 000 for radio and the printed media. The resulting sales were encouraging; Green was now anxious to expand Tootsizer sales to Saskatchewan and Alberta.

An advertising agency sold him on a $90 000 TV campaign covering six cities: Thunder Bay, Winnipeg, Regina, Saskatoon, Edmonton, and Calgary. The campaign would run for six weeks in May and June 1984, and feature 30-second spots once a week on local stations between 5 and 10 P.M. The agency estimated that these spots would reach about 90 percent of the watching public. Green was worried, but the agency convinced him that the idea was sound.

Mr. Green used the premise of this campaign, which included listings of local dealers under each commercial, to sell bookings for Tootsizer to the major chain stores.

The commercial was finished in mid-March, with a production cost of $20 000. Though it was professionally done and technically good, Green did not like it. Nevertheless, he could not drop the campaign because all his sales were tied to it, and he could not opt for a new commercial because there was not enough time.

Questions

1. Describe Tootsizer's overall marketing strategy for new-product production.
2. Evaluate the various elements of their marketing mix in light of this strategy.
3. What did the consultant's survey indicate to you about the plant food and fertilizer market in Winnipeg?
4. What problems was Tootsizer facing in 1984? If you were Green, what changes, if any, would you have made in the marketing program?

Source: M.D. Beckman and R. Lederman.

PART FIVE

Pricing

- CHAPTER 12 — PRICE DETERMINATION
- CHAPTER 13 — MANAGING THE PRICE FUNCTION

Case 9 — Jai Lai Restaurant
Case 10 — Dylex Ltd.

CHAPTER 12

Price Determination

CHAPTER OBJECTIVES

1. Define, explain, or describe the key terms listed under "Vocabulary and Key Terms."
2. Explain the concept of price and its role in the economic system and marketing strategy.
3. Explain the concept of elasticity and its relevance to marketing a product or service.
4. Outline and describe each of the objectives of pricing.
5. Discuss price determination in economic theory and price determination in practice.
6. Explain how break-even analysis, markups, mark-ons, turnover, and other criteria can be used in pricing strategy.
7. Illustrate the decision model for pricing strategy.
8. Apply your knowledge of Chapter 12 to the various activities provided in this chapter of the study guide.

VOCABULARY AND KEY TERMS

From the lettered terms listed below, select the one that best matches the meaning of each of the numbered statements that follows. Write the letter of that choice in the space provided.

a) price
b) utility
c) profit maximization
d) target return objective
e) sales maximization
f) market share objective
g) status quo objective
h) prestige goals
i) customary pricing
j) pure competition
k) monopolistic competition
l) average revenue
m) marginal revenue
n) average cost
o) fixed cost
p) variable cost
q) average variable cost
r) marginal cost
s) cost-plus pricing
t) incremental cost pricing
u) break-even analysis
v) markup

w)   mark-on
x)   stock turnover
y)   marginal analysis
z)   oligopoly
aa)   monopoly

1.   _____ In economic theory, a cost curve obtained by the total variable costs and dividing by the related quantity

2.   _____ The objective that emphasizes the maintenance of stable prices in order to allow a firm to concentrate its efforts in other areas of marketing

3.   _____ The exchange value of a good or service

4.   _____ The number of times an average inventory is sold annually

5.   _____ A market structure involving a heterogeneous product and geographic differentiation, allowing a marketer some degree of control over prices

6.   _____ An approach to profit maximization where the addition to total revenue is just balanced by an increase in total cost

7.   _____ In economic theory, the change in total cost that results from producing an additional unit of output

8.   _____ In economic theory, a revenue curve obtained by dividing total revenues by the quantity associated with these revenues

9.   _____ A market structure in which there are very few sellers, with no one seller controlling it

10.   _____ A market structure characterized by homogeneous products in which there are so many buyers and sellers that none has a significant influence on price

11.   _____ A pricing objective based on setting relatively high prices to maintain an image of quality

12.   _____ A pricing strategy based on the traditional costs of a product

13.   _____ A market structure with only one seller of a product with no close substitutes

14.   _____ In pricing theory, those costs that do not vary with difference in output

15.   _____ In pricing theory, those costs that change when the level of production is altered

16.   _____ A pricing policy that uses some base cost figures per unit to which are added a mark-up to cover unassigned costs and to provide a profit

17.   _____ A pricing objective linked to achieving and maintaining a stated percentage of the market for a firm's product or service

18.   _____ The want-satisfying power of a product or service

19.   _____ In economic theory, a cost curve obtained by dividing total cost by the quantity associated with these costs

20.   _____ In economic theory, the change in total revenue resulting from the sale of an incremental unit

21.   _____ A pricing objective that sets a minimum (floor) at what is considered the lowest acceptable profit level and then seeks to maximize sales within this framework

22.   _____ A pricing procedure in which only the costs directly attributable to a specific output are considered in setting a price

23.   _____ In pricing practice, the amount that is added to cost to determine a selling price

24.   _____ In pricing practice, the markup based on costs

25.   _____ A pricing tool for testing the financial implications of possible price decisions before they are actually implemented

26.   _____ A profitability objective usually stated as a percentage of sales or profits

27.   _____ In pricing theory, the point at which the addition to total revenue is balanced by an increase in total costs

PRACTICE TEST

True-False: In the space to the right of each statement, check the appropriate line to indicate whether the statement is true or false.

		True	**False**
1.	The rent for your apartment and tuition for your education are examples of price.		
2.	Marketing objectives are decided upon once pricing objectives have been determined.		
3.	Price policies and procedures are developed after the company has determined its pricing objectives.		
4.	Based on the percentage of respondents ranking the item, the top overall pricing objective is the creation of an identifiable image for the firm.		
5.	The primary objective used by most firms is that of achieving a specified return on investment.		
6.	In classical economic theory, the traditional pricing objective has been to maximize sales.		
7.	Target objectives are long-term in nature and are a specified return on sales or investment.		
8.	A company with a large share of a market will likely have the objective of retaining its market share.		
9.	The two most important factors influencing profitability are market share and quality.		
10.	The status quo objective stems from a desire to minimize competitive pricing action.		
11.	Status quo objectives are no longer a significant factor in pricing.		
12.	A large percentage of businesses follow economic theory in setting prices.		
13.	An oligopoly is a market structure with only one seller of a product with no close substitutes.		
14.	Average variable cost is simply the total variable cost divided by the related quantity.		
15.	Elasticity is a measure of the responsiveness of purchasers and suppliers to changes in price.		
16.	For manufacturers of luxury products, sales volume will climb drastically with a slight decrease in price.		
17.	One factor determining the elasticity of demand is the availability of substitutes.		
18.	The two most common cost-oriented pricing procedures are the full-cost approach and target-return pricing.		
19.	Incremental pricing attempts to overcome some of the problems of allocating fixed expenses.		
20.	Cost-oriented pricing adequately accounts for product demand.		

21.   A very low price may cause a price war in an oligopoly.

22.   The formula for determining break-even in units is to divide the per-unit contribution to fixed costs by the total fixed costs.

23.   Total costs is equal to total fixed cost plus total variable costs.

24.   Above average turnover, such as for grocery products, is generally associated with relatively high markup percentages.

25.   Full-cost pricing uses all relevant variable costs and fixed costs in setting the product's price.

Multiple Choice: Choose the expression that best answers the question or best completes the sentence.

26.   The most commonly reported primary pricing objective is to
  a.   meet competitive price levels
  b.   meet specified rate of return on investments
  c.   meet specified total profit level
  d.   increase market share
  e.   serve selected market segments

27.   The most commonly reported secondary pricing objective is to
  a.   meet competitive price levels
  b.   meet specified rate of return on investments
  c.   meet specified total profit level
  d.   increase market share
  e.   serve selected market segments

28.   In classical economic theory, the traditional pricing objective has been to
  a.   increase market share
  b.   achieve a specified return on investments
  c.   meet competition pricing practices
  d.   maximize profits
  e.   maximize sales

29.   Which of the following is not a volume objective?
  a.   maximization of sales within a given profit constraint
  b.   target return on sales
  c.   retaining market share
  d.   increasing market share
  e.   none of the above

30.   Profitability pricing objectives include
  a.   target return on sales
  b.   maximization of sales
  c.   increasing market share
  d.   status quo
  e.   prestige

31.   The most commonly mentioned primary and secondary pricing objective in a recent survey of businesses was
  a.   target return on sales
  b.   sales maximization subject to profit constraints
  c.   meeting competitors' prices
  d.   increasing market share
  e.   establishing relatively high prices to maintain a prestige image

32. Marginal cost is the
a. result of demand curves from which break-even analysis is calculated
b. differences between total costs (TC) and total revenue (TR)
c. change in total cost resulting from an additional unit of output
d. composition of fixed and variable components of revenue
e. formula TC+TR

33. The most commonly used method for setting prices today is
a. incremental pricing
b. marginal analysis
c. break-even analysis
d. cost-plus pricing
e. market-inspired pricing

34. The Melvin Manufacturing Company makes metal castings for the plumbing industry. This firm is planning to introduce a new manhole cover assembly and is wondering how many units it will have to sell to break even on the deal. Fixed costs to tool up to make this assembly are $100 000. Variable costs for each unit produced will be $20. At the price of $45 per assembly, how many units must be sold to break even?
a. 2500
b. 4000
c. 5000
d. 8000
e. 7500

35. John Franklin is a retailer who buys goods from Martin Manufacturing. The manufacturers selling price to this retailer is $50. The markup to the consumer is 40 percent of the retail price. The price the consumer pays will be
a. $125
b. $83.33
c. $75
d. $98
e. Not enough information is available to determine the price.

36. What is the "off-retail percentage" markdown on an item marked down from $125 to $100?
a. 25 percent
b. 33.33 percent
c. 20 percent
d. 15 percent
e. 28 percent

37. What is the markdown from the perspective of the department manager based on internal control procedures?
a. 25 percent
b. 33.33 percent
c. 20 percent
d. 15 percent
e. 28 percent

38. If a company has sales of $150 000 and an average inventory at cost of $50 000, its stock turnover is
a. 5
b. 4
c. 3.333

d. 3
e. 10

39. A major factor influencing the elasticity of demand is the
a. decrease in price of the product
b. drop in demand for its substitutes or complements
c. availability of substitutes or complements
d. increase of supply of the product
e. constant demand for the product

40. A product is priced to sell for $12 with average variable costs of $8. The company expects to earn a profit of $400 000 with its total fixed costs of $120 000. What is the minimum number of units that must be sold in order to reach this target return?
a. 400 000
b. 130 000
c. 120 000
d. 80 000
e. 50 000

41. John bought a bike from a retailer for $141.50. The retailer bought it from a manufacturer for $85. What was the markup on the bike?
a. 50 percent
b. 45 percent
c. 40 percent
d. 80 percent
e. 35 percent

42. If a firm has a marketing objective of increasing market share by 10 percent, the price objective would be
a. profitability
b. volume
c. social
d. prestige
e. none of the above

43. By using a market-share objective in pricing strategy, a firm may
a. be subject to regulations by the government
b. realize high profits
c. gain a more competitive position in the industry
d. develop a monopoly
e. all of the above

44. Which of the following statements is not derived from William Baumol's theory of pricing behaviour?
a. Firms set a minimum at what they consider the lowest acceptable profit level.
b. Firms should set price at a point where the addition to total revenue is just balanced by the increase in total cost.
c. Companies should maximize sales subject to a profit constraint.
d. Firms continue to expand sales as long as total profits do not drop below the minimum return level.
e. all of the above

45. Monopolistic competition is characterized by all of the following except
a. product differentiation

   b.   a market somewhat easy to enter
   c.   control over prices
   d.   a market somewhat difficult to enter

46.   In the short run, a firm will halt production in order to minimize its losses if
   a.   price falls below AC
   b.   price falls below AC, but remains above AVC
   c.   price exceeds AVC
   d.   price falls below AVC
   e.   none of the above

47.   Oligopoly is not characterized by which of the following?
   a.   control over price
   b.   a relatively small number of buyers and sellers
   c.   difficulty in entering the market
   d.   common in auto industry
   e.   none of the above

48.   The point of profit maximization is
   a.   MR = MC
   b.   the point where the MC curve intersects the AVC curve and the AC curve at the minimum points
   c.   the lowest point on the AFC curve
   d.   the lowest point on the AVC curve
   e.   the midpoint on the quality axis of the curve

49.   Price theory concepts are difficult to apply in practice because of
   a.   difficulty in estimating demand curves
   b.   social pressure
   c.   firms not attempting to maximize profits
   d.   inadequate communication
   e.   all of the above

50.   Which of the following relationships is true at the break-even point?
   a.   Profit is maximized.
   b   Price is minimized.
   c.   Variable costs are covered, but fixed costs are not.
   d.   Fixed costs are covered, but variable costs are not.
   e.   Total variable costs and total fixed costs are covered.

ANSWER KEY: CHAPTER 12

Vocabulary and Key Terms	True-False	Multiple Choice
1. q	1. T	26. b
2. g	2. F	27. a
3. a	3. T	28. d
4. x	4. F	29. b
5. k	5. T	30. a
6. y	6. T	31. c
7. r	7. F	32. c
8. l	8. T	33. d
9. z	9. T	34. b
10. j	10. T	35. b
11. h	11. F	36. c
12. i	12. F	37. a
13. aa	13. F	38. d
14. o	14. T	39. c
15. p	15. T	40. b
16. s	16. F	41. c
17. f	17. T	42. b
18. b	18. F	43. e
19. n	19. T	44. b
20. m	20. F	45. b
21. e	21. T	46. d
22. t	22. F	47. a
23. v	23. T	48. a
24. w	24. F	49. e
25. u	25. T	50. e
26. d		
27. c		

EXERCISE 12.1: FROBISHER MANUFACTURING COMPANY

Frobisher Manufacturing Company produces one product, a Myrna armchair, described as follows: classic design; comfortable; supporting fabric of pure, sand-coloured linen; seat and back wound at the front and attached with leather straps at the back of the seat; frame of solid pine with a clear lacquer finish. The chair is to be sold at a very affordable price, but the company must determine the specific price after conducting break-even and profitability analyses. The following information was used by the company.

1. *Fixed Cost.* The fixed cost for the year was estimated at $400 000. Included in the cost figure were administrative salaries and insurance premiums, rent, utilities, depreciation of machinery, telephone expense, supplies expense, advertising expense, and marketing costs.
2. *Variable Cost.* The variable cost per unit (for each chair produced) was estimated at $40. Included in the direct materials cost were the linen fabric, leather straps, foam, pine wood, and lacquer finish. Direct labour cost was also allocated and included in this figure.
3. *Factory Selling Price.* The factory selling price is to be one of four possible prices — $65, $80, $100, $120.

4. *Market Demand.* A market research report indicates the following demand for the chairs at the above price levels:

Price	Market Demand (in units)
$65	15 000
80	12 000
100	10 000
120	7 000

Questions

1. Determine the break-even point in units at each price level.

(1) Unit Price	(2) Unit Variable Cost	(3) Contribution to Overhead (1) – (2)	(4) Total Fixed Cost per Annum	(5) Break-even Point (in units) (4) ÷ (3)
$ 65				
80				
100				
120				

2. Develop a profitability analysis chart showing your computations at each price level.

(1) Unit Price	(2) Market Demand (in units)	(3) Total Revenue (1) × (2)	(4) Total Fixed Cost	(5) Total Variable Cost	(6) Total Cost (4) + (5)	(7) Total Profits (3) – (6)
$ 65						
80						
100						
120						

3. On the basis of the break-even and profitability analyses, arrive at the specific factory price to be charged for the chairs.

4. If the product is to be sold directly to specific furniture stores, what would be the suggested retail price if the trade discount to the retailer is 40 percent of the suggested retail price?

5. Complete the graph below using information obtained from your profitability and break-even analyses at the specific factory price to be charged for the chairs.

EXERCISE 12.2: ACHIEVING TARGET RETURN

Joseph Peacock is the Controller of Chief Mountain Food Company, a national company that man-ufactures food products, including a coffee line, a herbal-tea line, and a line of jams. Chief Mountain currently has a market share of only 2 percent, but it is growing and the company is positive about the future. A year ago, Joseph set a target-return-on-sales objective of 20 percent. He is now sitting down to analyze the results. The coffee line of products includes the Chinook, Buffalo, and Peacock brands. Sales, costs, and profits for the past year are as follows:

	Sales	Costs	Profits
Chinook	$700 000	$575 000	$125 000
Buffalo	500 000	400 000	100 000
Peacock	350 000	275 000	75 000

The company's herbal-tea line also includes three brands. The top brand by far is Mayflower. The other two brands, Three Hills and Big Mountain, were introduced two years ago. Sales, costs, and profits for the past year are as follows:

	Sales	Costs	Profits
Mayflower	$780 000	$660 000	$120 000
Three Hills	340 000	270 000	70 000
Big Mountain	200 000	175 000	25 000

Chief Mountain produces two brands of jam, Sun and Moon. Both include boysenberry, strawberry, and huckleberry jams, but the Moon-brand jams are lower in price and quality. Year-end results were as follows:

	Sales	Costs	Profits
Sun	$500 000	$400 000	$100 000
Moon	400 000	350 000	50 000

Joseph now must evaluate the overall success of the company over the past year, compared to the target-return-on-sales objective that was set at the beginning of the year. He will have to determine

EXHIBIT 12.1

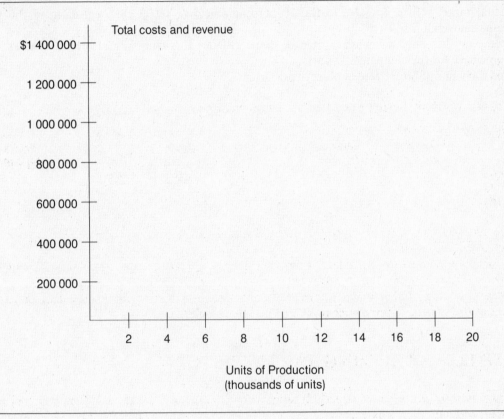

the success of each product in the line as well as the success of each line, then determine the overall target return on sales.

Questions

1. What was the target return on sales for each product in the coffee line? What was the target return on sales for the overall coffee line? Evaluate the results.

2. What was the target return on sales for each product in the herbal tea line? What was the target return on sales for the overall herbal tea line? Evaluate the results.

3. What was the target return on sales for each product in the jam line. What was the target return on sales for the overall jam line? Evaluate the results.

4. What was the overall target return on sales for the company (the product mix)? How close was the actual target return on sales to the 20-percent objective set at the beginning of the year? Evaluate the overall results.

5. The company has only a 2 percent market share. Should this company also have market share as an objective for the company? Discuss.

6. What is the value of target-return objectives. Discuss.

CHAPTER 13

Managing the Price Function

CHAPTER OBJECTIVES

1. Define, explain, or describe the key terms listed under "Vocabulary and Key Terms."
2. Explain the reasoning and methodology behind price quotations.
3. Explain the use of discounts and allowances and their effect on the list price of a good.
4. Outline the several alternatives to sellers of goods in handling transportation costs.
5. Explain why price policies are foundations on which pricing decisions are made.
6. Explain the relationship between price and the consumer's perception of a product's quality.
7. Discuss negotiated prices and competitive bidding, transfer pricing, and pricing in the public sector.
8. Explain the relationship between price levels, advertising expenditures, and profitability.
9. Apply your knowledge of Chapter 13 to the various activities included in this chapter of the study guide.

VOCABULARY AND KEY TERMS

From the lettered terms listed below, select the one that best matches the meaning of each of the numbered statements that follow. Write the letter of that choice in the space provided.

a) list price
b) cash discount
c) trade discount
d) noncumulative quantity discount
e) cumulative quantity discount
f) trade-in allowance
g) promotional allowance
h) brokerage allowances
i) F.O.B. plant
j) freight absorption
k) uniform delivered price
l) zone pricing
m) psychological pricing
n) unit pricing
o) skimming pricing
p) penetration pricing
q) flexible pricing
r) price lining
s) loss leader
t) transfer price
u) odd pricing

v) promotional price
w) profit centre
x) price limit

1. _____ The practice of marketing merchandise at a limited number of prices

2. _____ A price policy based upon the belief that certain prices are more appealing to buyers than others

3. _____ A price policy that refers to the charges for goods sent from one profit centre to another within the same company

4. _____ A psychological pricing technique in which prices are set ending in numbers not commonly used for price quotations

5. _____ Those rates that are normally quoted to potential buyers

6. _____ An advertising or sales promotional grant by a manufacturer to other channel members to integrate promotional strategy within a channel

7. _____ A pricing policy whereby a seller permits a buyer to subtract transportation expenses from the bill

8. _____ The pricing practice of offering payments to channel members or buyers for performing marketing functions normally required by a manufacturer

9. _____ Prices stated in terms of some recognized unit of measurement or a standard numerical count

10. _____ Quantity discounts that are one-time reductions in list price

11. _____ A price policy whereby the same price (including transportation expenses) is quoted to all buyers regardless of where they are located

12. _____ Those reductions in price that are given for prompt payment of a bill

13. _____ A lower-than-normal price used as an ingredient in a firm's selling strategy

14. _____ Any part of an organization to which revenue and controllable costs can be assigned

15. _____ The price policy requiring a buyer to pay all shipping charges

16. _____ A price policy setting an entry price for a product lower than what is expected to be the long-term price

17. _____ A price policy offering different prices to similar buyers who purchase similar quantities of merchandise

18. _____ A price policy whereby retailers price goods very low to attract customers, in the hope that they will buy other regularly priced merchandise

19. _____ A price policy that attempts to maximize the revenue from sales of a new product before the entry of competition

20. _____ A uniform delivered price quoted by geographical region

21. _____ A price policy that permits reduction, without altering the basic list price, by deducting from an item's price an amount for an old item a customer is replacing

22. _____ Quantity discounts that are reductions determined by purchasers of goods over a stated time period

23. _____ Payments, similar to trade or functional discounts, offered to certain channel members for special functions they have performed

24. _____ The belief that consumers regard perceived quality to vary directly with price, within a specified range

PRACTICE TEST

True-False: In the space to the right of each statement, check the appropriate line to indicate whether the statement is true or false.

	True	**False**
1. Payment terms such as 2/10, n/30 are examples of functional discounts.	_____	_____

2. Automobile manufacturers quote the list of a car sold to dealers throughout the country on the basis of a freight absorption price.

3. Unit pricing has been effective in improving the shopping habits of the urban poor.

4. A one-price policy is common in Canada because it facilitates mass merchandising.

5. "Buy one tire at the regular price, get the second for one cent" is an example of psychological pricing.

6. Skimming pricing policy is the most commonly used pricing technique.

7. A penetration policy attempts to maximize the revenue received from the sale of a new product before the entry of competition.

8. A skimming policy permits the marketer to control demand in the introductory stages of a product's life cycle.

9. A skimming policy's major disadvantage is that it will attract competition to the market.

10. A marketer of a new technological product is likely to price it at a lower price than its long-term price.

11. Penetration pricing is likely to be used in instances where demand for the new product or service is highly elastic and where consumers are price-sensitive.

12. The most difficult part of skimming and penetration pricing is deciding when to move the price to its intended level.

13. A variable price policy is more common in Canadian retailing than in industrial marketing.

14. A one-price policy adds flexibility to selling at the retail level.

15. Following the competition is one way of making pricing secondary to other elements in the marketing mix.

16. Price lining is the practice of marketing merchandise at a limited number of prices.

17. Most promotional pricing is done at the industrial level.

18. The use of loss leaders is a good example of the application of psychological pricing.

19. Most consumers have limits within which product quality perception varies directly with price.

20. Noncumulative quantity discounts are reductions determined by purchases over a stated time period.

21. Promotional allowances are attempts to integrate promotional strategy in the channel.

22. F.O.B. plant means the seller must pay all the freight charges.

23. There is a move today toward more user-paid systems for public services such as education.

24. In bidding for contracts, the most difficult task is estimating the probability that a certain bid will be accepted.

25. The transfer price is the price for sending goods from one
company profit centre to another.   _____ _____

Multiple Choice: Choose the expression that best answers the question or completes the sentence.

26. The pricing policy used to introduce the first ballpoint pen to the market after World War II
was a
  a. skimming policy
  b. penetration policy
  c. competitive policy
  d. cost-plus policy
  e. market-inspired policy

27. The pricing policy used by a food manufacturer to introduce a new-to-the-company canned fruit
product is likely to be a
  a. skimming strategy
  b. penetration strategy
  c. competitive pricing strategy
  d. cost-plus pricing strategy
  e. market-inspired strategy

28. In introducing to the market a distinctive, new toothpaste that will fight tooth decay and ensure
bright white teeth, Procter & Gamble is likely to follow a
  a. skimming-pricing policy
  b. penetration-price policy
  c. competitive-pricing policy
  d. costing policy
  e. market-inspired policy

29. The major disadvantage of a skimming-price policy is that it
  a. does not permit a company to recover its development cost quickly
  b. concentrates on costs rather than sales
  c. attracts competition
  d. is not effective for selling new, distinctive products
  e. lacks incentives for stimulating demand

30. A penetration price policy is used when
  a. prices are set high initially with the intent of dropping them later on to stimulate further demand
  b. the product is unique or different and a company wants to stimulate sales initially
  c. the premise is that an initially lower price will help secure market acceptance
  d. the product or service is highly inelastic
  e. potential competitors see the innovating company make large returns and are encouraged to enter
     the market

31. More than half of the respondents to a recent survey indicated that in pricing new products
they used a
  a. skimming strategy
  b. penetration strategy
  c. price at the level of comparable products
  d. competitive pricing strategy
  e. c and d

32. A one-price policy is common in
  a. retailing

b. wholesaling
c. industrial marketing
d. international marketing
e. institutional marketing

33. When a dress manufacturer prices its dresses at four price levels, it is using a policy of
a. variable pricing
b. psychological pricing
c. loss-leader pricing
d. price lining
e. promotional pricing

34. Ethical and moral implications surround the pricing practice of
a. flexible pricing
b. psychological pricing
c. loss-leader pricing
d. price lining
e. promotional pricing

35. Prestige pricing and odd pricing are associated with
a. flexible pricing
b. psychological pricing
c. loss-leader pricing
d. price lining
e. promotional pricing

36. Functional discounts are payments made to channel members or buyers for performing some marketing function for the manufacturer. Manufacturers refer to these discounts as trade discounts and they are determined through the use of
a. cash discounts
b. sales turnover calculations
c. markdowns
d. rebates
e. markups

37. Discounts, or one-time reductions in list price, granted because of large purchases from a manufacturer are known as
a. cash discounts
b. cumulative quantity discounts
c. noncumulative quantity discounts
d. rebates
e. trade discounts

38. Price limits basically mean that
a. people consciously limit their spending to goods that do not affect their consumption patterns
b. a firm may encounter legal opposition if the prices of its products exceed certain limits
c. the relationship between price and sales volume is limited to values greater than 2
d. consumers have limits within which their product-quality perceptions vary directly with price
e. reasonable individuals expect to be able to limit spending to necessities and a few luxuries, even in bad times

39. Phantom freight occurs when a business pays the majority of transportation costs, even though it may be located closer to the seller than a more distant buyer. This practice is associated with
a. F.O.B. plant pricing

b.   zone pricing
c.   F.O.B. mill pricing
d.   uniform-delivered pricing
e.   basing-point pricing

40.   A major problem facing company decision makers who transfer prices is
a.   how to determine the product-service attributes
b.   when to complete the transfer
c.   how to assign the controllable costs
d.   what rate to charge
e.   that no market price exists for transferred products and services

41.   A method of handling transportation costs that is often referred to as postage-stamp pricing is
a.   freight absorption pricing
b.   F.O.B. plant pricing
c.   basing-point pricing
d.   uniform-delivered pricing
e.   zone pricing

42.   Discounts that are also called functional discounts are
a.   cash discounts
b.   cumulative quantity discounts
c.   trade discounts
d.   promotional allowances
e.   noncumulative quantity discounts

43.   Which of the following is not a consideration when the marketer is dealing with shipping costs that are a high percentage of total costs?
a.   determining the geographic scope the firm can serve
b.   net margins earned
c.   the ability of the firm to control or influence resale prices of distributors
d.   delivery terms to potential customers
e.   all of the above

44.   The price policy that markets merchandise of a limited number of lines and identifies the market segment to which a firm is appealing is
a.   loss-leader pricing
b.   flexible pricing
c.   unit pricing
d.   price lining
e.   psychological pricing

45.   A key factor in using penetration pricing is
a.   the size of the market share desired
b.   whether the product is a consumer or industrial good
c.   the amount of competition
d.   the size of the product line
e.   when to move the price up

46.   Which pricing strategy is used to allow a firm to recover its sunk costs quickly?
a.   penetration pricing
b.   odd pricing
c.   price lining

   d.   skimming pricing
   e.   loss-leader pricing

47. The pricing policy based on the belief that certain prices are more appealing to buyers than others is
   a.   psychological pricing
   b.   penetration pricing
   c.   skimming pricing
   d.   price lining
   e.   unit pricing

48. Which of the following is not a consideration when using promotional pricing?
   a.   The consumer may have misconceptions about the prices.
   b.   Loss of profits could result from prolonged use.
   c.   Some consumers are not influenced by price appeals.
   d.   It may violate the Competition Act.
   e.   all of the above

49. Which of the following is not a pricing consideration in the public sector?
   a.   It is best to use the full-cost approach.
   b.   Taxes act as an indirect price.
   c.   It is best to use an ability-to-pay base.
   d.   The price should function as an instrument to recover costs.
   e.   none of the above

50. A firm is going to submit a bid for a job that it estimates will cost $35 000. One executive has proposed a bid of $60 000, another a bid of $50 000. There is a 40-percent chance of the buyer accepting the first bid and a 60-percent chance of the buyer accepting the second bid. From the expected net profit, which bid should the firm submit?
   a.   the first bid
   b.   the second bid
   c.   neither, because both will generate a low profit
   d.   either, because both bids generate the same expected net profit
   e.   The problem cannot be solved without additional information.

ANSWER KEY: CHAPTER 13

Vocabulary and Key Terms	True-False	Multiple Choice
1. r	1. F	26. a
2. m	2. F	27. c
3. t	3. F	28. b
4. u	4. T	29. c
5. a	5. F	30. c
6. g	6. F	31. e
7. j	7. F	32. a
8. c	8. T	33. d
9. n	9. T	34. c
10. d	10. F	35. b
11. k	11. T	36. e
12. b	12. T	37. c
13. v	13. F	38. d
14. w	14. F	39. d
15. i	15. T	40. d
16. p	16. T	41. d
17. q	17. F	42. c
18. s	18. F	43. e
19. o	19. T	44. d
20. l	20. F	45. e
21. f	21. T	46. d
22. e	22. F	47. a
23. h	23. T	48. e
24. x	24. T	49. a
	25. T	50. a

EXERCISE 13.1: FRIDAY

Waterloo Electronics of Ontario has invented and produced a computerized robot named Friday, whose 256 K memory can be easily programmed to do household chores. The housekeeper simply inserts a software disk into the mechanical robot and uses a detached keyboard to select the appropriate program. Friday then completes the required activity with amazing efficiency.

Ube Hess, marketing manager for Waterloo, wonders whether he should use a penetration or a skimming-price policy in selling this product. He knows that the software package is quite sophisticated, and that it will take even a shrewd competitor at least a year or more before it could come up with a similar robot. Waterloo has patent protection, but Ube knows that a competitor could circumvent that protection by developing a robot with a different design and method of operating. The robot must be priced at $2000 in order to cover all costs and provide a reasonable profit margin.

Ube is currently negotiating an exclusive distribution contract with Eaton's, which will market the robot in Canada. Jorge Martinez, representing Eaton's, has suggested that Eaton's will want a markup of at least 50 percent on the retail selling price. The department store has also indicated that it will promote the robot in its flyers and provide some limited local advertising. Ube realizes that he has a number of questions to answer before he can decide whether or not to market this product through this department store.

Questions

1. When should a company employ a skimming pricing policy? When should a company use a penetration pricing policy? Would a penetration or a skimming pricing policy be more appropriate in setting a price for the robots? Why?

2. Would the initial price set for Friday be a short-term or a long-term price? When would Ube change the price on the robot?

3. What price should be set for Friday? Back up your answer with sound arguments and necessary calculations.

4. Are there any other pricing moves the company should consider at this time?

5. Should Ube sell Friday only through Eaton's? Discuss.

EXERCISE 13.2: PRICING THE EXCALIBUR WATCH

Rebecca Hummel, marketing manager of Enchant Watch Company, is holding a high-level executive meeting to review some critical decisions made by the company two months ago. At that time, Enchant agreed to market its new Excalibur quartz watch only through select jewellery stores in cities with at least 25 000 people. The company currently markets men's and women's watches in three lines, priced at $69.95, $89.95, and $129.95. The Excalibur watch will be marketed to both the male and the female market, and is of slightly higher quality than the Marquis Royal men's and women's watch, currently the company's top-of-the-line offering. The company had been using psychological pricing, but Rebecca wants to discuss the validity of odd pricing. "The consumer is no longer sensitive to odd pricing," she says. "Is it wise for us to continue with this policy? Furthermore, what should the specific price be for this watch, and how will this new brand affect the company's price lines?" Enchant currently sells through a national specialty wholesaler who is provided a markup of 20 percent of the price to the retailer. The recommended markup to the jewellery stores was 60 percent of the suggested retail price. Joe Murphy, the company's production manager, says, "The prices we charge for the Excalibur watches should take into consideration the current markups to the trade, but the bottom line is, we must get back $45 per watch to recoup our manufacturing and shipping costs and permit a minimum 10 percent profit."

The meeting ends without any final decisions being made. Hummel realizes that the pricing policy is only one of several factors that will determine the success or failure of the Excalibur watch; pricing will have to be co-ordinated with specific product, distribution, and promotion strategies.

Questions

1. What factors should Hummel and her committee consider in establishing a pricing policy for the Excalibur watch?

2. Is psychological pricing important in marketing watches? Explain.

3. Using the current markup structure offered to the trade and taking into consideration the company's factory cost, what price should be set for the product? What other factors should the company take into consideration before making a final decision on price?

4. Where should the Excalibur watch fit in the price-line structure? Is price lining important in the sale of watches from the point of view of the manufacturer and the consumer? What problems are associated with price lining?

Case 9

JAI LAI RESTAURANT

The Jai Lai Restaurant is a large, high-quality, "cloth tablecloth and napkins" establishment. Its colourful history dates back to 1933, when Jasper E. Wottring founded the original cafe. He conceived the name from the game jai alai, which he observed being played while visiting Florida. The *a* was removed from *alai* in the belief it would make the name easier to recognize and remember.

In the early 1950s, the Jai Lai was moved to a new building with a seating capacity of 600. The large dining area was separated into five rooms by Spanish-style open arches and the interior included such interesting touches as reproductions of Spanish masters and exotic fish in lighted aquariums mounted in the perimeter walls.

The present owner and president of the corporation, Ted Girves, bought out one of the partners in 1963 and became a 50-percent shareholder. Mr. Wottring had died in the late 1950s. His son Dave is general manager. This new management team has been responsible for several changes, including hiring more waitresses instead of waiters and expanding the menu.

Slow Business during the Week

In early 1980, management decided to tackle a problem which seems to plague the restaurant business in general — how to generate more business on the slow weekdays (Monday-Thursday). The Jai Lai had no trouble drawing turn-away crowds on the weekends, yet weekday patronage was disappointing. Whereas they would typically serve 1200–1300 people on Saturday night, the average Monday crowd would total only 350–400 people.

Management examined certain approaches, such as outright discounting and coupons, which had been adopted by competitors, and concluded that such programs might harm the restaurant's quality image and convey the impression that they were "hurting" for business. Any program they adopted would have to be distinctive and effective, yet not jeopardize the quality image they had worked so long and hard to achieve.

Proposal — A Rebate Program

The automotive rebate programs then in progress inspired the idea of a similar "rebate" on selected dinners. Customers purchasing the selected dinners on Monday through Thursday evenings would receive the rebate in the form of silver dollars at the time the bill was paid.

There was a certain logic behind the rebate format:

- *A silver dollar rebate, as opposed to a simple discount or paper-money rebate, would be much more distinctive, stimulating conversation and recall.*
- *While other programs such as coupons or discounts actually reduced the amount of the bill and thus tended to reduce tip income and hurt employee morale, a rebate would have but a limited effect in this direction.*
- *By getting a full-priced check, the customer would see that prices were not high normally.*
- *Management could vary the dinners eligible for rebate and observe the resulting customer behaviour.*

It was decided that the program would have the following objectives:

1. to utilize the restaurant's capacity better during the week
2. to increase profitability[1]
3. to broaden its customer base, i.e., to attract new, regular customers.

The last objective was considered particularly important. The management felt that even if the restaurant only broke even on the incremental weekday business, the program would still be worthwhile if it attracted new, regular clientele. Such people might return on a weekend or on a weekday (ordering a dinner not eligible for rebate) and thus improve overall profitability. The management felt particularly confident that the restaurant's quality food and atmosphere would induce many of the first-time visitors to return.

Implementation of the Program

The rebate program was initiated in early March, coupled with weekend newspaper advertising to build awareness of the program. The headline of the advertisements read, "Get Back 2 Silver Dollars... And Enjoy a Great Dinner, Too!" The advertisements also featured three dinner options at competitive prices.

After seven months, management decided to see if the size of rebate influenced sales. In October, therefore, the rebate was changed from $2.00 to $1.00 on selected items.

Although dollar value per check decreased slightly, revenue overall rose substantially. The restaurant was able to handle the increased number of patrons with only a 20 percent increase in the weekday work force.

Review of the Program

Management, although encouraged by the response to the rebate program, had several misgivings at the end of the program's first three months. First, weekend business had hardly been affected by the program. Second, management had noted that as soon as a dinner was no longer eligible for rebate, its sales immediately plummeted to pre-rebate levels. (Of course, sales of dinners newly placed on rebate immediately rose.) Third, the incremental sales of a dinner placed on rebate seemed to be greatly affected by the original price of the dinner.

Inexpensive dinners placed on rebate suddenly became extremely popular, whereas expensive dinners experienced relatively modest increases. The Club Steak Dinner ($6.95) went from average Monday-Thursday sales of 45 weekly to 600–700

weekly within two weeks of being made eligible for rebate. After four weeks, the Porterhouse Steak Dinner ($9.75) replaced the Club Steak Dinner on the list of eligible rebate dinners. The result: Club Steak sales immediately slipped to Monday-Thursday sales of 50 weekly; Porterhouse sales increased, but not so dramatically — from Monday-Thursday sales of 20 weekly to about 210 weekly.

In conclusion, management began to view their new Monday-Thursday trade not as new, regular customers, but more as bargain hunting "opportunists" who would not patronize the restaurant except as induced by the rebate. At this point in time they are trying to evaluate the merits of continuing the rebate program.

Questions

1. Should the rebate program continue?
2. What other options are available to management in its attempt to increase Monday-Thursday business?

Source: From W. Wayne Talarzyk, *Cases for Analysis in Marketing*, 2nd ed. (Dryden Press, 1980). Reprinted by permission.

Note

1. In order to increase profitability, there would have to be a substantial sales increase of relatively expensive dinners. Jai Lai's total direct costs amounted to about 67–75 percent of the menu price with 40–50 percent being direct food costs and 27–30 percent being direct labour costs.

EXHIBIT C9-1 EXAMPLES OF NEWSPAPER ADVERTISEMENTS FOR REBATE PROGRAM

Case 10

DYLEX LTD.

What stops you dead is the look. The Fairweather store in Toronto's Eaton Centre fairly breathes serious money and haute class. The broad, black-and-grey marble aisle and elegant Greek columns evoke the cold glamour of art deco mansions; the lavish folds of burgundy velvet suggest a film star's boudoir. The mannequins have such a devastatingly icy presence that you scarcely notice what they're wearing. "It's gorgeous," sighs one woman. "It looks like Holt Renfrew."

Welcome to Fairweather, the next generation. The 130-store chain, owned by troubled retail giant Dylex Ltd., used to sell fun fashion; hip, low-priced, seasonal throwaways snapped up by trend-conscious teens and style-hungry secretaries. But there are 600 000 fewer teens today than a decade ago. The boomers — the original Dylex clientele — are getting older, and all of them want to dress *up*. The executives at Dylex finally got the demographic message: Fairweather needed a new image.

The result is a $1 million facelift, a fantasia of marble, chrome, velvet and gleaming wood. And the clothes? Well, call them *material working girl*. "It's the same cheap stuff they've always sold," says a woman passing through. "The buttonholes are frayed and these seams are puckering. And the cloth on these blazers is really thin."

New Product Strategy

In retailing, as in other businesses, the product is much more than the merchandise being sold. The product includes store location, interior decor, the sales staff, and the quality of service, as well as the items offered for sale. The Fairweather strategy of combining uptown decor with middle-rent fashion is deliberate. Secretaries read Danielle Steel and yearn to be rich but their paycheques don't stretch very far. Fairweather will give them their dreams, at least for the half-hour they go shopping. "Why can't the working girl making $20 000 or $30 000 a year be surrounded by the luxury of the very wealthy woman?" asks Lynn Posluns, the highly stylish 32-year-old president of Fairweather.

Lynn Posluns understands the very wealthy woman. She is one. Her father is Wilfred Posluns, the tough, secretive multimillionaire who is the chairman, chief executive officer, president, and co-founder of Dylex. Lynn is the rising star of her father's company. She's overseeing the Fairweather repositioning and she's gambling that lots of secretaries will fall for those velvet drapings, that rich marble, those cool columns — that look.

Dylex has more than money riding on Lynn Poslun's expensively padded shoulders. The Fairweather revamp — coming soon to a mall near you — is designed to show that Dylex can still conjure a retail miracle, just as it used to do. But if the miracle fails, one thing is certain: Lynn Posluns won't be the one out of a job.

The Dylex Family

Wilfred Posluns is an intensely private man dedicated to two things: his family and his company. His two loves are closely intertwined. Posluns and his elder brother Irving, who runs one of the Dylex clothing manufacturing companies, own the majority of Dylex's voting shares. Poslun's three children, Wendy, Lynn, and David, are all involved in the company. Wendy, the eldest, is a lawyer and sits on the board of directors. David, 30, is president of the Club Monaco chain in the United States. The way Wilf Posluns sees it, any threat to Dylex is a threat to his family's well-being.

Problems and Opportunities

Wilfred Posluns has a whole plateful of problems. He's locked in a bitter court battle with Jimmy Kay, his former friend and partner, for control of the company they co-founded in 1966. And Posluns and Kay's disastrous acquisitions in the United States — the worst moves in Dylex's history — continue to bleed money. Before the red ink is stanched, the company will have lost well over $200 million. But what galls him most is that Dylex, once Canada's red-hot retailer, has lost its touch. And it will be years before the picture improves. "They don't have much momentum at all," says a retail consultant. "They had their best year in 1985. Since then, they seemed perplexed about what to do next." If his family didn't control the company, Wilfred Posluns would probably be history.

Dylex is still king of the mall, with 1350 stores in Canada under such names as Braemar, Town & Country, Tip Top, Harry Rosen, Thrifty's, and Bi-Way. About $1 in every $10 that Canadians spend on clothes goes into a cash register in a store in one of the 15 retail chains owned by Dylex. But the profits are slipping. In 1988, Dylex earned $30 million on revenue of $2 billion, compared with a profit of $47 million on revenue of $1.6 billion three years earlier. The market segmentation Dylex pioneered — separate chains for different age, style, and mass market income groups — is old hat. This is the age of high-concept retailing, where stores project a picture of a way of life consumers would like to enjoy, and consumers buy image, shopping environment, and merchandise in equal parts.

The competition is stores such as Randy River and Willow Ridge, which sell a hip, global-traveller image, and the clothes to match. Dylex is stuck with Suzy Shier, a retrograde *bimboesque* name from the '60s. The competition is Brettons, a hugely successful chain that sells Ralph Lauren-style clothes for the whole family with terrific service. Dylex is still pushing unisex at Thrifty's, years after the concept went the way of shag haircuts.

The mass market for retail clothing is fragmenting fast. The new buzzword in the rag trade is *micromarketing*. "That," says retail researcher Len Kubas, "means designing the store and stocking merchandise to appeal to customers in the immediate neighbourhood. That works against the mass-market chain retailer. The big chains are just not geared to buying that way."

Company History

It was so much simpler back in the 1960s and 1970s, when Kay and Posluns made retailing magic through potent blend of entrepreneurial dynamism and corporate organization. The two men brought up a raft of chains operating in different segments of the mass market. They left in charge the people who had started them, with huge performance bonuses as incentives. Dylex was a silent partner offering efficient, centralized services such as warehousing, shipping, computers, financing, and real estate. Its 10 manufacturing divisions made many of the clothes the chains sold.

Together Posluns and Kay saw the future of retailing and its name was *shopping mall*. With their dozens of specialty stores, the malls broke the stranglehold the department stores had on shoppers. "We made the decision right from the start we'd go into every regional mall in Canada that had two department stores, no matter where it was, with all our chains," Posluns says. In return for renting so much space, Dylex got long leases at good rates, prime locations, and financial help in building the stores. "Essentially, we were a department store with our departments spread down the spine of the mall," says Kay.

For years, Posluns and Kay relied on the market smarts of their chain operators to keep the company nimble. Dylex was an association of partners; it was never as tightly directed as outsiders believed. "Our roles were to communicate with the chains and watch the bottom line," Posluns says. "My attitude was, 'You've built the chain, you run it.' I never got involved."

Problems in the 1980s

The formula worked, until the mid-1980s, when retailing hit the skids. Mall rents skyrocketed, the competition among the increasing number of specialty stores got ugly, and the women's apparel market, where Dylex does 40% of its business, dissolved into confusion. The company got stuck in a rut, unable to react to the changing mass market. There were fewer young women buying clothes, yet Dylex had three chains — Fairweather, Suzy Shier, and B.H. Emporium — competing for the same shrinking market.

Dylex fumbled new ventures. Harry Rosen Women flopped. Dylex then bought Rubys, which operated 54 high-fashion shoe stores for women under four different names. That, too, was a disaster, and the stores were sold.

As its chains matured and retailing grew more complex and less profitable, Dylex failed to respond. Success had bred complacency. Added to that, the men at the top had their minds on other matters. Posluns admits that Dylex has fallen behind in computer technology, merchandising, marketing strategies, even advertising techniques. "There are a lot of things we've recently started looking at that we didn't pay enough attention to before," he says.

Expansion to the United States

Like most partners who were once close, Kay and Posluns were loath to call it quits. If they gave it one more shot, maybe things would work out. In this atmosphere of hope and mistrust, the two men took their biggest gamble: they announced that Dylex had run out of expansion opportunities in Canada and would go south of the border. That was only partly true. "By going into the United States, Jimmy and I were trying something new," Posluns says. "It reminds me of a couple that has a child to save a marriage."

Posluns and Kay started off cautiously, buying control of two small retail chains in 1984. Then, only months after entering an intensely competitive market in which adventurous Canadian retailers have invariably lost their shirts, Posluns and Kay jettisoned their financial conservatism. They borrowed heavily to buy into a $450 million joint acquisition of Brooks Fashions and T. Edwards, two medium-priced women's clothing chains. The following year they purchased a 600-store chain called Foxmoor aimed at the teenage market, and became the proud co-owners of 1500 stores across the United States.

It was a high-risk move, quite out of character for the two men. They may have been dazzled by their big-name partners. Posluns and Kay had teamed up with AEA Investors Inc., a high-powered acquisitions and leveraged-buyout firm whose funds came from a group of very wealthy executives, men such as the former chairmen of American Express and RCA. "They were supposed to be the leveraged-buyout experts," grumbles Posluns. Kay allows that "we didn't spend enough time taking a close enough look. The management of the chains looked good, but it wasn't. We didn't do enough homework."

And so they failed. Soft sales across all three chains meant that interest costs were impossible to meet. Posluns was soon spending part of every week in New York trying to turn things around. In 1987, after two years of losses, Dylex wrote off its $118 million investment in Brooks and T. Edwards and placed the two chains in bankruptcy. Posluns spent two more years and another $100 million trying to turn around Foxmoor. He gave up in the summer of 1989 and announced that these stores would be sold or shut. "It was a terrible five years," Posluns says, "A fiasco." Dylex's U.S. stores were a black hole into which more than $200 million had disappeared.

The fiasco cost Dylex's Canadian operations their momentum, and Posluns knows it. "We should have started changing things in Canada four or five years ago, because the old way wasn't working anymore," he says. "Part of the reason we didn't was that I was so busy trying to make things work in the United States. Then there was the fighting between me and Jim. Things started happening to us, instead of us being in charge of our own destiny."

New Management Structure

Posluns was too distracted to recognize that if Dylex was going to regain its former glory, it needed a new management structure. It took a beating in the U.S. market to make him realize that he's not a retailer (something Posluns's senior managers have known all along) and Kay's departure to show him that he can't direct a $2-billion conglomerate by himself. Until 1989, Dylex didn't even have a squad of merchandisers to chart the company's course. The vice-presidents in charge of the chains ran their own shows and reported directly to Posluns. "Jim and I were the only people doing strategic level thinking," he says.

Posluns broke the logjam at the top, freeing key chain-store executives from day-to-day operations and forming a nine-member executive committee of vice-presidents and heads of divisions in charge of strategic planning. Top managers like Don Evans, Gord Edelstone, and Irving Teitelbaum immediately set to work on repositioning Dylex's stores and forcing up profits. Dylex's new president, Lionel Robins, was promoted from his position as executive vice-president of womenswear to run this committee. Chairman and majority owner Wilfred Posluns has handed Robins the task of utterly transforming the way Dylex does business.

Questions

1. What do you see as the basic marketing problems facing Dylex Ltd.?
2. What type of marketing research would be helpful to Mr. Posluns and his management team in marketing their stores?
3. What kinds of product extensions and product expansions should Dylex consider?
4. Do you think it is wise for Dylex to change the marketing of their Fairweather stores? Please support your recommendations.

Sources: Material presented here has been adapted from Michael Salter, "On the Rack," *Report on Business Magazine*, February 1990, p. 54, and Jan Matthews and Greg Boyd, "Can Lionel Robins Rescue Dylex?" *Canadian Business*, November 1990, p. 106. Reprinted by permission.

PART SIX

Distribution

- CHAPTER 14 — CHANNEL AND DISTRIBUTION STRATEGY
- CHAPTER 15 — WHOLESALING
- CHAPTER 16 — RETAILING

CASE 11 — *Murphy's Snack Foods*
CASE 12 — *Lucas Foods*

CHAPTER 14

Channel and Distribution Strategy

CHAPTER OBJECTIVES

1. Relate channel strategy to the other variables of the marketing mix.
2. Relate channel strategy to the concept of total quality management.
3. Explain the role of distribution channels in marketing strategy.
4. Describe the various types of distribution channels.
5. Outline the major channel strategy decisions.
6. Discuss conflict and co-operation in the distribution channel.
7. Integrate operations within a physical distribution system to the functioning of marketing channels.
8. Apply your knowledge of Chapter 14 to the various activities included in this chapter of the study guide.

VOCABULARY AND KEY WORDS

From the lettered terms listed below, select the one that best matches the meaning of each of the numbered statements that follows. Write the letter of that choice in the space provided.

a) distribution channel
b) intermediary
c) wholesaling
d) retailing
e) industrial distributor
f) agents
g) intensive distribution
h) selective distribution
i) exclusive distribution
j) TQM
k) EOQ
l) vertical marketing systems (VMS)
m) corporate VMS
n) administered VMS
o) contractual VMS
p) wholesaler-sponsored chain
q) retail co-operative chain
r) franchise
s) physical distribution
t) common carrier
u) contract carrier
v) containerization
w) unitization

1. _____ A business firm operating between a producer and a consumer or industrial purchaser
2. _____ Wholesalers who are involved in the marketing of small accessory equipment and operating supplies
3. _____ Involves the selection of a small number of retailers to handle a firm's product line
4. _____ Organizations recognizing that what they do prior to supplying the customer has a tremendous influence on performances, measured by cost or customer responsiveness
5. _____ Involves a broad range of activities concerned with the efficient movement of finished products from the source of raw materials to the production line and, ultimately, to the consumer
6. _____ A single ownership of each stage of a marketing channel
7. _____ An agreement whereby dealers contract to meet the operating requirements of a manufacturer or other franchisor
8. _____ Transportation carriers that serve the general public for a fee
9. _____ A technique that emphasizes a cost trade-off between two fundamental costs involved with inventory
10. _____ Transportation carriers that enter into contractual arrangements with select customers
11. _____ Channel co-ordination achieved through the exercise of economic and political power by a dominant channel member
12. _____ The activities of persons or firms selling to retailers and other wholesalers or to industrial users, but not in significant amounts to ultimate consumers
13. _____ The path that goods, and title to these goods, follow from producer to consumer
14. _____ Manufacturers of convenience goods who attempt to provide saturation coverage of potential markets
15. _____ A group of retailers who set up a wholesale operation to better compete with chains
16. _____ The selling of products that are purchased by persons for their own use and not for resale
17. _____ An innovation in materials handling that allows for the practice of combining several unitized loads
18. _____ Wholesaling intermediaries who do not take title to the goods they handle
19. _____ A technique whereby manufacturers grant their exclusive rights to a wholesaler or retailer to sell in a geographic location
20. _____ A technique by which wholesalers enter into a formal agreement with a group of retailers to operate under a franchise sponsored by the wholesalers
21. _____ A form of vertical marketing characterized by formal agreements between channel members
22. _____ Professionally managed and centrally programmed networks pre-engineered to achieve operating economies and maximize impact
23. _____ An innovation in materials handling that allows for the practice of combining as many packages as possible into one load

PRACTICE TEST

True-False: In the space to the right of each statement, check the appropriate line to indicate whether the statement is true or false.

		True	False
1.	Distribution channels create time and place utility but not possession utility.	_____	_____
2.	The term "intermediary" refers to both retailers and wholesalers.	_____	_____
3.	Confusion can result from the practices of some firms that operate both wholesaling and retailing operations.	_____	_____

4. If a firm sells 51 percent of its goods to the final consumer and 49 percent to retailers, that firm is still classified as a wholesaler.

5. While marketing channels do not create form utility, they are instrumental in providing time, place, and ownership utility.

6. An essential function of the distribution channel is to adjust discrepancies in assortment.

7. Distribution channel members hold large inventories to account for economies of scale in transporting.

8. Approximately 25 percent of all consumer goods are sold through the producer-to-consumer channel.

9. Agents are more commonly found in the all-aboard channel of distribution.

10. The traditional channel for consumer goods is from producer to agent to wholesaler to retailer to consumer.

11. The term "industrial distributor" is used in the industrial market to refer to those wholesalers who take title to the goods they handle.

12. Distributing services to both consumer and industrial users is usually more complex and more indirect than distributing consumer or industrial goods.

13. An increasingly common trend is the use of more than one distribution channel for similar products.

14. A travel agent in a service channel is an example of a facilitating agency.

15. Contract carriers offer their services to the public at large.

16. Private carriers provide transportation for a market fee.

17. Water carriers are the largest transporters and are considered the most efficient mode by which to move bulk commodities over long distances.

18. Trucking companies' main advantage is being able to haul high-valued goods over short to intermediate distances.

19. EOQ stands for easy order quantity.

20. The idea behind just-in-time inventory systems is to identify stocking levels that meet peak efficiency minimums and to balance higher transportation expenses against reduced inventory-holding expenses.

21. Distribution warehouses receive consolidated shipments from a central distribution centre and distribute smaller shipments to individual customers in more limited areas.

22. Soft drinks, cigarettes, and candy bars are usually distributed selectively.

23. Automobile manufacturers use exclusive distribution to sell their vehicles.

24. Exclusive dealing prohibits a marketing intermediary from handling competing products.

25. When there is single ownership of each stage of the distribution channel, an administered vertical marketing system exists.

Multiple Choice: Choose the expression that best answers the question or best completes the sentence.

26. Wholesalers generally do not sell in significant quantities to
   a. other wholesalers
   b. retailers
   c. industrial users
   d. service organizations
   e. ultimate consumers

27. What type of utility is created if distribution channels make a product available when consumers want to buy it?
   a. time utility
   b. place utility
   c. ownership utility
   d. form utility
   e. awareness utility

28. A business firm operating between the producer and the consumer or industrial producer is referred to as a
   a. marketing intermediary
   b. middleman
   c. facilitating agency
   d. vertical marketing system
   e. a and b

29. The process that alleviates discrepancies in assortment by reallocating the outputs of various producers into assortments desired by individual purchasers is referred to as
   a. assortment
   b. sorting
   c. breaking bulk
   d. the accumulation process
   e. standardizing the transaction

30. What percentage of all consumer goods are sold through the producer to consumer channel?
   a. 25 percent
   b. 50 percent
   c. 5 percent
   d. 33 percent
   e. 17 percent

31. Channels that are established by service providers
   a. tend to be longer than those usually used for tangible goods
   b. are usually more impersonal than those used for tangibles
   c. usually include industrial distributors
   d. are usually shorter than those used for tangible goods
   e. are typically free of horizontal and vertical conflict

32. For recycling to succeed, which of the following conditions must exist?
   a. A new product must be available for the consumer to start the process.
   b. A substantial and continuing quantity of secondary products must be available, such as recyclable aluminium and paper.
   c. There should be a technology to categorize and inventory the material being recycled.
   d. There should be franchises for intermediaries to start recycling new products.
   e. The material to be reprocessed must be metallic or ceramic material, such as glass or steel.

33. The term "industrial distributor" is commonly used in the industrial market to refer to
   a. intermediaries who sell accessory equipment and operating supplies to other wholesalers and retailers
   b. wholesalers who represent a select group of customers
   c. wholesalers who take title to the goods they handle
   d. the sales force of industrial users selling to other industrial users
   e. facilitating agencies representing industrial users

34. Relatively long channels of distribution are utilized for products such as
   a. detergents and hand soap
   b. automobiles
   c. high-fashion clothing
   d. furniture
   e. industrial goods

35. The most common channel used by industrial goods manufacturers is the
   a. agent/wholesaler channel
   b. agent channel
   c. traditional channel
   d. direct channel

36. The most common channel used in the sale of consumer goods is the
   a. all-aboard channel
   b. traditional channel
   c. one-step channel
   d. direct channel

37. A business that provides specialized assistance for regular channel members in moving products from producer to consumer is
   a. franchise
   b. an industrial distributor
   c. a facilitating agency
   d. a marketing specialist
   e. an agent or broker

38. The lower the unit value of the product, the
   a. shorter the channel
   b. longer the channel
   c. more likelihood the shopping goods will be distributed
   d. greater is the necessity for the use of market specialists in the channel
   e. greater the complexity in channel distribution

39. Channels tend to be shorter when
   a. users are in the industrial market
   b. customers are geographically concentrated
   c. specialized knowledge, technical know-how, and regular service needs are present
   d. customers place relatively small numbers of large orders
   e. all of the above

40. Industrial products channels tend to be shorter than consumer channels because
   a. retailers are found only in consumer goods channels
   b. industrial buyers tend to form concentrated markets
   c. there are a limited number of customers
   d. all of the above

e. None of the above; consumer goods channels tend to be shorter than channels for industrial products.

41. Producers of convenience goods who attempt to provide saturation coverage of their potential markets are the prime users of
  a. intensive distribution
  b. selective distribution
  c. exclusive distribution
  d. exclusive dealings
  e. market restriction practices

42. Selective distribution will normally be used
  a. in order to give retailers incentives to push the product at the retail level
  b. when product service is important to the customer
  c. when a manufacturer wishes to reduce its total manufacturing costs
  d. to avoid selling to marginal retailers
  e. all of the above

43. A supplier might force a dealer who wishes to handle a specific line of products to also carry other of the supplier's products or to refrain from purchasing from other suppliers. This practice is known as
  a. market restriction
  b. tied selling
  c. exclusive dealings
  d. resale price maintenance
  e. price discrimination

44. Horne & Pitfield, a wholesaler, has the right in some western provinces to enter into contractual arrangements as a representative of IGA franchises, with specific independent retailers. The franchise is sponsored by Horne & Pitfield and the retailers operate under the IGA banner. This is an example of a
  a. franchise
  b. retailer co-operative
  c. wholesaler-sponsored voluntary chain
  d. corporate chain
  e. consumer co-operative

45. Suboptimization is likely to occur when
  a. each physical distribution function attempts to minimize its own costs
  b. there are unrealistic customer service standards
  c. there is a physical distribution system with centralized control
  d. there are shortages of raw materials and component parts
  e. each manager is shortsighted in functional operations

46. Transport carriers that do not offer their services to the public at large are
  a. common carriers
  b. contract carriers
  c. private carriers
  d. regulated carriers
  e. government carriers

47. Which transportation alternative is considered the largest transporter and the most efficient method of moving bulky products over long distances?
  a. air freight
  b. pipelines

c.   water carriers
d.   trucking
e.   railways

48. Which transportation alternative has the lowest rates per tonne per kilometre?
a.   air freight
b.   pipelines
c.   water carriers
d.   trucking
e.   railways

49. The economic order quantity (EOQ) is based on the premise that
a.   the total costs of inventory goods will be at a minimum when the costs associated both with holding goods and with ordering goods are at a minimum
b.   the total costs of inventory goods will be minimized if a single order is placed for the entire year's requirement
c.   the more orders placed, the less the total cost of maintaining an inventory
d.   the fewer goods held in inventory at any given time, the lower the total inventory costs
e.   it is not the cost of holding or ordering goods that runs up inventory costs, but the actual cost of buying goods

50. The basic ideal of identifying stocking levels that meet peak efficiency minimums and balancing higher transportation costs against reduced inventory expenditures for inventory holding is known as
a.   EOQ
b.   TQM
c.   suboptimization
d.   containerization
e.   JIT

ANSWER KEY: CHAPTER 14

Vocabulary and Key Terms	True-False	Multiple Choice
1. b	1. F	26. e
2. e	2. T	27. a
3. h	3. T	28. e
4. j	4. F	29. b
5. s	5. T	30. c
6. m	6. T	31. d
7. r	7. F	32. b
8. t	8. F	33. c
9. k	9. T	34. a
10. u	10. F	35. d
11. n	11. T	36. b
12. c	12. F	37. c
13. a	13. T	38. b
14. g	14. F	39. e
15. q	15. T	40. d
16. d	16. F	41. a
17. v	17. F	42. e
18. f	18. T	43. b
19. i	19. F	44. c
20. p	20. T	45. a
21. o	21. F	46. b
22. l	22. F	47. c
23. w	23. T	48. e
	24. T	49. a
	25. F	50. e

EXERCISE 14.1: THE FISH MARKET

Abe Morrisey, the proprietor of the Fish Market on Water Street in downtown Halifax, Nova Scotia, has established a reputation in the area as a dynamic businessman. While his main market for fish is Halifax-Dartmouth, he sells fish, especially lobster, across Canada. The Fish Market's customers include moderately expensive and expensive restaurants, restaurants in tourist resorts and high-priced hotels, and retail fish markets in various provinces. Included in the retail market are food chains such as Safeway, Steinberg, IGA, and Super Value. Although Abe does not usually sell through independent wholesalers, he has recently been using the services of Horace Bentley, a fish broker who has both a reputation for efficient service and contacts with retail buyers across the country.

The live lobsters are packed with ice and seaweed in crates and delivered F.O.B. The Fish Market to the Halifax airport on the dates of the orders. Abe has orders for boiled lobsters (pre-cooked) and for canners (small lobsters) as well. These are shipped by air to markets outside Nova Scotia. Other fish such as cod and halibut are also sold across Canada and the same method of packing and shipping is used.

Recently, a number of inquiries about buying lobster have come from Europe. The annual catch of lobster in North America is 30 000 tonnes. European lobsters lack the enlarged claws of the true lobster, and the annual catch in Europe is only 3600 tonnes. Abe wonders whether or not he should enter this market, and if so, whether he should ship via air or water.

Questions

1. What are the advantages and disadvantages of sending lobster by air in Canada?
2. Would shipping by rail be a viable alternative to shipping by air? Why or why not?

3. Should the Fish Market sell lobster to the European market? What factors should be considered before making this move?
4. If Mr. Morrisey decides to enter this market, which of water or air transportation would be the best alternative for shipping lobster to Europe? Why?
5. Does Abe gain any advantages by selling through a fish broker?

EXERCISE 14.2: FEDERAL EXPRESS

In 1973 Fred Smith decided that big airlines could not be relied upon to transport air freight in their cargo hulls. He began to envision an air service that would guarantee customers "absolutely, positively overnight" door-to-door delivery. Smith risked $4 million to purchase a small fleet of jets, which he had painted orange, white, and purple, so that they would be recognizable: thus began the delivery service known as Federal Express.

Smith's initial system was to have parcels picked up in the evening, flown by jet to a single destination sorting centre, and rerouted to their final destination before sunrise. Federal Express was not an instant success, but since overcoming a few early losses, the company has indeed prospered. In *Winning the Innovative Game*, Waitley and Tucker quote Fred Smith:

> The people who were the big forces in the airplane business missed the forest for the trees. They were so steeped in their own rules about how you had to operate that they missed this entire (electronics) revolution. I knew that the United States was going to be relying on the computer for its economic prosperity. The electronic and computer age had to have a specialized transport system to support it. Just as railroads bring coal to the steel companies and take steel to the automobile companies, the electronics industry had to have specialized transportation systems to keep it supplied and supported.

Smith has always been on the lookout for new ideas. In 1984, Federal Express started ZapMail, an electronic mail service. According to Waitley and Tucker, "Zap enables a customer to send a copy of a document to someone in another city and have it delivered within two hours by courier, or instantly, if the sender and receiver both have ZapMailer facsimile machines in their offices." In a stroke of innovation, satellite transmissions and facsimile machines could be used to transport documents. Unfortunately, ZapMail ran into problems from the start. Customers did not feel comfortable with the system, and the company had trouble meeting its delivery schedules. Also, the price tag ($25 for ten pages) was too high for the market. The company decided to discontinue the service before it had an effect on their primary business. However, never let it be said that Federal Express would not take a chance on a new idea.

Questions

1. What customer-service standards did Federal Express meet with their overnight small parcel service? Discuss. Why do you think the company was successful with this service?
2. Was ZapMail an idea before its time? Would a system similar to ZapMail succeed today or has the appearance of fax machines in businesses and homes eliminated the need for a commercial service of this nature?

Source: Denis E. Waitley and Robert B. Tucker, *Winning the Innovative Game* (New Jersey: Fleming H. Revell, 1986), pp. 30–1, 237–40. Reprinted by permission.

CHAPTER 15

Wholesaling

CHAPTER OBJECTIVES

1. Define, explain, or describe the key terms listed under "Vocabulary and Key Terms."
2. Relate wholesaling to the other variables of the marketing mix.
3. Describe and identify the functions performed by wholesaling intermediaries.
4. Distinguish between wholesaling and retailing.
5. Explain the channel options available to a manufacturer who desires to bypass independent wholesaling intermediaries.
6. Identify the conditions under which a manufacturer is likely to assume the wholesaling function rather than use independents.
7. Discuss the major distinction between merchant wholesalers and agents and brokers.
8. Identify the major types of merchant wholesalers and the instances in which each type might be used.
9. Identify and discuss the major types of agents and brokers.
10. Apply your knowledge of Chapter 15 to the various activities in this chapter of the study guide.

VOCABULARY AND KEY TERMS

From the lettered terms listed below, select the one that best matches the meaning of each of the numbered statements that follows. Write the letter of that choice in the space provided.
a) wholesaler
b) wholesaling intermediaries
c) sales branch
d) sales office
e) public warehouse
f) trade fairs or trade exhibitions
g) merchandise marts
h) merchant wholesaler
i) full-function wholesaler
j) rack jobber
k) cash-and-carry wholesaler
l) truck wholesaler
m) drop shipper
n) commission merchant
o) auction house
p) brokers
q) selling agent
r) manufacturer's agent

1. _____ Includes intermediaries who take title to goods that they handle and those who do not take title

2. _____ Prevails in industries where retailers are small and carry large numbers of relatively inexpensive items, none of which is stocked in depth

3. _____ An independent salesperson who works for a number of manufacturers of related but noncompeting products and receives a commission based on a specified percentage of sales

4. _____ Bringing buyers and sellers together in one location and allowing potential buyers physically to inspect the merchandise before purchasing

5. _____ A wholesaler who sells large lot orders to customers and places them with producers who ship directly to customers

6. _____ Provides space for permanent exhibition where manufacturers rent showcases for their product offerings

7. _____ Wholesaling intermediaries who take title to the products that they handle

8. _____ Independently owned storage facilities

9. _____ A wholesaler who provides the racks, stocks the merchandise, prices the goods, and makes regular visits to refill the shelves

10. _____ An agent intermediary who brings buyers and sellers together but rarely serves a manufacturer on a continuing basis

11. _____ An agent intermediary who predominates in the marketing of agricultural products

12. _____ An establishment, maintained by a manufacturer that does not carry stock, serving a regional office for the firm's sales personnel

13. _____ Wholesaling intermediaries who market the products of a manufacturer and who are often referred to as the firm's marketing department

14. _____ A wholesaling intermediary who specializes in marketing perishable food items and performs the sales, delivery, and collection functions

15. _____ An establishment, maintained by a manufacturer, that serves as a warehouse for a particular sales territory

16. _____ Periodic shows where manufacturers in a particular industry display their wares for visiting retail and wholesale buyers

17. _____ A wholesaling intermediary who reduces the number of services provided to retail customers and also reduces the costs of serving such customers

18. _____ Wholesaling intermediaries who take title to the goods they handle

PRACTICE TEST

True-False: In the space to the right of each statement, check the appropriate line to indicate whether the statement is true or false.

	True	False
1. The term "wholesaler" is applied to all wholesaling intermediaries in the channel of distribution.	_____	_____
2. "Wholesaling intermediaries" is a broader term than the term "wholesaler."	_____	_____
3. Agents and brokers are examples of wholesalers.	_____	_____
4. Chain stores often assume wholesaling functions and bypass independent wholesalers.	_____	_____
5. Increased market contacts in the channel of distribution can lead to lowered marketing costs.	_____	_____
6. Intermediaries can be eliminated from the channel of distribution, but the channel functions must be performed by someone else in the channel.	_____	_____

7. Less than 25 percent of all industrial goods are sold directly to users by manufacturers.

8. Manufacturers prefer to distribute wholesale through their own facilities.

9. A sales branch will carry inventory, and orders will be processed to customers from that branch.

10. By maintaining sales offices in close proximity to customers, firms can reduce their selling costs as well as improve their customer service.

11. Public warehouses are warehouses, funded and supported by large retail chains, that distribute manufactured goods to these chains.

12. A merchandise mart provides space for permanent exhibitions at which manufacturers can rent showcases for their product offerings.

13. Trade fairs are year-round shows at which manufacturers show their wares to visiting retail buyers.

14. Place Bonaventure in Montreal is a good example of a trade fair.

15. Agents and wholesalers take title to and possession of the goods they handle.

16. The rack jobber is an example of a full-function wholesaler.

17. Rack jobbers predominate in the coal, lumber, and woollen goods industries.

18. Costco Wholesale Corporation is an example of a rack jobber.

19. Cash-and-carry wholesalers are the most commonly found merchant wholesalers in Canada today.

20. The drop shipper takes orders from customers and places them with producers who ship directly to the customers.

21. The drop shipper operates in fields in which the product is bulky and customers make purchases in carload lots.

22. The commission merchant acts as the producer's agent and receives an agreed-upon fee when the sale is made.

23. The most common type of broker is the real-estate agent.

24. Manufacturer's agents are company sales representatives who have complete authority over the terms of sales to customers.

25. Selling agents are common in the textile, coal, sulphur, and lumber industries.

Multiple Choice: Choose the expression that best answers the question or best completes the sentence.

26. The term that is attached to only those wholesaling intermediaries who take title to the products they produce is
a. wholesaling intermediaries
b. wholesaler
c. wholesaling
d. wholesaling middlemen
e. merchant intermediary

27. What term describes not only intermediaries who assume title, but also agent intermediaries who perform wholesaling functions but do not take title?
   a. wholesaling intermediaries
   b. wholesaler
   c. wholesaling
   d. wholesaling middlemen
   e. merchant intermediary

28. A full-function merchant wholesaler will perform the marketing function of
   a. storage
   b. transportation
   c. selling and buying
   d. shipping
   e. all of the above and more

29. The fundamental marketing principle is that
   a. some member in the channel must assume the risk if the goods do not sell
   b. ownership is the key to the success of any business enterprise
   c. marketing functions must be performed by some member of the channel of distribution; they may be shifted but not eliminated
   d. the "bottom line" will determine the long-term success of each member in the channel of distribution
   e. none of the above

30. In a channel of distribution that includes four manufacturers and four retailers, the existence of a wholesaler could reduce the number of transactions from sixteen to
   a. four
   b. twelve
   c. nine
   d. eight
   e. five

31. What percentage of all industrial goods are sold directly to users by the manufacturer?
   a. 25 percent
   b. 40 percent
   c. 50 percent
   d. 35 percent
   e. 5 percent

32. Sales offices and branches are examples of
   a. independently owned merchant wholesalers
   b. public warehouses
   c. buying offices (retailer-owned)
   d. manufacturer-owned facilities
   e. agent wholesaling intermediaries

33. Which one of the following intermediaries will never take possession of the goods but will take title?
   a. rack jobber
   b. commission merchant
   c. merchant wholesaler
   d. drop shipper
   e. selling agent

34. Trade fairs are
   a. periodic shows where manufacturers display their goods
   b. year-round shows where manufacturers display their goods
   c. permanent exhibitions where manufacturers rent showcases
   d. agricultural fairs and garden shows
   e. none of the above

35. Costco Wholesale would be classified as a
   a. full-function wholesaler
   b. limited-function wholesaler
   c. rack jobber
   d. agent wholesaling intermediary
   e. sales office

36. Rack jobbers
   a. are limited-function wholesalers
   b. take orders from customers and place them with producers who ship directly to the customer
   c. are agent wholesaling intermediaries
   d. stock the merchandise, price the goods, and make regular visits to the retail stores to refill the shelves
   e. market perishable food items

37. Truck wholesalers
   a. take orders from customers and place them with producers who ship directly to the customer
   b. are agent wholesaling intermediaries
   c. are full-function wholesalers
   d. stock the merchandise, price the goods, and make regular visits to the retail store to refill the shelves
   e. market perishable items

38. Cash-and-carry wholesalers perform most wholesaling functions except
   a. taking title
   b. storage and transportation
   c. financing and delivery
   d. financing and risk taking
   e. collecting market information

39. The direct-response wholesaler
   a. stocks the merchandise, prices the goods, and makes regular visits to the retail stores to refill the shelves
   b. deals in perishable items
   c. takes possession when the producer ships the goods to a central market for sales
   d. relies on catalogues rather than a sales force to contact retail, industrial, and institutional customers
   e. brings buyers and sellers together

40. Of the following wholesale intermediaries, the one with the lowest operating expenses as a percentage of sales, is the
   a. broker
   b. selling agent
   c. manufacturer's agent
   d. cash-and-carry wholesaler
   e. direct-response wholesaler

41. Wholesalers are firms that sell to all the following customers except
    a. retailers
    b. other wholesalers
    c. industrial users
    d. ultimate consumers
    e. other intermediaries

42. Which of the following services is not normally performed by full-function merchant wholesalers?
    a. storing merchandise in convenient locations
    b. maintaining sales forces to call regularly on retailers
    c. making deliveries
    d. extending credit to qualified buyers
    e. All of the above are commonly done by full-function merchant wholesalers.

43. Wholesaling intermediaries can be bypassed if the manufacturers are willing to
    a. lose sales
    b. limit their product lines
    c. lower prices
    d. assume the functions they perform
    e. all of the above

44. Electronics Corporation of Canada is a small firm with limited financial resources and virtually no marketing capability. Its sole product is a low-price telephone answering/recording device. Which of the following wholesalers appears most appropriate?
    a. auction company
    b. selling agent
    c. merchant wholesaler
    d. broker
    e. commission merchant

45. Which of the following statements about drop shippers is not true?
    a. They take title to the goods.
    b. They store the goods.
    c. They receive orders from customers.
    d. They operate in fields in which products are bulky.
    e. They do not maintain an inventory.

46. All of the following take title to the goods they handle except
    a. rack jobbers
    b. drop shippers
    c. selling agents
    d. merchant wholesalers

47. All of the following are limited function wholesalers except
    a. truck jobbers
    b. rack jobbers
    c. drop shippers
    d. cash-and-carry wholesalers

48. Which intermediary is commonly found in the textile, coal, and lumber industries?
    a. drop shipper
    b. selling agent
    c. manufacturers' agent
    d. commission merchant

49. Manufacturers' agents are used to develop channels for several reasons. Which of the following is not one of the reasons given in the text?
a. They reduce selling costs by spreading the cost over several different products.
b. They take possession of the products and provide storage.
c. Agents are paid on a commission basis and often cost less than a sales force.
d. Firms with unrelated lines typically need more than one channel.
e. They provide access to the market for small firms with no sales force.

50. Which statement about commission merchants is not true?
a. They have little latitude in their decisions.
b. They predominate in agricultural products marketing.
c. They take possession of the goods.
d. They act as the producer's agent.
e. They receive an agreed-upon fee.

ANSWER KEY: CHAPTER 15

Vocabulary and Key Terms	True-False	Multiple Choice
1. b	1. F	26. b
2. i	2. T	27. a or d
3. r	3. F	28. e
4. o	4. T	29. c
5. m	5. F	30. d
6. g	6. T	31. c
7. a	7. F	32. d
8. e	8. F	33. d
9. j	9. T	34. a
10. p	10. T	35. b
11. n	11. F	36. d
12. d	12. T	37. e
13. q	13. F	38. c
14. l	14. F	39. d
15. c	15. F	40. a
16. f	16. T	41. d
17. k	17. F	42. e
18. h	18. F	43. d
	19. F	44. b
	20. T	45. b
	21. T	46. c
	22. T	47. b
	23. T	48. a
	24. F	49. b
	25. T	50. a

EXERCISE 15.1: EXPANDING A BUSINESS TO A NEW TERRITORY

Barrett, Inc., a manufacturer of patio furniture in Oakville, Ontario, operates with a small sales force: Two salespeople working out of an office in Ottawa cover northern Ontario; four other salespeople working out of the company's Oakville plant cover southern Ontario. The company's sales volume surpassed $25 million last year.

At the company's annual meeting, June Barrett, the president and owner of the company, expresses interest in expanding distribution of the patio furniture to the western provinces. She feels that the West, because of its outdoor lifestyle, would be a lucrative market for the company. Barrett needs only to figure out the logistics of distribution.

June says to Malcolm McKenzie, the marketing manager, "I don't think we are big enough to set up sales branches in Vancouver and Winnipeg. We only sell patio equipment, and the volume of sales would likely be insufficient to cover our costs." Malcolm replies, "It seems to me that we have a choice of selling through manufacturers' agents, selling agents, or our own sales force from a sales branch or sales office. If we were to sell through sales offices, let's say in Winnipeg, Calgary, and Vancouver, the cost that would be incurred through the sales branch would be eliminated. We would still have to determine the size of the sales force and the method of compensation, that is, straight commission or salary plus commission. The cost of running the offices and the ways and means of economically handling distribution from Oakville to our intermediaries in the West are other problems. Distribution can be facilitated by using public warehouses."

"Let's not get ahead of ourselves," June says. "Selling from a company-owned sales office may not be the best solution. Selling through manufacturers' agents who are already established in the West is a good alternative. The advantage of using manufacturers' agents is that you have to pay them only if they sell the goods. They are experienced in dealing with companies similar to ours and we could use these manufacturers' agents to develop the territory for us. In a year or two, once our patio furniture is accepted by the retail trade, we could discontinue our relationship with the agents and set up our own sales offices or perhaps even sales branches."

"Perhaps we better call an executive meeting," says Malcolm. "There appear to be a number of ways we could go — sales office, sales branch, manufacturers' agents, independent wholesalers, or selling agents. We haven't even examined the last two as possible options and these are good choices as well." June agrees with Malcolm and a meeting is called for the following Tuesday to deal with the distribution alternatives.

Questions

1. What territorial decisions must first be resolved?
2. Should the company sell through its own sales force (from either sales branches or sales offices) in the West or sell through independent wholesaling intermediaries (e.g., manufacturers' agents, selling agents, merchant wholesalers, brokers)? Support your position.
3. If the company should decide against selling through its own sales force, what specific wholesaling intermediaries would best serve the needs of Barrett, Inc.?
4. In answering 1, 2, and 3 above, your decision on the approach to be used by Barrett, Inc., may be facilitated if you first consider the functions to be performed by either the sales force or the intermediaries in the western territory. Clarify this statement.

EXERCISE 15.2: THE HIGH COST OF DISTRIBUTION

Why does a videocassette recorder made in Asia cost less in Seattle than it costs in Vancouver, B.C.? An article in the *Globe and Mail* points out that "an Asian company charges its Canadian subsidiary handling distribution as much as 10% more than it charges its subsidiary south of the border — even before tariffs and transportation are added. The difference stems from the enormous sales volume possible in the United States, coupled with that market's strategic importance for global manufacturers. If VCR makers hope to dominate the world market, they have to dominate the United States first." The accounting firm Ernst & Young, which tracked several products through various distribution channels in both the United States and Canada, uncovered a number of differences in product-distribution and industry practices. These differences were outlined in the *Globe and Mail* as follows:

> Prices are often lower in the United States because all links in the distribution chain benefit from economies of scale unavailable in Canada. Price competition on a given product is more intense south of the border because the players at any one level of distribution — retailers,

for instance — compete not only among themselves, but with players from other levels, such as manufacturers who operate retail factory outlets. U.S. retailers have lower gross margins than their Canadian counterparts, partly because they have to cover lower wholesale and operating costs, including taxes and wages. Canadian prices are higher in part because of duties, costlier transportation and different labelling requirements.

It is considerably less expensive to distribute goods in the United States than it is in Canada. Ernst & Young also determined that 70 percent of manufacturers in the United States used independent sales representatives (such as brokers and manufacturers' agents) rather than in-house staff for distribution. A broker will charge a commission on sales of less than 3 percent, a small amount when compared with the cost of operating a sales force. In Canada, where large manufacturers dominate the marketing of goods, only 30 percent of manufacturers use independent salespeople; full-function wholesalers are more commonly employed. These wholesalers' margins of markup are higher because of the many services they offer (financing, storage, transportation, etc.). In Canada, according to *The Globe and Mail*, "Ernst & Young found that the revenue generated by wholesale merchants equalled 41.1% of Canada's gross national product. But south of the border, wholesale merchants accounted for only 32.7 percent of the economy." It was also noted that "individual wholesale merchants are much smaller in [Canada], and relatively more numerous. The average wholesale merchant in Canada had annual sales of $3.63 million in 1987 compared with $5.05 million for similar operations in the United States."

In summary, because of differences in the two countries' distribution systems, Canadians pay more than Americans for most products shipped from foreign markets. These price differences, in conjunction with the exchange rate and the GST, have driven Canadian consumers in increasing numbers south of the border in search of deals on a host of products. Thus, marketing today is a greater challenge than ever for Canadian retailers.

Questions

1. Why are wholesaling and retailing costs lower south of the border?
2. How are wholesaling practices in Canada different from those in the United States?
3. What recommendations would you make to the government or to Canadian industry to resolve our distribution problems?

Source: Kenneth Kidd, "Price Gaps That Drive Canadians to U.S. Shops Start in Far East," *Globe and Mail*, 23 April 1991.

CHAPTER 16

Retailing

CHAPTER OBJECTIVES

1. Define, explain, or describe the key terms listed under "Vocabulary and Key Terms."
2. Relate retailing to the other variables of the marketing mix.
3. Describe early Canadian retailing.
4. Describe the major types of retail stores and the characteristics of each type.
5. Identify the major types of mass merchandisers.
6. Explain the forms of non-store retailing.
7. Compare and contrast the chain store with the independent retailer, and identify the industries dominated by chains.
8. Identify the three types of planned shopping centres and distinguish planned shopping centres from downtown retailing districts.
9. Apply your knowledge of Chapter 16 to the various activities in this chapter of the study guide.

VOCABULARY AND KEY TERMS

From the lettered terms listed below, select the one that best matches the meaning of each of the numbered statements that follows. Write the letter of that choice in the space provided.

a) retailing
b) general store
c) supermarket
d) single-line and limited-line store
e) specialty store
f) general merchandise store
g) department store
h) discount house
i) hypermarket
j) house-to-house retailing
k) mail-order retailing
l) automatic vending machines
m) chain stores
n) suburban shopping centres
o) neighbourhood shopping centres
p) community shopping centres
q) regional shopping centres
r) scrambled merchandising
s) wheel of retailing
t) teleshopping
u) mass merchandiser
v) catalogue retailer

1. _____ A shopping centre complex composed of a supermarket and a group of smaller stores
2. _____ A type of retailer who handles a large assortment of one-line products or a few related lines of goods
3. _____ Retail stores, similar to department stores, that sacrifice credit, clerical assistance, and delivery services in exchange for lower prices
4. _____ A retailing method in which there is direct contract between a retailer and a customer at the home of the customer
5. _____ Planned retailing centres normally located in the suburbs of cities
6. _____ Large-scale departmentalized retail stores offering a large variety of food products
7. _____ A retailing method in which a customer can order merchandise by mail, by telephone, or by visiting the mail order desk of a retail store
8. _____ A shopping centre complex that includes a branch of a local department store and a variety store, in addition to other stores
9. _____ A giant mass-merchandiser who operates on a low-price, self-service basis and carries a wide range of products from soft goods and groceries to automobile parts and some service outlets
10. _____ A retailing method that allows consumers to order merchandise that has been displayed on television
11. _____ The retail practice of carrying dissimilar items in an attempt to generate added sales volume
12. _____ A general merchandise store stocked to meet the needs of a small community or rural area
13. _____ A large retail firm handling a variety of merchandise and employing at least 25 people
14. _____ A true robot store for a wide range of convenience goods
15. _____ Groups of retail stores that are centrally owned and managed and handle the same line of products
16. _____ Giant shopping districts of at least 100 000 square metres of shopping space built around one or two department stores and as many as 100 other smaller stores
17. _____ A hypothesis developed by M.P. McNair to explain the pattern of change in retailing
18. _____ Retailers who carry a wide variety of product lines, all of which are stocked in some depth
19. _____ All of the activities involved in the sale of products and services to an ultimate consumer for his or her own use
20. _____ A retailer who typically handles only part of a single line of products
21. _____ Stores emphasizing brand-name products at low prices, high turnover, reduced services, and a wide range of products
22. _____ A retailer who presents a customer with printed descriptions of products and a showroom display, and fills orders from a backroom warehouse

PRACTICE TEST

True-False: In the space to the right of each statement, check the appropriate line to indicate whether the statement is true or false.

		True	False
1.	Retailing is one of the most dynamic aspects of marketing.	_____	_____
2.	Retailing is the last step of the marketing channel for the consumer goods manufacturer.	_____	_____
3.	Retailing involves sales made solely from retail stores.	_____	_____
4.	A general store is in the decline stage of the retail life cycle.	_____	_____
5.	The success of Safeway's large Food-for-Less stores forced Loblaws to open their Superstores.	_____	_____

6. Retail trade area analysis refers to studies that assess the relative drawing power of alternative retail locations.

7. The law of retail gravitation delineates the retail trade area of a potential site on the basis of distance between alternative locations and relative populations.

8. This chapter of the text provides three categories under which to classify retailers.

9. Convenience stores typically include furniture stores, appliance stores, and grocery stores.

10. Specialty retailers provide some combination of product lines, service, and reputation that results in consumers' being willing to expend considerable effort to shop at the specialty stores.

11. A variety store is an example of a self-service retailer.

12. Specialty stores and department stores are examples of full-service retailers.

13. The full-service retail store focuses on convenience goods and offers a full line of services.

14. All supermarkets are also chain stores.

15. Supermarkets operate on very low profit margins.

16. Supermarkets have diversified by adding nonfood lines, which tend to produce higher profit margins than food lines.

17. The fastest growing retailer today is the specialty store retailer.

18. Department stores have suffered shrinking profits because of their high-cost locations and method of operations.

19. There is very little distinction today between the department store and the discount houses (e.g., Woolco and Kmart).

20. Mass merchandisers often stock a more limited line of products than department stores.

21. Hypermarkets are more common in Europe than in Canada.

22. The house-to-house method of selling is a low-cost method of retailing.

23. Chains account for approximately one-third of all retail stores and 32 percent of all retail sales.

24. The largest type of planned shopping centre is the community shopping centre.

25. Scrambled merchandising is the retail practice of carrying dissimilar lines to generate added sales volume.

Multiple Choice: Choose the expression that best answers the question or best completes the sentence.

26. After the trading-post days, the Hudson's Bay Company and other retailers evolved into the institution known as the
   a. specialty store
   b. department store
   c. discount house
   d. general store
   e. general-line store

27. Retailers must determine and evaluate their offerings with respect to
a. general goods/services categories
b. specific lines and products
c. inventory depth
d. width of assortment
e. all of the above

28. Which of the following is an example of a convenience retailer?
a. an appliance store
b. a furniture store
c. gasoline retailers
d. a women's boutique
e. an automobile dealer

29. Which of the following is an example of a shopping store?
a. an appliance store
b. a furniture store
c. an automobile dealer
d. a women's boutique
e. all of the above

30. Based on classification of retailers by services provided, which of the following would be classified as a self-service retailer?
a. automated vending
b. discount retailing
c. variety stores
d. department stores
e. specialty stores

31. Based on classification of retailers by services provided, which of the following would be classified as a limited service retailer?
a. automated vending
b. discount retailing
c. variety stores
d. department stores
e. specialty stores

32. A large assortment of a single line of products or a few related lines of goods are offered by
a. specialty stores
b. department stores
c. discount houses
d. limited-line retailers
e. hypermarkets

33. What retail store operates on razor-thin profits, a high inventory turnover of 20–26 times per year, and a self-service basis?
a. the department store
b. the hypermarket
c. the supermarket
d. the limited-line store
e. the specialty store

34. The retail store that handles only part of a single line of products is the
a. department store
b. hypermarket
c. supermarket
d. limited-line store
e. specialty store

35. The distinguishing feature of department stores is that they
a. operate many leased departments
b. are organized around departments for the purpose of service, promotion, and control
c. are managed by chain-store organizations to provide for efficiency, promotional advantage, and management expertise
d. are located in downtown areas or suburban shopping centres
e. handle a wide variety of merchandise

36. All but one of the following are examples of mass merchandisers.
a. department stores
b. sporting goods store
c. hypermarkets
d. discount houses
e. catalogue retailers

37. The largest catalogue retailer in Canada is
a. Sears
b. Canadian Tire
c. Eaton's
d. Consumer Distributing
e. Sony

38. The customers of mail-order merchandisers can order merchandise by all the following means except
a. by mail
b. by visiting the mail-order desk of a retail store
c. by telephone
d. from a catalogue retailer

39. Chain stores are groups of stores that are
a. operated by a manufacturer or wholesaler
b. franchised by a specific company
c. centrally owned and managed and handle the same line of products
d. operated principally by food and shoe stores
e. independently owned but handling the same line of products

40. The largest consumer product retailer in Canada based on revenues earned in 1989 was
a. Hudson's Bay Co.
b. Dylex, Ltd.
c. Provigo, Inc.
d. Canada Safeway, Ltd.
e. Loblaw Companies, Ltd.

41. The practice of scrambled merchandising is carried out by the following retailer:
a. the drugstore
b. the supermarket
c. the gasoline retailer

   d.   all of the above
   e.   none of the above

42. All of the following are examples of retail transactions except
   a.   purchase of fresh vegetables at a roadside stand
   b.   purchase of this book at the university bookstore
   c.   preparation of personal income tax report by a local accounting firm
   d.   purchase of paint by a contractor
   e.   All of the above are retail transactions.

43. The reason for the general store's virtual extinction is
   a.   high prices resulting from inefficient order quantities
   b.   poor service
   c.   inability to compete with specialized stores
   d.   all of the above
   e.   none of the above

44. An example of a limited-line retailer would be a
   a.   furniture store
   b.   hardware store
   c.   sporting goods store
   d.   appliance store
   e.   all of the above

45. Which of the following does not characterize a supermarket?
   a.   large profit margin
   b.   departmentalized
   c.   adequate parking facilities
   d.   low prices
   e.   self-service

46. Which of the following characteristics best describes department stores?
   a.   buyers running their departments almost as independent businesses
   b.   a willingness to adapt to changing consumer desires
   c.   limited number of services
   d.   a and b
   e.   b and c

47. Which of the following is not classified as a general merchandise retailer?
   a.   discount house
   b.   department store
   c.   supermarket
   d.   variety store

48. Which of the following is not a characteristic of house-to-house retailing?
   a.   direct contact between seller and customer
   b.   a low-cost method of distribution
   c.   maximum consumer convenience
   d.   manufacturers controlling the marketing channels
   e.   its use by firms emphasizing product demonstrations

49. The main advantage possessed by chain operations over independent retailers is
   a.   convenience of location
   b.   economies of scale
   c.   personalized service

d. a and b
e. all of the above

50. A shopping centre containing at least 100 000 square metres of shopping space and as many as 100 or more stores built around two or more department stores is a
a. community shopping centre
b. suburban shopping centre
c. regional shopping centre
d. neighbourhood shopping centre

ANSWER KEY: CHAPTER 16

Vocabulary and Key Terms	True-False	Multiple Choice
1. o	1. T	26. d
2. d	2. T	27. e
3. h	3. F	28. c
4. j	4. T	29. e
5. n	5. F	30. a
6. c	6. T	31. c
7. k	7. T	32. d
8. p	8. F	33. c
9. i	9. F	34. e
10. t	10. T	35. b
11. r	11. F	36. b
12. b	12. T	37. d
13. g	13. F	38. d
14. l	14. F	39. c
15. m	15. T	40. e
16. q	16. T	41. d
17. s	17. T	42. d
18. f	18. T	43. c
19. a	19. T	44. e
20. e	20. F	45. a
21. u	21. T	46. d
22. v	22. F	47. c
	23. T	48. b
	24. F	49. b
	25. T	50. c

EXERCISE 16.1: THE WHOLESALER-SPONSORED VOLUNTARY CHAIN

Pierre and Marnie Lemieux operate a medium-sized food store in a medium-sized town in Alberta. Business was good up until 1986, when Safeway opened up a store in town; since then, sales have steadily tailed off. Pierre and Marnie have been approached by Franklin Szabo, a marketing representative from Horne & Pitfield, about the possibility of joining the Independent Grocers Association (IGA).

"The IGA is a wholesaler-sponsored voluntary chain," says Franklin. "Horne & Pitfield has been granted the rights to offer franchise privileges to retailers who are willing to enter into a formal agreement setting out the obligations of both parties to the agreement." "Is there an advantage to joining the IGA?" asks Marnie. "Will we lose our independence as merchants by belonging to this organization? Will we be better off than we are now?"

"These are all good questions, Marnie," Franklin responds. "Let me answer this way. You are beginning to hurt because of the increase in competition. By joining the IGA you will be more competitive with Safeway and others in the trade. With our company-owned trucks, we distribute over 12 000 varied products from national manufacturers and suppliers to the retailers who are a part of our organization. Because of the large number of stores that are franchised members, we are able to offer everyone a cost advantage. We buy in large quantities from manufacturers, taking advantage of quantity discounts and other benefits and passing these savings on to our member customers. We also have specialists who will call on you on a regular basis, and offer you advice on store layout, inventory controls, personnel problems, and promotional plans. Furthermore, what you sell will be IGA-branded products that can be purchased only from your store, and customers will develop loyalty to these quality brands."

"What will be our obligation to Horne & Pitfield?" asks Pierre.

"You have five obligations as a member of the IGA family," continues Franklin. "The IGA name must be on the building and in your promotion. Also, you will have to participate 100 percent in all IGA merchandising programs and carry all IGA brands. Likewise, you will be expected to participate in Horne & Pitfield's advertising and promotional programs. This will cost you roughly 1 percent of your sales. The advertising programs help to build the franchise name and customer awareness of our products. As a member you will buy most of your merchandise from us. These obligations are not hard to live with; furthermore, while you will still be an independent owner, you will also have the advantage of being able to compete more effectively with large chains, such as Safeway."

At the end of the meeting, Franklin invites Pierre and Marnie to Edmonton to talk to other officials of Horne & Pitfield. Unsure of whether they should pursue this option further, the two decide to attend the meeting in Edmonton and see what transpires.

Questions

1. What advantages does an independent retail business gain by joining a wholesaler-sponsored voluntary chain?
2. What factors should Pierre and Marnie consider before joining a franchise?
3. Why would a wholesaler (e.g., Horne & Pitfield) be willing to serve as an IGA franchiser?
4. How does a wholesaler-sponsored voluntary chain differ from a retail co-operative?
5. What is the difference between the two contractual systems in question 4 and a franchise?

EXERCISE 16.2: THE EVOLUTION OF THE STORE

First, there was the general store; then the general-line store arrived on the scene, soon followed by the specialty store. Originally, all food purchases were made at full-service grocery stores, but in accordance with the wheel-of-retailing hypothesis, the supermarket appeared. The department store was the predominant mass merchandiser during the first half of the twentieth century, and still is, although the discount house gave them a scare in the 1950s. (Again, the wheel-of-retailing hypothesis was vindicated — the consumers still considered price and selection of merchandise important.) Today, discount houses are similar to department stores. Another mass merchandiser, the variety store, is in the decline stage of the retail life cycle. In recent years, we have witnessed the rise of the superstore, catalogue retailers, and new types of general line and specialty stores. The specialty store has taken new roots with broad merchandise selection, hurting in the process comparable lines sold by department stores. The department stores have run into hard times although they should survive in the long run. An increasingly familiar retailer on the scene since the late 1980s has been the warehouse retailer. A common sight now is the scrambled merchandising practice carried out by limited-line merchandisers such as drugstores and supermarkets. In order to serve shoppers' needs better, malls have brought together all these stores in one location. What of the future?

Questions

1. Explain the wheel-of-retailing hypothesis.
2. Explain the practice of scrambled merchandising.

3. Why have specialty stores regained prominence on the retail scene?
4. Will the department store continue to meet the needs of fickle consumers? What are the strengths that may allow department stores to stay competitive in the marketplace? What is the difference, if any, between department stores and discount houses?
5. What are warehouse stores?
6. What types of retailers are in the decline stage of the life cycle? Why? What types of retailers are in the growth stage of the life cycle? Why?
7. Use your imagination to think of new types of retailers that may enter the marketplace between now and the year 2000.

Case 11

MURPHY'S SNACK FOODS

Murphy's Snack Foods began in 1979. For a decade it was a small fry in Canada's $600-million-a-year potato chip and corn snack industry. In competed only in the corn snacks segment of the industry (see the accompanying table), using a single plant in Concord, Ontario, to produce items for other snack food companies and for some private label brands for chain stores, such as Loblaws (no-name products) and Marks and Spencer.

The situation changed drastically in April 1989, when Murphy's acquired a Frito-Lay plant in nearby Kitchener and the rights to six of that well-known firm's brand names in Canada.

The reason for the change began in January 1988, when Hostess Food Products Ltd., a wholly owned subsidiary of General Foods Inc., and the Frito-Lay Division of Pepsi-Cola Canada Ltd. announced plans for a merger. Hostess was the industry leader in Canada; Frito-Lay ranked fourth with a market share of 9.4 percent. The Competition Tribunal reviewed the merger, under the Competition Act, and concluded that it would reduce competition if allowed to proceed as planned. The tribunal approved a restructured deal that included divesting part of Frito-Lay to Murphy's Snack Foods. In April 1989, Murphy's Potato Chips acquired the plant, six brand names (O'Grady's, Laurentide, Adams, Ridgies, Jacks, and Tostitos), and a fleet of delivery trucks.

For the once-tiny firm, the acquisition meant a huge commitment of resources, both financial and human. The risk seems to be paying off (see the accompanying sales history), but the rapid transition has left problems, many of which involve distribution and production levels.

EXHIBIT C11-1

The Canadian Potato Chip and Corn Snack Industry

Product	% of Retail Sales
Potato chips	75%
Corn Snacks	
Extruded corn*	5
Popcorn	3
Tortilla chips	12
Corn chips	5
*Cheese twists, cheese balls, and so on.	

EXHIBIT C11-2

Recent Sales History of Murphy's Snack Foods

Year	Gross Sales
1985	$ 2 500 000
1986	3 000 000
1987	4 000 000
1988	5 500 000
1989	32 000 000
1990	35 000 000

Channels of Distribution

Moving to the sale of brand-name products required Murphy's to change its channels of distribution. It also had to develop new packaging and truck maintenance systems while addressing all the issues associated with running a larger organization.

Before

Before April 1989, Murphy's usual way of doing business in Ontario was to take customer orders over the phone and arrange for either customer pick-up or drop shipment. A small portion of sales went to wholesale merchants, which serviced the smaller stores. In Quebec, a distributor placed truckload orders and warehoused them until they were sold. These methods were cost-effective, although they eliminated customers that required merchandising assistance.

With the 1984 introduction of Murphy's Good Value Snacks line, sold primarily to small chains and department stores such as Kmart and Zellers, came a significant increase in sales volume. Nevertheless, Murphy's traditional distribution channels continued to satisfy the needs of its customers.

After

The accepted industry practice for branded products is a route sales distribution system (rack jobbers). To survive at this level, Murphy's was forced to change channels to serve its new market.

Murphy's had only a few months to develop a sales team, including 75 route salespeople, and the routes and remuneration packages. It also had to restructure its accounting system to handle route sales. Frito-Lay had used a manual system; Murphy's opted to move immediately to an automated system with computerized hand-held order-entry units.

Murphy's has continued to use drop shipments for situations in which merchandising is not required or permitted. (Chain stores such as Loblaws, A&P, and IGA have union restrictions against merchandising by a supplier.)

Physical Distribution System

Murphy's Potato Chips services a market located primarily (about 95 percent) in Ontario, with the remainder spread among Quebec, Newfoundland, and the Maritimes. After it acquired the Frito-Lay brands, its physical distribution system changed significantly.

Before

All production for Murphy's corn snacks items used to originate from its Concord plant, and all distribution was handled from one warehouse there for customer pick-up or for delivery by one of Murphy's two trucks. Once orders were delivered, the responsibility for organizing stock and reordering was left with the customer.

Orders were taken over the phone for delivery from stock, typically within two days. Production was scheduled to maintain stock levels which were dictated by the sales history of the various products. Producing to stock created no problems with the main sellers (cheese balls and cheese twists) since inventory turnover was high. For the slower moving items, however, production was scheduled each ten-day period to allow larger production runs. This cost-minimizing procedure sometimes resulted in stockouts or in overstocks in which the product became stale and had to be rejected.

Murphy's production volume required the full capacity of its two delivery trucks. The trucks were not fully utilized, however. Inefficiencies developed because of the improper supervision of drivers, the inability to plan shipments to maximize truck use (since notice was often very short), and the necessity of short-shipping customers because of stockouts. It was often necessary to hire expensive carriers to make additional deliveries.

After

Since acquiring the Frito-Lay brands, Murphy's has moved all production to the facility in Kitchener, where the production scheduled is based on orders. A one-week lead time for shipment is now required. Salespeople, who visit their accounts weekly or biweekly, service the racks, remove stale products, and replenish the stock.

Within the plant, the inventory turns over in less than a week. Ideally, goods move out of production straight onto a truck. The firm has a total of 11 highway trailers and 75 route sales vans, as well as its two original delivery trucks.

Under the April 1989 plan, most of which Murphy's adapted from Frito-Lay, shipments would go to two kinds of distribution facilities:

• Warehouses, in Ottawa, Scarborough (an eastern borough of Toronto), and Concord, sites central to sizeable populations. Each such facility can service the needs of six to eleven route salespeople. All are operated by a warehouse manager, who is responsible for maintaining stock levels.

- Bin locations, in areas of fairly low population density. Each bin is a smaller facility, with one or two sales people operating out of it. These salespeople are responsible for all goods delivered to their bin as well as for stock replenishment. The original plan called for 25 bins.

With this seemingly well-organized system in place, Murphy's distribution costs have proved to be approximately 300 percent of the industry standard. The firm attributes part of this high cost to the fact that the acquired fleet of trucks needed major repairs and some even had to be replaced. Furthermore, the organization of the warehousing system was not optimal, but when Murphy's took over the operations at Kitchener there was no time to analyze its efficiency. Since then, the warehouse in Concord has been closed and another facility opened in Mississauga (a western suburb of Metropolitan Toronto). Five bins have been closed in the Hamilton and Kitchener districts and replaced by two centrally located warehouses.

At the Retailer

Before Murphy's acquired major brands, it was essentially a production facility supplying low-end product lines to retailers and wholesalers. Its customers did not require, and it was not structured to provide, merchandising services such as stock reordering, stock rotation, or display maintenance. New merchandising has become critically important — hence its use of rack jobbers to maintain displays. Struggling to keep sales at levels that justify its greatly enlarged production facilities has become a treadmill that management has not found a way to get off.

The Battle for Shelf Space

Gaining shelf space is an important part of competition of this level of the industry. The major supermarket and convenience store chains, such as Loblaws, A&P, and Beckers, negotiate shelf space at the head office level. By industry custom, a seller may offer

1. *Superior service* — which stresses that the physical distribution system be able to supply all of a chain's outlets.

2. *Listing allowances* — which are payments for the opportunity to put the product on the shelf.

3. *Selling price incentives* — which are "off invoice" deals such as
    - Case allowances — a fixed allowance per case for promoting the product. For example, if the item normally retails at $1.99 per bag, it will sell at $1.79 with a case allowance of $0.20 a bag.
    - Volume rebates.
    - Co-op advertising.

Case allowances are the most important of these tactics since chips are very price sensitive. About 75 percent of the total sales volume sells at less than retail price. Sometimes there are bidding wars to secure space during special occasions, such as New Year's and Superbowl Sunday.

Murphy's Tactics

This game is hardball, and Murphy's management sometimes wonders if it has the money to play. So far it has managed to avoid listing allowances, which are very costly. It cannot avoid case allowances, given their importance, but it has chosen to be selective about who gets them when. This approach has dangers, however. Since its sales volume is lower than that of its competitors, which use case allowances, Murphy's is continually at risk of losing shelf space (or its position on the shelf).

Murphy's is also trying some other tactics. It has introduced products that no one else can provide. It is, for example, the sole Canadian distributor of Cape Cod chips, manufactured by Eagle Snacks in the United States. Finally, it is pursuing chains' private-label business, which is very low margin but brings up production volumes and gives leverage for negotiating shelf space for the branded products.

Sales to Independent Stores

Murphy's approach to mom and pop and convenience stores must be a bit different. Product approval is gained through selling at head office to convenience store chains, but it is the individual operators that decide how much of a product to order. These sales have a higher margin (more small bags and higher selling prices), but they require more work from the route salespeople, who make the actual sales. It is thus important to design the right remuneration package to motivate the sales force properly.

Some case allowances are used, but there are rarely volume rebates or co-op advertising deductions.

For stores in which Murphy's has not obtained shelf space, sales people are encouraged to set up temporary cardboard displays for an initial trial. If it is successful, the store owner may decided to grant shelf space for the product. Another method Murphy's is using is the introduction of the bonus bag (25 percent more). Promotions appeal to the retailer and also to the salespeople, who now have something new to offer.

A Catch-22 Situation

Murphy's is continually faced with the problem of acquiring and maintaining shelf space for all its products. Its financial position does not allow for a national advertising program. Neither can it offer case allowances to the extent of its competitors. Yet it must increase its sales volumes if it is to operate the Kitchener production facility efficiently. Its managers feel they are in a Catch-22 situation.

Questions

1. What do you think Murphy's should do to utilize its delivery trucks more efficiently?
2. What channel strategies should Murphy's employ to expand to the western Canadian market?
3. What effect might requiring a one-week lead time for delivery or a minimum order quantity have on the efficiency of the distribution system? What are some of the risks?
4. Evaluate the risks Murphy's faced at the time of the acquisition.
5. Distribution costs are the highest component in the price of snack foods. With the increasing costs of operating fleet trucks and increasing demand for more and better service by retailers, what can Murphy's do to reduce physical distribution costs?
6. Why are snack foods so price sensitive?
7. What recommendations can you give Murphy's for increasing sales volumes?
8. What do you see as the future of Murphy's Snack Foods?

Source: Case developed by Bill Crowe, St. Lawrence College, Kingston, Ontario, and Mark Siemonsen, marketing consultant. Information and photo supplied by Murphy's Potato Chips, Kitchener, Ontario. Reprinted by permission.

Case 12

LUCAS FOODS

Harold Riley was marketing manager of Lucas Foods, a diversified food manufacturing and wholesaling company based in Winnipeg. The company had recently had some success with a new product, Gold Medal Crumpettes. Jerry Lucas, president of Lucas Foods, asked his marketing manager to recommend an appropriate strategy for the new product that would best capture the available opportunity and support the mission of the company.

The Industry

Lucas Foods was in the food manufacturing and wholesaling business, marketing a broad product line that included frozen egg products, shortening, flour, baking mixes, spices, and bulk ingredients. Its primary customers were the five major national food wholesalers, with smaller regional wholesalers and independent grocery stores accounting for a smaller portion of their sales.

Gold Medal Crumpettes was a recent entry in Lucas Foods' bakery products group. This product fell into the product class commonly known as *biscuits*. Competitive products in this class included crumpets, scones, English muffins, and tea biscuits. Competition also came from a variety of substitute products such as toast, donuts, and muffins. Biscuit producers included such prominent names as Weston Bakeries and McGavin Foods Ltd. domestically, as well as the American firm of S.B. Thomas, which concentrated on English muffins, and dominated the market for that product.

Lucas Foods estimated that the product life cycle for specialty bakery goods was from five to seven years. Generally, if a new product was going to be successful, it enjoyed quick acceptance in the marketplace. Introduced in 1984, Gold Medal

Crumpettes at first had limited distribution. They had been sold in Manitoba and Saskatchewan, had recently been introduced in Alberta and Minnesota. Safeway was presently the only major chain to carry the product, but sales growth had been steady to date.

History of Lucas Foods

The company was originally formed under another name over 50 years previously. It specialized at first in frozen egg products, and later diversified into cabbage rolls and frozen meat products. The company was purchased by a major brewery in 1972, but the frozen egg portion of the business was sold back to the original owner six years later. They sold the business to Jerry Lucas in 1979. Since then sales have doubled to their present annual level of $12 million.

The company followed a "portfolio approach" to its product line, regularly adding or deleting items according to established criteria with respect to the marketing cycle. With the single exception of frozen egg products, no specific product or product family dominated their overall product offering. (An exception was made for frozen egg products because of their unique life-cycle and recession-proof qualities.)

In its business mission statement, Lucas Foods indicated a desire to grow to an annual sales level of $50 million and to become a major national food manufacturer and wholesaler, as well as an exporter. Its major competitive weapons were believed to be its excellent reputation, product knowledge, marketing expertise, and level of customer service.

Marketing Gold Medal Crumpettes

Lucas Foods believed that the consumption of biscuit products was uniform across age groups, seasons, and geographic locations. It was a mature market. The product itself was targeted toward the "upscale buyer." Package design, pricing policy, and product ingredients positioned Gold Medal as high-priced and high-quality relative to the competition. Therefore, the primary variables for segmenting the market were socio-economic: Gold Medal Crumpettes were a luxury item.

The Crumpettes were designed to incorporate the taste and texture of scones, English muffins, and biscuits. They could be eaten with or without butter, either toasted or untoasted. They were available in four flavours — plain, raisin, cheese, and onion — and the company had plans to add three more flavours, including pizza. The product could be stored frozen. The name, Gold Medal Crumpettes, was specifically selected to imply a connotation of quality.

Since wholesale food distribution in Canada was dominated by relatively few firms, management felt that it had little choice in the distribution of its products. Lucas Foods did not own a large warehouse to store its finished baked goods. It manufactured Gold Medal Crumpettes to order. The merchandise was then transported by common carrier to various customers under net 30 days credit terms.

The goal of the company's promotional efforts was to stimulate and encourage consumer trial of the product. There was some radio advertising when the product was first introduced. Although Lucas suggested the retail price, the distributor, especially in the case of Safeway, did most of the promotion. Typical promotions included:

- hostesses distributing free samples of the product in supermarkets
- crossover coupon promotions with jam companies
- mailout coupons to consumers
- free products to stores
- temporary price reductions for distributors

So far, $50 000 dollars had been spent on the promotion of Gold Medal Crumpettes. To complement these promotional efforts, Lucas Foods had three salespersons, who, along with the marketing manager, regularly called on all major accounts.

Gold Medal's high price was consistent with its positioning, and was arrived at after evaluating consumer surveys and the company's production costs. The expected price sensitivity of the market was also considered. A package of eight biscuits retailed for $1.89. The product was sold to supermarket chains in a case of twelve packages, with a factory price of $12.00 per case. Manufacturing costs, including allocated overhead, were $8.40 per case. This provides a contribution margin of $3.60 per case, or 30 percent. Production capacity was available for up to 16 000 cases per month.

Capturing the Opportunity

The estimated total potential market for Gold Medal Crumpettes is shown in Figure C12-1. Ha-

FIGURE C12-1

Total Potential Market for Gold Medal Crumpettes
(Yearly Sales)

	Cases	Volume
Manitoba	43 000	$ 520 000
Canada	960 000	11 500 000
United States	9 600 000	115 000 000

rold Riley felt that Lucas Foods held a 16 percent share of the Manitoba market.

The Manitoba consumer had been very receptive to the product. However, outside Manitoba, the company had only a limited reputation and was not well known as a wholesale food supplier. This lack of awareness made it more difficult for the product to obtain the acceptance of retailers. Also, the company faced an almost total lack of consumer awareness outside the province.

If Gold Medal succeeded in obtaining quick acceptance in new markets, competitors might view the development of a similar product as an attractive proposition. This could be particularly distressing if the competitor taking such an action was a major producer with an existing broad distribution system. Therefore, the speed with which Gold Medal Crumpettes could be introduced and developed into a dominant market position was very important to the long-term survival and profitability of the product. There was also the question of whether or not the degree of consumer acceptance the product had achieved in Manitoba could be repeated in new markets.

Pricing research conducted by the company indicated that consumers were not prepared to cross the $2.00 price level at retail to purchase the product. If production costs were to rise and force an increase in selling price, sales might decline. Also, while the current exchange rate allowed Lucas to be quite competitive in the U.S. market, a strengthening of the Canadian dollar could damage the company's export position.

Selecting a Strategy

Harold Riley had to propose a marketing strategy to Jerry Lucas that he felt would best take advantage of the opportunity available to Gold Medal Crumpettes. He was considering three alternatives:

1. Maintain the product's existing market coverage and strategy. This implied limiting distribution of the product and focusing the company's efforts on the Prairie provinces and the state of Minnesota.

2. Phased Expansion. This would involve expanding across Canada, region by region, to become a major force in the Canadian biscuit market and begin selective entry into the U.S. market.

3. Rapid Expansion. This approach would involve an attempt to expand rapidly in both countries, to precede and preferably pre-empt competitive products in all markets, and to seek a dominant position in the North American biscuit market.

During their early discussions, Jerry had pointed out that the company had the financial capacity to undertake any of these options. It was a question of how best to focus the available resources.

Before evaluating his alternatives, Harold drew up the following list of criteria to guide him in coming to an appropriate decision:

- The alternative should be feasible.
- The alternative should be profitable.
- The market opportunity should be exploited as far as possible while still meeting the first two criteria.
- The alternative should fit into the activities of the company.
- The alternative should be consistent with the mission of the company.
- The alternative should be consistent with Lucas Foods' portfolio management approach concerning return, risk, and diversity.
- There should be early evidence to support the alternative.

Questions

1. How would you evaluate each of the three alternatives suggested by Harold Riley against the stated criteria? Identify at least three pros and three cons for each alternative.
2. Which alternative should Harold Riley recommend to Jerry Lucas? Why?
3. Outline a basic marketing plan of action for your chosen strategy.

Source: Prepared by John Fallows under the direction of Walter S. Good, as a basis for classroom discussion rather than to illustrate either effective or ineffective handling of an administrative situation. Reprinted by permission of the Case Development Program, Faculty of Management, University of Manitoba. Support for the development of this case was provided by the Canadian Studies Program, Secretary of State, Government of Canada.

PART SEVEN

Marketing Communications

- CHAPTER 17 — MARKETING COMMUNICATIONS
- CHAPTER 18 — APPLYING MARKETING COMMUNICATIONS

Case 13 — Bounce-a-Roo, Inc.: New Product Advertising
Case 14 — Advertising — Chinese Style

CHAPTER 17

Marketing Communications

CHAPTER OBJECTIVES

1. Define, explain, or describe the key terms listed under "Vocabulary and Key Terms."
2. Describe the concept of the marketing communication process.
3. Outline and discuss the components of the marketing communication mix.
4. List and discuss the five objectives of promotion.
5. Explain how a firm should budget for its marketing communication strategy.
6. Explain how a marketing communication plan can be integrated appropriately.
7. Examine the business, economic, and social importance of promotion.
8. Apply your knowledge of Chapter 17 to the various activities in this chapter of the study guide.

VOCABULARY AND KEY TERMS

From the lettered terms listed below, select the one that best matches the meaning of each of the numbered statements that follows. Write the letter of that choice in the space provided.
a) marketing communication
b) marketing communications process
c) message
d) sender
e) receiver
f) encoding
g) decoding
h) feedback
i) noise
j) transfer mechanism
k) personal selling
l) advertising
m) sales promotion
n) public relations
o) publicity
p) pulling strategy
q) pushing strategy
r) percentage of sales
s) meet competition
t) task objective method
u) fixed sum per unit
v) direct-sales results test

1. _____ A firm's communications and relationships with its various publics
2. _____ A budget allocation method, under which a predetermined promotional amount is allocated on either a historical or a forecasted basis
3. _____ The receiver's interpretation of a message
4. _____ A budget allocation method, under which a firm defines its goals and then determines the amount needed to accomplish them
5. _____ Interference with the transmission of a message
6. _____ All the marketing activities (other than personal selling, advertising, and publicity) that stimulate consumer purchasing and dealer effectiveness
7. _____ The translation of a message into understandable terms, and its transmittal through a communication medium
8. _____ A nonpersonal sales presentation usually directed to a large number of potential customers
9. _____ A promotional effort by a seller to stimulate final user demand, which then exerts pressure on a distribution channel
10. _____ A budget allocation method under which a fixed percentage of funds, based on past or forecasted sales volume, is allocated for promotion
11. _____ The source of a message in the communication system
12. _____ A seller's promotional presentation, conducted on a person-to-person basis with a buyer
13. _____ A promotional effort directed at members of a marketing channel rather than a final user
14. _____ The means used to convey a message to a receiver (e.g., salesperson, advertisements)
15. _____ The segment of public relations directly related to promoting a company's products or services
16. _____ An inclusive term that encompasses advertising, personal selling, and sales promotion
17. _____ A budget allocation method that simply attempts to match competitor's promotion expenditures
18. _____ The postcommunication reaction to a message
19. _____ The decoder of a message
20. _____ The transmission of a message from a sender to a receiver that deals with buyer-seller relationships
21. _____ Information transmitted by a (marketing) communication system
22. _____ A method of ascertaining for each dollar of promotional outlay the corresponding increase in revenue

PRACTICE TEST

True-False: In the space to the right of each statement, check the appropriate line to indicate whether the statement is true or false.

	True	False
1. Marketing communications is defined by the author as all messages designed to persuade the consumer to buy.	_____	_____
2. The sender is the source of the communication system.	_____	_____
3. Encoding is the receiver's interpretation of the message.	_____	_____
4. Decoding is the most troublesome aspect of the communication process.	_____	_____
5. Nonpurchases can serve as feedback to the sender.	_____	_____
6. Personal selling is the most significant element in a firm's marketing communication expenditures.	_____	_____
7. Today fewer than 500 000 people in Canada are engaged in personal selling.	_____	_____

8. Sales promotion is the most important form of nonpersonal selling.

9. Mass consumption makes advertising appropriate for products that rely on sending the same message to large audiences.

10. Advertising is most appropriate where markets are concentrated in specific locations.

11. Installations rely more heavily on personal selling than on the marketing of operating supplies.

12. Advertising is more heavily used in the introduction stage of the life cycle than in the growth or maturity stages.

13. Advertising is an important mix component for low-unit-value products because of the high costs per contact for personal sales.

14. The cost of an industrial sale is now estimated to be approximately $230.

15. A pulling strategy is a promotional effort designed to stimulate final-user demand.

16. Personal selling is the main ingredient in the mix when using a pulling strategy.

17. Co-operative advertising, trade discounts, and personal selling are commonly used with a pushing strategy.

18. In the post-transactional phase, advertising is more important to the program than personal selling.

19. The "Thick" bars advertising on television is a good example of efforts by an advertiser to differentiate its product.

20. The threshold effect occurs when there are no sales but lots of initial investment in advertising.

21. The fixed sum per unit is the most common way of allocating budgets.

22. Most advertisers prefer to use a direct-sales results test to measure the effectiveness of a promotion.

23. Evaluation of the effectiveness of advertising is a simpler process than determining the effectiveness of the company's sales force effort.

24. The Canadian government is the largest advertiser in Canada.

25. Advertising has become an important factor in the campaign to achieve socially oriented objectives.

Multiple Choice: Choose the expression that best answers the question or best completes the sentence.

26. The source of the marketing communications is called the
a. go-getter
b. decoder
c. sender
d. encoder
e. interpreter

27. The receiver's interpretation of the message is referred to as
   a. decoding
   b. encoding
   c. transmission
   d. go-getterism
   e. sending

28. The receiver's response to the message is called
   a. decoding
   b. encoding
   c. feedback
   d. the transfer mechanism
   e. communication

29. All messages that inform, persuade, and influence the consumer to buy are a part of the marketer's
   a. marketing mix
   b. feedback mechanisms
   c. marketing communications
   d. public relations
   e. publicity

30. John Widmer is a salesperson for AV Datatron. He has prepared a sales presentation on a new computer software package. In the process of marketing communications John would be the
   a. encoder
   b. decoder
   c. feedback mechanism
   d. transfer mechanism
   e. receiver

31. The market for light bulbs is widely scattered. The GBC Corporation is marketing these light bulbs to varied retail outlets in every province in Canada. The most effective way to present the message on the product is to
   a. employ a hard-working sales force to contact retail accounts
   b. use a pulling strategy to make consumers aware of the brand
   c. use a pushing strategy
   d. use sales promotion at the retail level
   e. use free publicity to build the brand name

32. In selling heavy machinery to the industrial market, the most effective marketing communication element is
   a. advertising
   b. personal selling
   c. sales promotion
   d. public relations
   e. publicity

33. When a marketer advertises with the objective of increasing the demand for a product without having to lower the price, an effort is being made to
   a. stabilize sales
   b. differentiate the product
   c. accentuate the value of the product
   d. stimulate the demand for the product
   e. none of the above

34. McCain's is a producer of high-quality frozen vegetables and fruit juices. When it advertises the dependable high quality of its products its objective is to
a. stabilize sales
b. differentiate the product
c. accentuate the value of the product
d. stimulate the demand for the product
e. none of the above

35. A small steel company follows a policy of pricing its steel products just a fraction lower than the leader in the industry. This policy has been operative for years. Its objective is to
a. stabilize sales
b. differentiate the product
c. accentuate the value of the product
d. stimulate the demand for the product
e. none of the above

36. Displays, trade shows, product demonstrations, coupons, and contests are all examples of
a. advertising
b. personal selling
c. sales promotion
d. publicity
e. public relations

37. In the maturity stage of the product life cycle, heavy emphasis is placed on
a. advertising
b. personal selling
c. sales promotion
d. personal selling and sales promotion
e. publicity

38. The most commonly used marketing communications component for low-unit value products is
a. publicity
b. public relations
c. sales promotion
d. personal selling
e. advertising

39. The most expensive form of marketing communications is
a. publicity
b. public relations
c. sales promotion
d. personal selling
e. advertising

40. A manufacturer of salt will package this product and distribute it to various grocery wholesalers across the country. What type of marketing communications would be most effective in eliciting brand recognition from the ultimate consumer?
a. heavy advertising over TV to create brand awareness
b. a pulling strategy
c. an extensive publicity campaign
d. a strategy to obtain shelf space at the retail level and heavy reliance on the package to sell the product
e. hiring a large sales force to push the product on retailers

41. The Xerox Corporation provides funds for scholarships and social aid projects. Feature stories about charitable projects on the part of Xerox are examples of
   a. public relations
   b. sales promotion
   c. noise
   d. marginal analysis

42. Which of the following tasks must be accomplished if a marketing communication message is to be considered effective?
   a. It must gain the attention of the receiver.
   b. It must stimulate the needs of the receiver.
   c. It must be understood by both the receiver and the sender.
   d. It must suggest an appropriate method of satisfying the needs that have been stimulated in the receiver.
   e. all of the above

43. A pulling strategy is best illustrated by
   a. offering intermediaries bonuses for above-average sales
   b. heavy advertising aimed at consumers
   c. co-operative advertising
   d. sales-training programs for retail sales personnel
   e. discounts for additional shelf space and sizable retail orders

44. A pushing strategy relies mainly upon
   a. personal selling
   b. trade discounts
   c. consumer advertising
   d. a and b
   e. a and c

45. Which of the following is the crucial assumption underlying the task objective approach?
   a. The firm can afford to spend as much as its competition.
   b. The productivity of each promotional dollar is measurable.
   c. The emphasis will always fall upon advertising.
   d. A computer is available for the task.
   e. all of the above

46. The fixed-sum-per-unit approach differs from percentage of sales in only one respect:
   a. It assumes that the productivity of each dollar is measurable.
   b. It assumes that some of the promotional dollar will be wasted.
   c. It applies a predetermined dollar amount to each sales or product unit.
   d. It requires the use of a computer.
   e. It assumes that each sales unit contributes the same amount.

47. The most common approach to allocating a marketing communication budget is the
   a. task-objective method
   b. percentage-of-sales method
   c. fixed-sum-per-unit approach
   d. meet-competition approach

48. Advertising should be the main element of the marketing communication budget when
   a. the product has hidden qualities
   b. the primary demand for the product is on the upswing
   c. there is an opportunity to differentiate the product

d. the company has sufficient money to cover the cost of advertising
e. all of the above

49. Advertising is used primarily in marketing
a. high-value products
b. industrial goods
c. low-value goods
d. services

50. Which of the following is a reason for the economic importance of marketing communications?
a. It is responsible for the employment of millions of people.
b. It increases units sold, thereby assisting in reducing production costs and prices.
c. It subsidizes the informational content of newspapers and broadcast media.
d. all of the above
e. a and c

ANSWER KEY: CHAPTER 17

Vocabulary and Key Terms	True-False	Multiple Choice
1. n	1. F	26. c
2. u	2. T	27. a
3. g	3. F	28. c
4. t	4. T	29. c
5. i	5. T	30. d
6. m	6. F	31. b
7. f	7. F	32. b
8. l	8. F	33. d
9. p	9. T	34. b
10. r	10. F	35. a
11. d	11. T	36. c
12. k	12. F	37. a
13. q	13. T	38. e
14. j	14. T	39. e
15. o	15. T	40. d
16. a	16. F	41. a
17. s	17. T	42. e
18. h	18. F	43. b
19. e	19. F	44. d
20. b	20. T	45. b
21. c	21. F	46. c
22. v	22. T	47. b
	23. F	48. e
	24. T	49. c
	25. T	50. d

EXERCISE 17.1: COMMERCIALS THAT SELL

Consumers are bombarded daily with a myriad of advertising stimuli. It is said that the average consumer is exposed to more than a thousand ads daily from the various media but that very few of these messages are absorbed fully by the central processing unit within our brains. If you want to use TV to sell your products, what type of commercials will do the job most effectively?

In the book *Ogilvy on Advertising*, David Ogilvy analyzes commercials that he found to have above-average ability to change a consumer's brand preference, and ranks humour as the number-one approach to take. (He also warns that commercials must genuinely be funny for consumers to respond positively to them.) He ranks the slice-of-life approach number two: "In these commercials one actor argues with another about the merits of a product, in a setting which approximates real life. In the end the doubter is converted — your toothpaste really does give children healthier teeth" (p. 105). Ogilvy also feels that some testimonials, such as ones by loyal users who state the virtues of the product, are very effective. He is not sold on the ability of testimonials by celebrities to change brand preference, however. Commercials by celebrities are the most expensive form of advertising, and if they are not particularly effective, one might wonder why so many sponsors use them. In the book *Of Women and Advertising*, John Straiton writes, "Commercials using well-known celebrities are among the best remembered of all. However, recent measurement techniques show that they are low in ability to persuade people to switch brands" (p. 88). In other words, using celebrities in commercials may promote brand recognition, but accomplish little else.

Straiton thinks advertisers should spend less time trying to entertain consumers, and more time demonstrating products and explaining how consumers can benefit from using them: "A demonstration is powerful because it can show you 'texture' — the thickness of the ketchup, the body in hair, the bubbles in tonic water, the feel of a Mercedes swerving at eighty miles an hour to avoid a truck, the smoothness of an instant pudding, the fluffiness of Minute Rice. When you demonstrate the product, you help the consumer rehearse using it" (p. 81).

According to a June 12, 1989, article in *Maclean's*, advertisers are increasingly using sex to sell products. While some advertisers criticize the use of sexually aggressive promotions such as certain beer ads and the Beemans chewing gum ads,

> the advertising industry executives and their critics alike also predict that advertisements aimed at your male consumers — who still dominate the markets for products ranging from beer to auto parts — will continue to become more explicit. For their part, advertisers say that they have to use graphic, sexually charged images to capture the attention of the so-called grazers — people with remote channel changers who flip to other programs during commercials. (p. 34)

The author of this article points out that the market is changing and a larger percentage of consumers of products in the marketplace are women. Thus, many ads that feature stereotypes, such as the woman scraping and cleaning her oven or discussing her preference for detergent or floor wax brands, are beginning to disappear. Straiton also suggests that there is a place for sex in advertising — when sex is the consumer benefit being sold. For example, he notes, perfume advertisements seem to suggest there is a reason for smelling nice, and that some suntan-lotion and skin-softener advertisers make relevant use of a woman's body to sell their products. According to the *Maclean's* article, "the increasingly graphic sexual images are not aimed only at young men — sex is also used to sell a variety of products to women" (p. 35). Perfume, for example, is a sexual product, is promoted that way, and is aimed at the female audience. It is likely that advertisers will continue to use sex as a lure in their advertising.

Questions

1. Give examples of TV commercials you have viewed that make use of the following techniques in advertising their products:
   a. humour
   b. slice of life
   c. celebrities
   d. testimonials by ordinary people
   e. demonstrations
   f. sex
2. What type of commercials are most likely to get your attention? The advertiser is concerned that viewers will zap its commercial with the remote. What might be done to address this problem?

3. Although sex is now used to promote a much narrower range of products than in the past, it is still a powerful advertising tool. Who are the main target market(s) of sex in advertising? Is sex in advertising likely to continue to be a hot sell in the future? What is your reaction to this advertising technique?
4. How effective is the use of celebrities in advertising? What are the primary advantages and disadvantages of using celebrities in advertising? What principles should advertisers follow when considering using celebrities in advertising?

Sources: David Ogilvy, *Ogilvy on Advertising* (New York: Crown, 1983), pp. 103–9. Reprinted by permission.
John Straiton, *Of Women and Advertising* (Toronto: McClelland and Stewart, 1984), pp. 81–93, 138. Reprinted by permission.
"The Hot Sell," *Maclean's*, 12 June 1989, pp. 34–5.

EXERCISE 17.2: MARISSA KRUPPKE, COGNIZANT CAR SALESPERSON

Marissa Kruppke has been the top car salesperson at BC Motors in Vancouver, BC, for the past five years, and the reason for her success is her friendly personality, knowledge of the car industry, and desire to provide good service to her customers.

Marissa has just completed a course in consumer behaviour at BC Institute of Technology and is excited about the possibilities of applying Festinger's theory of postcognitive dissonance to the car business. Cognitive dissonance, as Marissa understands it, is simply the postdecision anxiety that a consumer experiences in purchasing an item. It is generally conceded that postcognitive dissonance increases when the dollar value of an item increases, when the item is a major purchase requiring much thought and deliberation, or when the item purchased lacks features that are present in items not selected. A customer will show dissonance simply because he or she can't buy everything and rejected alternatives are likely to have features not present in the chosen alternative. Marissa has reflected that when a customer purchases a car, that customer may feel some anxiety or uncertainty about whether or not the right decision has been made. Therefore, it is unwise to fast-talk a consumer into buying, as this is forced compliance, and buyer remorse will likely follow.

Marissa realizes that postcognitive dissonance may lead a consumer to have second thoughts about a purchase contract. If not allowed to back out of the contract, the consumer will be unhappy and unlikely to buy from her or her company again. She reflects that if she had a better idea of how consumers handled cognitive dissonance, then she could use this information to provide better service and increase her chances of having return customers. Upon doing further reading, Marissa discovers that customers who make a purchase usually search for information that supports the decision they have made. Talking to friends about what a good buy they made helps them to deal with their anxiety. At the same time, these customers will often ignore, discount, or simply fail to deal with information that does not support the decision they made. If in the back of their mind they feel that this information confirms that they made a wrong choice, they will likely buy another brand the next time around. How can a salesperson avoid having this happen?

Marissa feels that she will have to spend more time thinking about this subject before attempting to apply what she knows about it to her business. Maybe, she thinks, she will also discuss the subject with her professor.

Questions

1. From the information given in this exercise, explain cognitive dissonance.
2. Suggest ways in which Marissa can apply cognitive dissonance to her sales approach.
3. Relate cognitive dissonance to your own experience (e.g., purchasing a car, deciding on a university or college, buying a home, etc.).

CHAPTER 18

Applying Marketing Communications

CHAPTER OBJECTIVES

1. Define, explain, or describe the key terms listed under "Vocabulary and Key Terms."
2. Identify the different categories of advertisements.
3. Describe the process of creating an advertisement.
4. Identify the different categories of sales promotion.
5. Classify the three basic sales tasks.
6. Discuss the characteristics of successful salespeople.
7. Specify the functions of sales management.
8. Apply your knowledge of Chapter 18 to the various activities in this chapter of the study guide.

VOCABULARY AND KEY TERMS

From the lettered terms listed below, select the one that best matches the meaning of each of the numbered statements that follows. Write the letter of that choice in the space provided.

a) product advertising
b) institutional advertising
c) informative advertising
d) persuasive advertising
e) reminder-oriented advertising
f) advertising agency
g) comparative advertising
h) sales promotion
i) point-of-purchase advertising
j) specialty advertising
k) order processing
l) creative selling
m) missionary selling
n) prospecting
o) qualifying
p) presentation
q) closing
r) follow-up

1. _____ The sales task that has a salesperson identify a customer need and take orders for a firm's product or services

2. _____ Displays and demonstrations that seek to promote a product at a time and place closely associated with the actual decision to buy

3. _____ The step in the sales process that seeks to determine whether a prospect can become a customer

4. _____ Nonpersonal selling of a particular good or service

5. _____ A nonpersonal form of promotion that must be co-ordinated with advertising and personal selling as elements of the promotional mix

6. _____ The practice of making direct promotional comparisons with leading comparative brands

7. _____ Items carrying a firm's name that help reinforce previous or future advertising and sales messages

8. _____ The step in the sales process in which potential customers are identified

9. _____ The postsales activities that often determine whether a person will become a repeat customer

10. _____ A basic sales tasks employed by a seller to make a buyer see the worth of what he or she is attempting to sell

11. _____ An advertising method concerned with promoting a concept, idea, philosophy, or goodwill of an industry, or organization

12. _____ A form of advertising that seeks to develop demand through presenting factual information on the attributes of the product and/or service

13. _____ A marketing specialist firm that assists the advertiser in planning and preparing its advertisements

14. _____ A type of sales activity that involves selling the goodwill of a firm and provides a customer with technical or operational assistance

15. _____ A form of advertising in which the emphasis is on the use of words and/or images to try to create an image for a product and to influence attitudes about it

16. _____ The step in the sales process in which a salesperson tells his or her story to a potential customer

17. _____ A form of advertising that reinforces previous promotional activity by keeping the company name in front of the public

18. _____ The step in the sales process in which a salesperson must ask a prospect for an order

PRACTICE TEST

True-False: In the space to the right of each statement, check the appropriate line to indicate whether the statement is true or false.

	True	False
1. Procter & Gamble is the largest advertiser in Canada.		
2. Cosmetic firms spend more on advertising than on personal selling.		
3. Advertising expenditures can range from less than 1 percent of sales in the detergent industry to a high of 10 percent of sales for some industrial products.		
4. Advertising planning begins with effective research.		
5. Product advertising is concerned with developing an image for a company or an industry.		
6. Institutional advertising is closely related to the public-relations function of the enterprise.		

7. Informative advertising attempts to convince a customer to buy a specific brand by making comparisons with other leading brands.

8. Persuasive ads will make effective use of words and images to stimulate a buyer to try a certain brand.

9. Comparative advertising is not used as much today as it was in the 1970s.

10. The largest amount of advertising revenue is spent on television advertising.

11. The primary advantages of magazine advertising are selectivity, quality reproduction, and long life.

12. A primary disadvantage of radio advertising is its high cost.

13. The main advantages of television advertising are high impact, mass coverage, and flexibility.

14. The main disadvantages of newspaper advertising are short lifespan, hasty readers, and poor reproduction.

15. A company may have an internal advertising department or use an outside agency, but it will never use both.

16. Comparative advertising is best employed by firms that lead the market for a certain product or service.

17. Co-operative advertising is the sharing of advertising costs between the retailer and the manufacturer or wholesaler.

18. Post-testing is the assessment of an advertisement's effectiveness before it is actually used.

19. The three sales tasks are order processing, creative selling, and customer follow-up.

20. Missionary selling is a direct type of selling.

21. The saying "Salespeople are born, not made" is basically true.

22. The final step in the sales process is follow-up.

23. Displays and demonstrations that seek to promote the product are good examples of specialty advertising.

24. Sales promotional techniques may be used by all members of a marketing channel.

25. Order processing is most often typified by selling at the wholesale and retail levels.

Multiple Choice: Choose the expression that best answers the question or best completes the sentence.

26. The total number of people employed in advertising is approximately
   a. 5000
   b. 10 400
   c. 8500
   d. 75 000
   e. 100

27. Which of the following is a good example of positioning by attributes of the product?
   a. Sears is a value store.

b. We do it all for you at McDonald's.
c. Crest is a cavity fighter.
d. Mercedes-Benz automobile is for the discriminating executive.
e. Are you up for it? 7-Up.

28. Which type of advertising attempts to develop demand for a particular product or service?
a. product advertising
b. institutional advertising
c. image advertising
d. cause advertising
e. specialty advertising

29. Which type of advertising is concerned with promoting a concept, idea, or philosophy of a company or industry?
a. product advertising
b. institutional advertising
c. image advertising
d. cause advertising
e. specialty advertising

30. Informative advertising is normally found in the
a. introductory stage of the product life cycle
b. growth stage of the product life cycle
c. maturity stage of the product life cycle
d. decline stage of the product life cycle
e. b and c

31. Informative advertising tends to be used
a. in situations in which the advertiser wishes to compare its brand with competitive brands
b. to reinforce previous promotional activity
c. to promote a concept, idea, or philosophy of a company or industry
d. in the promotion of new products
e. in the early maturity stage of the product life cycle

32. A company that uses comparative advertising in most cases is also using
a. informative product advertising
b. persuasive product advertising
c. reminder-oriented product advertising
d. institutional advertising
e. cause advertising

33. Canadian Tire in its advertising presents the message that "Canadian Tire means more than tires." This is an example of
a. informative product advertising
b. persuasive product advertising
c. reminder-oriented product advertising
d. institutional advertising
e. cause advertising

34. Which of the following is a disadvantage of television advertising?
a. temporary nature of the message
b. high cost
c. high mortality rate for commercials
d. evidence of public lack of selectivity
e. all of the above

35. Which of the following is an advantage of magazine advertising?
a. flexibility
b. intense coverage
c. repetition
d. community prestige
e. selectivity

36. Which of the following is an example of specialty advertising?
a. point-of-purchase advertising
b. co-operative advertising
c. coupons and premiums
d. items carrying a firm's name, such as calendars and pencils
e. free distribution of an item door to door (sampling)

37. A salesperson who tries innovative selling techniques to make the buyer see the worth of a product, is likely using the sales task of
a. order processing
b. creative selling
c. missionary sales
d. suggestive selling
e. none of the above

38. The moment of truth in selling is the
a. approach to the customer
b. qualifying the prospect
c. closing the sale
d. effectiveness of the presentation
e. follow-up with the customer after the sale

39. Salespeople engaged in order processing must
a. identify customer needs
b. create customer wants
c. point out the need to the customer
d. all of the above
e. a and c

40. All of the following are basic sales tasks that form the basis for a sales classification except
a. creative selling
b. suggestive selling
c. missionary sales
d. order processing

41. Originally, advertising agencies sold
a. copywriting
b. research
c. space
d. magazines and newspapers in addition to advertising
e. all of the above

42. All of the following are communication objectives of advertising except
a. to inform potential customers of the product
b. to remind potential customers that the company's product is available
c. to downgrade the quality of competitors' products and to accentuate the quality of the company's product
d. to persuade customers that they should buy the company's product

43. Positioning is especially important in advertising
a. products that are not leaders in their field
b. products that are leaders in their field
c. consumer products
d. industrial products
e. low-cost products

44. Informative product advertising seeks to
a. create goodwill
b. promote a philosophy
c. develop initial demand
d. remind former customers of a previously sampled product
e. reinforce previous buying behaviour

45. Comparative advertising is usually used by
a. firms leading the market
b. products that stress low cost
c. consumer products
d. firms not leading the market
e. none of the above

46. Institutional advertising deals with
a. nonpersonal selling of a good
b. personal selling of a service
c. promoting a philosophy
d. promoting goodwill
e. c and d

47. Persuasive product advertising is usually used in which stage of the product life cycle?
a. growth
b. maturity
c. introduction
d. decline
e. all of the above

48. Which of the following is not an advantage of newspaper advertising?
a. intense coverage
b. flexibility
c. reader control of exposure to the advertising message
d. selectivity of market targets
e. community prestige

49. Which of the following is not an advantage of television advertising?
a. high impact on audience
b. mass coverage
c. flexibility
d. low mortality rates for commercial

50. Which of the following is not an example of sales promotion?
a. specialty advertising
b. co-operative advertising
c. samples, coupons, and premiums
d. trade shows
e. trading stamps

ANSWER KEY: CHAPTER 18

Vocabulary and Key Terms	True-False	Multiple Choice
1. k	1. F	26. c
2. i	2. T	27. c
3. o	3. F	28. a
4. a	4. T	29. b
5. h	5. F	30. a
6. g	6. T	31. d
7. j	7. F	32. b
8. n	8. T	33. c
9. r	9. F	34. e
10. l	10. F	35. e
11. b	11. T	36. d
12. c	12. F	37. b
13. f	13. T	38. c
14. m	14. T	39. e
15. d	15. F	40. b
16. p	16. F	41. c
17. e	17. T	42. c
18. q	18. F	43. a
	19. F	44. c
	20. F	45. d
	21. F	46. e
	22. T	47. a
	23. F	48. d
	24. T	49. d
	25. T	50. b

EXERCISE 18.1: DETERMINING THE SIZE OF THE SALES FORCE

Aaron Appliance is a medium-sized manufacturer of small appliances in Hamilton, Ontario. Its primary market extends 300 km from Hamilton, but its secondary market covers major cities in Ontario beyond the 300-km radius. The company is currently reassessing the size of the sales force necessary to service the company's accounts in Ontario and to allow each salesperson time to do his or her assigned tasks. After completing a study that determined the total number of hours required for sales calls for each type of account, Chuck Breen, the sales manager, has calculated the time necessary for each salesperson to do the job. He figures that if each salesperson works 40 hours per week for 49 weeks, the average number of hours per year will be 1960. Each salesperson's time can thus be allocated to assigned tasks as follows:

Activity	Hours per year
Sales Calls on Accounts	980
Travel to and from Accounts	392
Nonselling Activities	588
Total	1960

Chuck now checks the records and determines that currently there are over 5000 accounts that require sales calls. To service each of these 5000 accounts would require (according to the study) an average of fifteen hours per year. At a sales seminar he attended last year in Toronto it was illustrated that in this industry the required number of salespersons was equal to the total number of hours required for servicing accounts divided by the total number of hours a salesperson actually spent on sales calls on accounts. He thus concludes that he now has all the information necessary for determining what size the sales force should be. The company currently has 82 salespeople covering Ontario. Is this too many or too few?

Chuck recognizes that the salesperson's job includes order processing, creative selling, and missionary sales. Salespeople are also involved with a number of nonselling activities, such as setting up retail displays for the manufacturer and doing credit checks on potential new accounts, as well as the usual paperwork on regular accounts. All sales staff are required to meet twice a year at regularly scheduled conferences, where they work on developing new and better techniques for selling products creatively. Compared with most other companies in the field, Aaron Appliance expects high standards of performance from its employees, who are expected to engage in a fair number of nonselling activities. Chuck feels that the salespeople are in general happy with the company and with their own performances.

Questions

1. What percentage of the salesperson's time can be allocated to the tasks listed above? What sort of nonselling activities would a salesperson be responsible for?

2. How many salespeople does Chuck Breen need in order to service the 5000 accounts in his company's market? From the above description, write out the formula for determining the required number of salespeople.

3. Based on your calculations, does the company have too few or too many salespeople? What other factors should Breen take into consideration before he either hires or fires salespeople?

4. What sales tasks are involved in selling small appliances to the retail trade? Allocate the percentage of time that you feel a salesperson on this job would spend on each of the three sales tasks.

EXERCISE 18.2: EVALUATION OF ADVERTISEMENTS

Included over the next few pages are a number of advertisements for analysis. Examine each advertisement carefully and answer the questions following the ads. The objective of this exercise is to give you experience in evaluating advertisements and relating these ads to principles in the text.

INTRODUCING A BETTER WAY

Now premeasured in its own Filter Packet! Rich Maxwell House* ground coffee, just drop it in your auto-drip coffee maker.

No more measuring, no more guesswork...just perfect Maxwell House* coffee everytime.
New Maxwell House* Filter Packets. A better way to enjoy great coffee.

NEW MAXWELL HOUSE* FILTER PACKETS.
Available in regular and naturally decaffeinated.
Hugga Mugga

*Registered trade-mark of Kraft General Foods Canada Inc.

Questions

1. What type of advertisement is this (i.e., informative, persuasive, or reminder-oriented product or institutional ad)?
2. Does this ad relate to the product–life cycle concept? Explain.

Questions

1. What type of advertisement is this (i.e., informative, persuasive, or reminder-oriented product or institutional ad)?
2. Is this an example of comparative advertising? What are the arguments given for using Kraft Free over Hellmann's?
3. Would a buyer be more willing to try the product based on the information provided in the ad? Why or why not?

Wilt Chamberlain. Cardmember since 1976.
Willie Shoemaker. Cardmember since 1966.

Membership
Has Its Privileges.™

Don't leave home without it.®
Call 1-800-668-AMEX to apply.

Questions

1. What type of advertisement is this (i.e., informative, persuasive, or reminder-oriented product or institutional ad)?
2. Can you relate this ad to your study of the chapter on consumer behaviour? What is the advertiser trying to accomplish with this ad?

"We're making important breakthroughs in understanding the nature of pain. And a big factor is the funding that pharmaceutical companies provide."

*Helen Bouman,
neurological researcher,
University of Calgary*

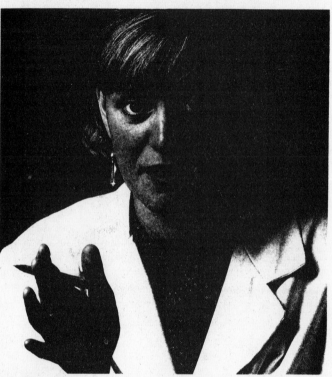

Helen Bouman's field of research is nerve cells and the way they transmit messages.

"Some years ago, it was found that the body has its own naturally occurring pain killers or opiates, called endorphins. This had enormous implications for pain relief: medicines could be designed to 'suit' particular opiates, and be targeted on them. This affects all areas of neurological research, including my own. I'm using inhibitors to turn neurons on and off, to see what they do. This work is revealing the secrets of both pain and pleasure."

What researchers in this field are embarked on is a total re-mapping of the brain – an exercise that will clearly take a great deal of time and money. Helen Bouman received a research award from the Health Research Foundation of the Pharmaceutical Manufacturers Association of Canada (PMAC). This award was co-funded with the Medical Research Council of Canada under the University-Industry Program.

"As a graduate student starting out, it wasn't easy getting funded. It isn't for anyone. So the kind of support we get from the pharmaceutical companies is very important. It helps keep basic research like mine alive. And that's where the search for cures *has* to begin – with basic, detailed research."

This area of study could eventually lead to treatment of conditions like Alzheimer's Disease and spinal paralysis. If so, it would join a long list of landmark therapeutic breakthroughs achieved by the pharmaceutical industry.

In fact, more than 90% of modern prescription medicines came from research undertaken by the innovative pharmaceutical companies.

Exactly who are the "innovative" pharmaceutical companies? We're the people who develop, manufacture and sell original *brand-name* prescription medicines. And each year, we invest hundreds of millions of dollars in our own research programs, as well as in grants and fellowships to researchers at universities across Canada.

So that every time a prescription is filled with an original brand-name medicine, another contribution is made to future research.

Research that could perhaps save a child from leukemia. Or give hope to an Alzheimer's patient. Or even enable a paraplegic to walk.

PHARMACEUTICAL MANUFACTURERS ASSOCIATION OF CANADA

Representing Canada's Innovative Pharmaceutical Companies

For more information, write:
PMAC, 302 – 1111 Prince of Wales Drive, Ottawa, Ontario K2C 3T2

Bringing Research to Life

Questions

1. What type of advertisement is this (i.e., informative, persuasive, or reminder-oriented product or institutional ad)?

2. What message is advocated with this ad? Why do you feel the Pharmaceutical Manufacturers Association has had to resort to advertising to present their message?

Questions

1. What type of advertisement is this (i.e., informative, persuasive, or reminder-oriented product or institutional ad)?
2. How do you react to the ad?
3. Who placed this ad? Does the advertiser spend a large amount of money on advertising? Give examples of other ads placed by this advertiser.

EVERY TIME SOMEONE CHOOSES NATURAL GAS, THE GUYS DOWN AT BINCHER'S POND SEEM TO SING A LITTLE LOUDER.

THE GUYS AT Bincher's Pond are an easy bunch to please.

All they ask for is fresh air, clean rain and an abundant supply of six-legged suppers.

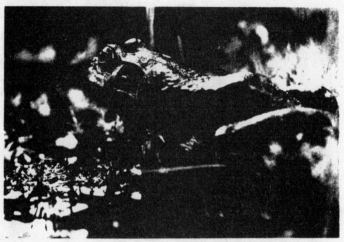

That simple request is getting harder to fulfill. Pollution is fouling the air and choking our rivers and lakes.

Our attitude about the environment must change.

We owe it not only to ourselves, but to our children and the songsters at the pond.

MAKE A CHANGE FOR THE BETTER.

Can one person really contribute to a cleaner environment? The answer is yes.

We can recycle more. We can use less paper and plastic disposables and grow more mindful of the energy we use to heat our homes and fuel our vehicles.

Part of the solution is a greater use of natural gas. It's abundant, efficient and the cleanest of fossil fuels.

FUEL FOR THOUGHT.

Natural gas can reduce air pollution, lessen the damage of acid rain and help moderate the greenhouse effect.

Look at the facts.

Industries that use natural gas in place of coal or oil can reduce the harmful emissions that contribute to our global warming.

Using natural gas, these same industries can eliminate their emissions of sulphur dioxide, the primary cause of acid rain.

Breathe deeply, there's more.

A vehicle fueled by natural gas produces fewer hydrocarbons – which means less smog – and 40% less carbon dioxide than a gasoline-powered vehicle.

Because North Americans buy over 725 million litres of gasoline a day, adapting our vehicles to natural gas could significantly clean up the air.

NOT PERFECT, BUT A GOOD START.

Natural gas is not the complete answer.

But when you compare it to coal, oil or gasoline, the advantages of natural gas outshine the alternatives.

So the next time you step outside, take a deep breath and remember the guys at the pond.

They'd appreciate your vocal support.

For a free booklet on how you can help the environment by the use of natural gas, call this toll-free number:

1-800-668-1503

Natural Gas.
The Natural Choice.

Questions

1. What type of advertisement is this (i.e., informative, persuasive, or reminder-oriented product or institutional ad)?
2. Is this an effective ad? What is your reaction to the message that is presented?

Case 13

BOUNCE-A-ROO, INC.: NEW PRODUCT ADVERTISING

Hi! My family and I are very proud to be introducing Bounce-a-Roos to the United States. They have been part of almost every baby's early life in Australia for many years. When our first baby was born, my mother, who lives in Australia, sent us one and we found it almost indispensable. As people saw our babies enjoying it they wanted one, and what started as my mother sending Bounce-a-Roos one at a time has grown to the point that we are now starting to market them on a wide scale in the United States.

This was the note, included with a product brochure, that Judyth Box, M.D., sent to people who inquired about purchasing a Bounce-a-Roo.

Product Description

First invented in Chicago about 20 years ago, the Bounce-a-Roo patent was sold to an Australian. In that country, the seats have been considered a necessity for babies for years. Bounce-a-Roos are very simple in design and consist of a spring steel frame with a cotton net. The gentle bouncing motion of the Bounce-a-Roo, brought about by baby's own movements or by someone else, is very soothing to a fussy baby and is also pleasing to a happy one. Bounce-a-Roos weigh only three pounds and slip over the arm for easy portability.

The net slips off to go into the washing machine and is available in many colours. The Bounce-a-Roo can be used for babies from birth to about one year old, depending on the nature of the baby. It is especially nice in hot weather. Mothers of babies who have used the Bounce-a-Roos are beginning to report a new use for the seats. According to several mothers, toddlers of 18 months to three years are using them as toys. "Christina sits on her Bounce-a-Roo and bounces, almost like it's a trampoline," says Melinda Newsome. Other mothers report older children using Bounce-a-Roos as backrests for watching television. While all these uses prolong the useful life of the Bounce-a-Roo, Judyth Box advises turning the net upside down so the children won't catch a foot in the baby strap.

Similar products are appearing on the market now, but they do not compare in quality with the Bounce-a-Roo. "We have been trying to have the frames made here in the United States, but our standard is that a ten-pound baby must be at a 45-degree angle to the floor when sitting on the Bounce-a-Roo. U.S. prototypes produced so far have a ten-pound baby lying flat, and so do the competitive products on the market," Box explained. Another feature of the Bounce-a-Roo not seen on the competing models is the netting. A ten-pound baby sinks into the netting and is kept in place by his or her own weight. Many of the competitive products have a denim seat cover and the baby is held in by, or hung up on, a strap. There is a strap on the Bounce-a-Roo for safety's sake, but it is not essential. "The Bounce-a-Roo will remain the Rolls-Royce of baby seats for some time yet," says Box.

Bounce-a-Roos cost $29 each and are available in nine colours: pink, red, green, gold, yellow, brown, royal blue, light blue, and white. There is no charge for shipping anywhere in the continental United States. The sunshade, in white or light blue, is available at a cost of $18. The company accepts cheques or money orders and Visa or MasterCard for purchases. A brochure describing the product is shown in Exhibit C13-1.

Sales Patterns

Sales for Bounce-a-Roos have been showing a steady increase overall since their introduction to the United States in April 1982. "There must be more babies born in the fall than at any other time of the year," says Box. "Or else people see our Bounce-a-Roos in campgrounds and at picnics during the summer and want one for the baby in their life. At any rate, we at Bounce-a-Roo notice a build-up in sales over the summer and early fall, then a tapering off for a brief period — and the Christmas rush hits."

Box notes that it seems popular for expectant grandparents and aunts to send a Bounce-a-Roo for a shower or baby gift. These types of customers especially appreciate the convenience of simply calling Bounce-a-Roo and having their gift shipped out of town or out of state. "As women are having their first baby at an older age today, friends and

EXHIBIT C13-1 PORTIONS OF BROCHURE FOR BOUNCE-A-ROO

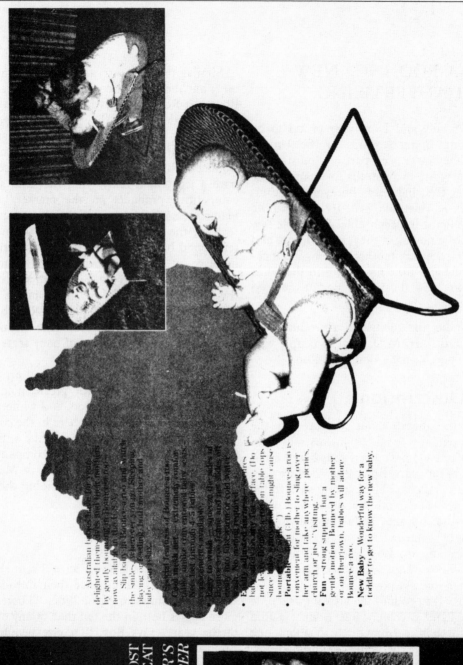

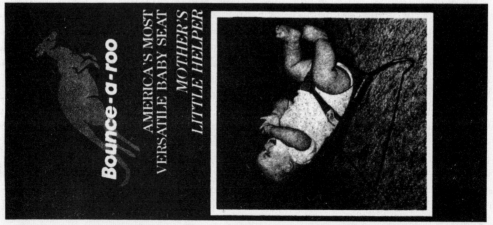

relatives seem even more excited," Box observes. "We often hear, 'She's having her first baby at 32, and she deserves something extra — a Bounce-a-Roo!' A new mother who receives a Bounce-a-Roo as a gift is frequently so excited about it that she buys them for her friends who have babies after her. The record so far is held by one young mother who gave five Bounce-a-Roos to friends within eight months of receiving her own at a baby shower."

Advertising Possibilities

Most of the sales of Bounce-a-Roos to date have come from new purchases by and referrals from previous customers. The company is currently considering ways in which it can effectively advertise to expand the market for Bounce-a-Roos. One alternative the company is exploring is advertising in a special section of the Saturday edition of a local newspaper. The following information describes this advertising opportunity.

> These "People, Products, and Business" pages are a very effective advertising medium for distributors, dealers, manufacturers, contractors, consultants, agencies, and other businesses that sell or service commercial accounts, as well as retail establishments. Businesses on these pages run a small advertisement each week for a period of one year. During that year, they receive free write-ups on a request basis. The write-ups appear similar to a news story and usually include a photograph. Each write-up is about one-sixteenth of a page in size. The smallest one-inch advertisement costs $20.95 weekly ($1089.40 yearly) and entitles the advertiser to a maximum of three write-ups. A two-inch

advertisement costs $40.70 weekly ($2116.40 yearly) and entitles the advertiser to a maximum of five write-ups. The paper has a readership of approximately 400 000 people. Write-ups on a business may emphasize its services, product line, personnel, newly introduced products, special capabilities, location changes or expansions, awards or recognitions, or any other aspect of the operation that the advertiser wishes to stress. An account executive can assist in the writing of the final draft of the story and a newspaper photographer can take any pictures necessary, all free of additional charge.

Questions

1. From an advertising perspective, what do you see as the basic problem facing Bounce-a-Roo?
2. What type of market research would be helpful to the firm at this time?
3. How would you segment the market for a product such as this?
4. Discuss the strengths and weaknesses of the various types of media for Bounce-a-Roo's advertising.
5. If you were going to use direct mail, who would you want to mail to and why?
6. Do you think that Bounce-a-Roo would be better off to use magazines, newspapers, or both as a medium for its advertising?

Source: W. Wayne Talarzyk, *Cases and Exercises in Marketing* (Chicago, Ill.: The Dryden Press, 1987), pp. 193–7. Reprinted by permission.

Case 14

ADVERTISING — CHINESE STYLE

Though Americans' national pride wouldn't readily allow them to admit it, one-fourth of the world's population is still unfamiliar with common ad names like "Coke" and "McDonald's." When the Communists took over mainland China in 1949

they abolished advertising as a capitalist weapon. Only in 1979 was advertising once again allowed as part of the new leadership's attempts to modernize the country and eliminate its "developing" nation status.

Advertising in China is not without its rules. Tobacco and liquor, for example, can be advertised only in hotels and stores where only foreigners shop. While there exists no central censorship committee, each medium is expected to ensure that advertising does not adversely affect the nation's social, political, or moral climate.

Since the rebirth of advertising is a recent phenomenon in China, many companies from outside the country must learn to adjust to a new market. Advertising tends to be literal. At Ogilvy & Mather, one of a number of firms operating in Hong Kong, clients are advised to keep things simple: Factual, straightforward presentations with little or no attempt at analogy or humour. The Chinese are traditionally suspicious, they feel, of foreign salespersons. Ads tend to emphasize quality, durability, and performance.

One American company, Eastman Kodak, has done well in China, with a multimedia ad campaign that has made film sales even greater than in Hong Kong. To suit the new market, the company had to adapt its selling themes. In Western countries the company's ads focus on saving memories. In China that would mean memories of the cultural revolution, which most Chinese would like to forget. Kodak's Chinese ads concentrate on saving only the present — today's memories of birthday parties or weddings.

While many Western companies are still in the planning stages for their products' ad campaigns, the Japanese dominate the market in China. The top ten advertisers in China are Japanese. Japanese products stress durability, unlike many American products, and that quality is important to the Chinese. Also, Japanese firms started advertising in China in 1979 before many of their products were even available in China. In that way they gained an edge over their competition, having had the advantage of getting their products' name known in advance. This method is recommended to Western companies since they have a difficult time understanding that no one in China has heard of them.

Advertising in China provides benefits in two ways. China's leaders claim that advertising helps the Chinese people learn about world developments of the past 30 years and helps the country's economy by stimulating sales. Product manufacturers and advertisers also benefit from the potential market of one billion new customers.

Questions

1. Why are Japanese marketers so successful in China?
2. Using the information presented in this case, develop an advertising strategy for a U.S. firm operating there. Examples of such companies include Bayer, Burroughs-Wellcome, Johnnie Walker, Compaq Computers, Doral cigarettes, General Foods, Gillette, IBM, and Philip Morris.

Source: Lynne Reaves, "China: A New Frontier for Advertisers," *Advertising Age*, 16 September 1985, pp. 74, 78.

PART EIGHT

Additional Marketing Management Considerations

- CHAPTER 19 — GLOBAL MARKETING
- CHAPTER 20 — NOT-FOR-PROFIT MARKETING
- CHAPTER 21 — TOTAL QUALITY MANAGEMENT IN MARKETING

Case 15 — Live Aid
Case 16 — Kellogg's Corn Flakes

CHAPTER 19

Global Marketing

CHAPTER OBJECTIVES

1. Define, explain, or describe the key terms listed under "Vocabulary and Key Terms."
2. Explain the importance of international marketing today.
3. Contrast the concepts of absolute advantage and comparative advantage.
4. Outline the environment for international business.
5. Discuss the basic concepts in international trade.
6. Compare and contrast buyer behaviour in international marketing with that in domestic marketing.
7. Discuss the marketing mix characteristics and strategies of international marketing.
8. Examine the importance of trade blocs.
9. Outline the various approaches to global marketing taken by companies.
10. Apply your knowledge of Chapter 19 to the various activities in this chapter of the study guide.

VOCABULARY AND KEY TERMS

From the lettered terms listed below, select the one that best matches the meaning of each of the numbered statements that follows. Write the letter of that choice in the space provided.

a) exporting
b) importing
c) balance of trade
d) balance of payments
e) exchange rate
f) devaluation
g) revaluation
h) geocentric
i) ethnocentric
j) polycentric
k) regiocentric
l) GATT (General Agreement on Tariffs and Trade)
m) import quota
n) embargo
o) cartels
p) local-content laws
q) FCN treaties
r) dumping
s) absolute advantage
t) comparative advantage
u) EDC (Export Development Corporation)
v) tariff

1. _____ Laws that specify the portion of a product that must come from domestic sources
2. _____ An international trade accord that has sponsored various trade negotiations
3. _____ A restriction on the amount of goods in a specific product category that may enter a country
4. _____ The purchasing of foreign goods and raw materials
5. _____ Selling goods and services abroad
6. _____ Assumes that its way of doing business in its home market is the proper way to operate, and tries to replicate this in foreign markets
7. _____ The money flow into or out of a country
8. _____ The relationship between a nation's imports and exports
9. _____ Held by a nation marketing a product for which it is the sole producer or the most economic producer
10. _____ A monopolistic organization of foreign firms
11. _____ A term applied to situations in which products are sold at significantly lower prices in a foreign market than in a nation's domestic market
12. _____ Held by a nation if it produces an item more efficiently than other products
13. _____ A complete ban on certain products
14. _____ The rate at which a nation's currency can be exchanged for other currencies or gold
15. _____ Friendship, commerce, and navigation treaties that include many aspects of international marketing
16. _____ Provides financial services to Canadian exporters and foreign buyers in order to facilitate and develop export trade
17. _____ Countries with similar cultures and economic conditions served with similar marketing mix
18. _____ The process of a nation's reducing the value of its currency in relation to gold or some other currency
19. _____ The assumption that every country is different and that specific market approaches should be developed for each separate country
20. _____ The process of a nation's adjusting its currency upward relative to gold or some other currency
21. _____ A tax levied against products imported from abroad
22. _____ Developing a marketing mix that meets the needs of target consumers in all markets

PRACTICE TEST

True-False: In the space to the right of each statement, check the appropriate line to indicate whether the statement is true or false.

	True	False
1. Some 40 000 new jobs are supported by every million export dollars.	_____	_____
2. Some two million Canadians work in areas directly or indirectly related to export trade.	_____	_____
3. Canada is more dependent than the United States on the export market.	_____	_____
4. A favourable balance of trade occurs when the value of a nation's imports exceeds its exports.	_____	_____
5. In recent years Canada has had a favourable balance of payments, even when the nation had an unfavourable balance of trade.	_____	_____

6. Devaluation occurs when a nation reduces the value of its currency in relation to gold or some other currency.

7. Revaluation occurs on a normal basis every five years to keep currency equal in relative terms to world markets.

8. A nation has an absolute advantage in the marketing of a product if that nation is the sole producer or can produce the product for less than anyone else.

9. Canada as a nation does not have a comparative advantage for any product that is exported to foreign markets.

10. Canada has a high volume of trade with Japan and a positive balance of trade.

11. Wheat is Canada's largest export in foreign trade.

12. Many companies have failed abroad because they tried to use the same marketing strategy that was successful at home.

13. Protective tariffs are usually lower than revenue tariffs.

14. Protective tariffs are designed to raise the retail price of imported goods to that of similar domestic products.

15. An exchange control sets limits on the amount of products in certain categories that may be imported.

16. Canada and the United States have both been guilty over the years of dumping their products over each other's borders.

17. A local content law specifies the portion of a product that must come from domestic sources.

18. A cartel is an organization set up by GATT to control the spread of dumping on foreign markets.

19. The EDC is a Canadian Crown corporation that provides financial services to Canadian exporters and foreign buyers in order to facilitate and develop export trade.

20. Coca-Cola and Rolex watches are examples of products that could be defined as global products.

21. Cost-plus pricing is more appropriate for global markets than for the domestic market.

22. There are many more distribution options available when marketing internationally.

23. A regiocentric approach to global marketing means developing a marketing mix that meets the needs of target consumers in all markets.

24. A custom union establishes a free-trade area plus a uniform tariff for trade with nonmember nations.

25. With the Europe of 1992, there is not only free flow of goods but also of people, capital, and services.

Multiple Choice: Choose the expression that best answers the question or completes the sentence.

26. Which of the following countries is least dependent on foreign trade?
a. Belgium
b. Canada

c. United States
d. United Kingdom
e. New Zealand

27. For Canada as a country, exports account for
a. 46 percent of our GNP
b. 7.7 percent of our GNP
c. 30 percent of our GNP
d. 23 percent of our GNP
e. 10.6 percent of our GNP

28. How many Canadians work in areas directly or indirectly related to export trade?
a. 200 000
b. 2000
c. 1 000 000
d. 2 000 000
e. 500 000

29. An unfavourable balance of trade occurs when
a. the value of a nation's exports exceeds its imports
b. the value of its imports are in excess of exports
c. exports and imports are equalized
d. a country's currency loses value due to the exchange rate
e. insufficient money comes into the country's economy via the sales abroad for a country's products

30. When a nation reduces the value of its currency in relation to gold or some other currency it is experiencing a(n)
a. unfavourable balance of trade
b. revaluation
c. comparative advantage
d. devaluation
e. exchange adjustment

31. When a country adjusts the value of its currency upwards, it is making a(n)
a. devaluation
b. exchange adjustment
c. revaluation
d. currency exchange
e. factor adjustment

32. The Nimba Company is the only producer of Whatchamacallits in the world. As a Canadian producer selling to the many countries that are unable to produce this product in their country, Nimba and Canada both have a(n)
a. unfavourable balance of trade
b. favourable balance of trade
c. comparative advantage
d. absolute advantage
e. positive advantage

33. If a nation can produce one product more efficiently than others, it is said to have a(n)
a. unfavourable balance of trade
b. favourable balance of trade
c. comparative advantage
d. absolute advantage
e. positive advantage

34. The leading commodity export in Canadian foreign trade in 1989 was
   a. wheat
   b. lumber
   c. motor vehicles
   d. pulp and paper products
   e. motor vehicle parts

35. The leading commodity import in Canadian foreign trade in 1989 was
   a. machinery, industrial and agricultural
   b. motor vehicles
   c. motor vehicle parts
   d. office machines and equipment
   e. chemical and related products

36. A tariff is a(n)
   a. practice in which products are sold at significantly lower prices in a foreign market than in a nation's own domestic market
   b. complete ban on importing certain products
   c. limit set on the amount of any given product that may be imported
   d. international trade accord
   e. tax levied against products imported from abroad

37. Dumping is a(n)
   a. practice in which products are sold at significantly lower prices in a foreign market than in a nation's own domestic market
   b. complete ban on importing certain products
   c. limit set on the amount of any given product that may be imported
   d. international trade accord
   e. tax levied against products imported from abroad

38. An import quota is a(n)
   a. practice in which products are sold at significantly lower prices in a foreign market than in a nation's own domestic market
   b. complete ban on importing certain products
   c. limit set on the amount of any given product that may be imported
   d. international trade accord
   e. tax levied against products imported from abroad

39. A trade embargo is a(n)
   a. practice in which products are sold at significantly lower prices in a foreign market than in a nation's own domestic market
   b. complete ban on importing certain products
   c. limit set on the amount of any given product that may be imported
   d. international trade accord
   e. tax levied against products imported from abroad

40. Which company approach to global marketing assumes that its way of doing business in its home market is the proper way to operate and therefore replicates this way of doing business in foreign markets?
   a. geocentric approach
   b. regiocentric approach
   c. polycentric approach
   d. ethnocentric approach
   e. none of the above

41. A company that recognizes that countries with similar cultures and economic conditions can be served with a similar marketing mix is assuming a(n)
    a. geocentric approach
    b. regiocentric approach
    c. polycentric approach
    d. ethnocentric approach
    e. none of the above

42. A company that develops a marketing mix that meets the needs of target consumers in all markets is assuming a(n)
    a. geocentric approach
    b. regiocentric approach
    c. polycentric approach
    d. ethnocentric approach
    e. none of the above

43. A company that assumes that every country is different and that a specific marketing approach should be developed for each separate country is using a(n)
    a. geocentric approach
    b. regiocentric approach
    c. polycentric approach
    d. ethnocentric approach
    e. none of the above

44. What is the purpose of revenue tariffs?
    a. to impose political sanctions
    b. to raise funds for the government of the importing nation
    c. to reduce trade activity
    d. to raise the price of imported products
    e. all of the above

45. Which of the following statements is true about protective tariffs?
    a. They raise the price of imported products.
    b. They are usually higher than revenue tariffs.
    c. They are usually lower than revenue tariffs.
    d. a and c
    e. a and b

46. Which of the following is not true concerning foreign promotional strategy?
    a. Many firms have taken a firm stand against illicit business practices.
    b. Overseas marketing practices by Canadian firms are not evaluated in terms of Canadian standards.
    c. Effective personal selling is still vital.
    d. Advertising has gained in importance.
    e. all of the above

47. Which of the following is not true about pricing strategies in foreign markets?
    a. Export pricing is the least affected of the marketing mix variables.
    b. Price strategies are affected by varying economic conditions in different nations.
    c. Pricing strategies are subject to competitive constraints.
    d. Pricing strategies are subject to political constraints.
    e. Pricing strategies are subject to legal constraints.

48. The Export Development Corporation serves
    a. Canadian importers

b. Canadian exporters
c. foreign purchasers of Canadian goods
d. foreign exporters
e. b and c

49. Which of the following is not related to free trade?
a. Europe 1992
b. Canada–U.S. Free Trade Agreement
c. a custom union
d. an economic union
e. the EDC

50. Which of the following is not a factor contributing directly to Canadian-foreign competition in the domestic market?
a. EDC
b. EEC
c. Canadian trade commission
d. Canadian political stability
e. a and b

ANSWER KEY: CHAPTER 19

Vocabulary and Key Terms	True-False	Multiple Choice
1. p	1. F	26. c
2. l	2. T	27. c
3. m	3. T	28. d
4. b	4. F	29. b
5. a	5. F	30. d
6. i	6. T	31. c
7. d	7. F	32. d
8. c	8. T	33. c
9. s	9. F	34. c
10. o	10. T	35. c
11. r	11. F	36. e
12. t	12. T	37. a
13. n	13. F	38. c
14. e	14. T	39. b
15. q	15. F	40. d
16. u	16. T	41. b
17. k	17. T	42. a
18. f	18. F	43. c
19. j	19. T	44. b
20. g	20. T	45. e
21. v	21. F	46. e
22. h	22. F	47. a
	23. F	48. e
	24. T	49. e
	25. T	50. b

EXERCISE 19.1: THE 1992 EUROPEAN COMMUNITY

The European Common Market was formed by six nations in 1957, and since then has grown to include twelve countries. The date that has been targeted for achieving a truly unified Europe is 1992. The long-term gains of this new market agreement will make the European Community (EC) competitive with the Japanese and American markets. As Quelch points out in *The Market Challenge of 1992*:

> Few of the gains are immediate or direct. One could think of the sources of the potential gains falling into five categories, only the first of which could be thought of as immediate or not contingent on subsequent company action:
>
> 1. Lower costs due to the elimination of frontier controls and the simplification of administrative procedures.
> 2. Lower costs and improved efficiency due to increased competition.
> 3. Lower costs due to improved exploitation of economies of scale.
> 4. Reallocation of resources and new patterns of competition, leading to a truer exploitation of comparative advantage.
> 5. Increased innovation and dynamism as a result of liberalization, freer competition, increased cross-border business, and so forth. (pp. 10–11)

The removal of frontier control barriers will both result in immediate cost advantage to companies and eliminate one of the major difficulties that the European Common Market now experiences — long lineups at border crossings. In the past, many companies have suffered costly delays at these crossings, so eliminating these barriers will benefit all members of the agreement.

Increased competition among producers within the EC will improve the bloc's efficiency; on the other hand, manufacturers of competing products in countries such as Canada will find it difficult to sell to this trading bloc. However, global manufacturers who already have manufacturing plants or joint ventures in the European Community (companies such as Canon, Kellogg, Fuji, IBM, and American Express) will not be negatively affected.

Nationals will have to reallocate their physical and human resources to gain a true comparative advantage over companies operating in another country within the EC. (A comparative advantage exists whenever the relative ability of countries to produce goods differs.) For example, a company producing plastic pipes in France will no longer be able to use trade barriers to protect itself against a competitor in Germany. If the German manufacturer operates more effectively and efficiently it will probably be able to outsell the French producer in both markets because it has a comparative advantage. The 1992 EC removes all barriers within the community and all companies must compete on an equal footing.

Lower costs will result from economies of scale (i.e., savings realized when applying a production or marketing technique to a larger number of products or services). Inefficient companies will eventually be absorbed by larger companies in mergers and acquisitions as the market becomes more competitive. The multinationals operating within the European Community already apply economies of scale on an international basis; in Europe they may set a standard for European producers to follow.

According to Quelch:

> the 1992 reforms will create significant opportunities and threats for companies both within and outside the EC. The completion of the program will "change the rules of the competitive game" in the EC marketplace. To take advantage of the opportunities and to guard against the threats, managers must reconsider all aspects of their strategies, including R&D, manufacturing, distribution and marketing. While all of these strategic dimensions are important, we believe that effective marketing will be especially critical to competitive success in the post–1992 EC arena. (p. iii)

Questions

1. For EC marketers, what are the advantages of operating within this trading bloc?
2. Will multinational companies currently operating within the European Community be adversely affected by the 1992 changes to the European Common Market?

3. What is meant by economies of scale? Give an example.
4. What is meant by comparative advantage? What role will this principle play in the post-1992 years in Europe?
5. Will a 1992 European Community hinder Canada's trade with EC countries?

Source: John Quelch, *The Marketing Challenge of 1992* (Toronto: Addison-Wesley Publishing Company, 1990), pp. iii, 9–13. Reprinted by permission.

EXERCISE 19.2: GLOBALIZATION

Multinational companies such as the Ford Motor Company manufacture and market products specifically designed for predetermined foreign target markets. In *The Marketing Imagination*, Theodore Levitt of the Harvard Business School endorses a globalization strategy of creating similar purchasing behaviour in diverse cultures. He contends that, in global markets, corporations as diverse as Revlon, Sony, and Toyota can standardize the manufacturing and distribution of their products. Levitt does not mean that minor changes in the product cannot be designed to meet the cultural needs of a country. For example, Toyota produces cars with the steering wheel on the right side to meet the needs of British consumers. However, apart from these minor changes, other features of the product will be the same.

Globalization is a concept that applies to corporations that sell standardized products worldwide. Black & Decker, who previously customized tools for the foreign market (designing them to meet special needs of customers in Italy, Germany, etc.), is converting to globalization and will soon market fifty standardized power tools worldwide. Strong competition from Mikita Electric Works, Ltd., of Japan was one reason for the move to globalization. Mikita has a global strategy and produces a low-priced drill similar to Black & Decker's for consumers in Germany, Italy, the United States, Canada, and many other countries. Black & Decker believes its change in strategy will help prevent Mikita, and others, from eroding its leading market share on the world market.

Black & Decker believes the globalization strategy is flexible enough to allow it to sell small appliances, as well as its power tools, abroad. To do this, the company would first have to buy an existing small appliance line and convert it to the Black & Decker label. One strategy being considered is to enter the high-price, high-quality market, now controlled by such European giants as Braun and Krups.

Questions

1. What is globalization? Why is it an effective strategy for Black & Decker to pursue at this time?
2. What problems may be encountered by Black & Decker with this strategy of global marketing?
3. Why do you agree or disagree with the global strategy of not recognizing the diverse cultural differences of countries in the design and marketing of products? Why would Black & Decker move from the traditional multinational approach of designing specific products for specific markets?

Source: Theodore Levitt, "The Marketing Imagination," *Fortune*, 14 May 1984.

CHAPTER 20

Not-for-Profit Marketing

CHAPTER OBJECTIVES

1. Define, explain, and describe the key terms listed under "Vocabulary and Key Terms."
2. Outline the primary characteristics of nonprofit organizations that distinguish them from profit organizations.
3. Identify the types of marketing in nonprofit settings.
4. Explain how a marketing mix might be developed in nonprofit settings.
5. Understand what variables might be used in the evolution and control of a nonprofit marketing program.
6. Apply your knowledge of Chapter 20 to the various activities in this chapter of the study guide.

VOCABULARY AND KEY TERMS

From the lettered terms listed below, select the one that best matches the meaning of each of the numbered statements that follows. Write the letter of that choice in the space provided.

a) nonprofit organization
b) bottom line
c) volunteer
d) cost recovery
e) person marketing
f) idea marketing
g) organization marketing
h) multiple publics

1. _____ Business jargon referring to the overall profitability measure of performance
2. _____ An organization whose primary objective is something other than returning a profit to its owners
3. _____ An attempt by a nonprofit organization to recover the actual cost of operating the unit
4. _____ Efforts designed to cultivate in a market target attention to, interest in, and preference for a particular person
5. _____ An attempt to influence others to accept the goals of an organization
6. _____ Identification of and marketing of a cause to chosen consumer segments
7. _____ A nonprofit organization works with several groups to accomplish its goal (e.g. their clients and funders)
8. _____ Individuals or groups who contribute their time and effort to the service of the nonprofit organization

PRACTICE TEST

True-False: In the space to the right of each statement, check the appropriate line to indicate whether the statement is true or false.

		True	False
1.	Nonprofit organizations are found only in the private sector.		
2.	The marketing mix can be applied only to profit marketing.		
3.	Marketing research is used more extensively in nonprofit marketing than in profit marketing.		
4.	Marketing research may be needed in nonprofit marketing in order to learn how to best communicate current findings.		
5.	A substantial portion of the Canadian economy is composed of nonprofit organizations.		
6.	It is estimated that 50 percent of service workers are employed in service marketing.		
7.	The market offerings of nonprofit organizations are more nebulous than the tangible goods or service offerings of profit-seeking organizations.		
8.	The product offered by nonprofit organizations is normally tangible in nature.		
9.	Nonprofit organizations normally have at least two major publics to work with from a marketing viewpoint.		
10.	Private sector businesses deal with multiple publics but tend to think about marketing to one of these publics, their customers.		
11.	One major problem of nonprofit organizations is their lack of efficiency in marketing.		
12.	Person marketing refers to efforts designed to cultivate the attention, interest, and preference of a market target toward a person.		
13.	Advocacy advertising is very closely associated with person marketing.		
14.	The success of antismoking campaigns is a good example of the success of idea marketing in a nonprofit setting.		
15.	Nonprofit organizations face different product decisions than would be expected from a profit-seeking business.		
16.	In nonprofit marketing a heavy promotional effort can often overcome a poor marketing strategy.		
17.	A nonprofit organization never considers profit maximizing a goal in marketing.		
18.	A common pricing goal of nonprofit organizations is cost recovery.		
19.	Distribution channels for nonprofit organizations tend to be short, simple, and direct.		
20.	Marketing communications is not an important element in the marketing mix of nonprofit organizations.		

Multiple Choice: Choose the expression that best answers the question or best completes the sentence.

21. Which of the following statements about nonprofit organizations is true?
a. They represent a substantial portion of the Canadian economy.
b. Their primary objective is something other than returning a profit.
c. Not all of the marketing mix variables are present.
d. all of the above
e. a and b

22. Which of the following is not a characteristic of nonprofit organizations?
a. Products offered are often intangible.
b. Service users exercise control over the organization's destiny.
c. Customers have little control over the organization's destiny.
d. They often have a monopoly in a given area.
e. Resource contributors can often interfere with the marketing program.

23. The current status of nonprofit marketing is the result of
a. new federal regulations
b. an evolutionary process
c. resistance from the profit sector
d. all of the above
e. none of the above

24. Nonprofit organizations can be found
a. in both public and private sectors of society
b. only in the private sector
c. only in the public sector
d. only in service industries in the private sector
e. only in charitable organizations

25. The term "myopia" as applied to nonprofit marketing means that
a. an organization recognizes its goals and strives to achieve them
b. planning is the critical factor in the success of the nonprofit organization
c. management fails to have the foresight to consider what business it is in
d. marketing research will lead the company toward the satisfaction of company goals and objectives
e. none of the above

26. Nonprofit organizations normally have at least two major publics to work with from a marketing point of view:
a. their customers and their sponsors
b. their shareholders and their funders
c. their employees and their funders
d. their clients and their funders
e. their employees and their shareholders

27. Perhaps the most common feature of a nonprofit organization is
a. its common goal of cost recovery
b. its interest in avoiding marketing myopia
c. its lack of a "bottom line"
d. the presence of shareholders
e. its lack of a common pricing policy

28. Nonprofit organizations
a. have a clear, simple organizational structure

    b.   lack a single, clear organizational structure
    c.   often have multiple organizational structures
    d.   b and c
    e.   none of the above

29.   Recent advertising on the importance of wearing seat belts and motorcycle helmets, and the campaign against smoking are all examples of
    a.   person marketing
    b.   idea marketing
    c.   organizational marketing
    d.   public sector marketing
    e.   test marketing

30.   Included in the category of mutual benefit organizations in nonprofit marketing are
    a.   colleges, universities, and hospitals
    b.   police and fire departments
    c.   churches, labour unions, and political parties
    d.   military services
    e.   charitable organizations

31.   A common failure among nonprofit organizations is
    a.   an inability to recognize the importance of marketing research
    b.   a lack of concern about the cost of operating the nonprofit organization
    c.   the assumption that heavy promotional efforts can overcome a poor product strategy or marketing mix
    d.   a and b
    e.   none of the above

32.   A political party offering a $1000-a-plate political fund-raiser is a good example of a
    a.   profit-maximization pricing strategy
    b.   cost-recovery pricing strategy
    c.   concerted effort to provide market incentives
    d.   market suppression
    e.   share-of-the-market pricing strategy

33.   Nonprofit groups that follow a penetration pricing policy to encourage increased usage of a product or service are using this pricing strategy to
    a.   maximize profits
    b.   cover the actual costs of operating the item
    c.   provide market usage incentives
    d.   discourage consumption
    e.   none of the above

34.   Distribution channels for nonprofit organizations tend to be
    a.   long because the market is widely distributed
    b.   short, simple, and direct because of the shortness of contact
    c.   cumbersome and generally badly organized
    d.   none of the above
    e.   a and c

35.   The most important element of the marketing mix from the nonprofit organization's point of view is
    a.   product
    b.   price

   c.   marketing communications
   d.   distribution
   e.   all of the above, as it is the coordination of all the elements of the mix that will determine
        its success

36.   Which of the following practices was implemented before marketing in nonprofit organizations?
   a.   strategic planning
   b.   personnel selection
   c.   accounting
   d.   a and b
   e.   all of the above

37.   According to the text, Kotler believes that the marketing director should report to
   a.   the vice-president designated by the president
   b.   the vice-president of marketing
   c.   the sales manager
   d.   the company president
   e.   none of the above

38.   Which of the following elements is not an element of the marketing mix in the nonprofit sector?
   a.   promotional strategy
   b.   product strategy
   c.   pricing strategy
   d.   distribution strategy
   e.   none of the above

39.   All of the following are examples of cost recovery ventures except
   a.   mass transit
   b.   publicly supported colleges
   c.   churches
   d.   bridges
   e.   All of the above are examples.

40.   Which of the following is an example of a private sector, nonprofit organization?
   a.   Acadia University football team
   b.   art institute
   c.   labour union
   d.   b and c
   e.   all of the above

ANSWER KEY: CHAPTER 20

Vocabulary and Key Terms	True-False	Multiple Choice
1. b	1. F	21. e
2. a	2. F	22. b
3. d	3. F	23. b
4. e	4. T	24. a
5. g	5. T	25. c
6. f	6. F	26. d
7. h	7. T	27. c
8. c	8. F	28. d
	9. T	29. b
	10. T	30. c
	11. T	31. c
	12. T	32. a
	13. F	33. c
	14. T	34. b
	15. F	35. e
	16. F	36. e
	17. F	37. a
	18. T	38. e
	19. T	39. e
	20. F	40. d

EXERCISE 20.1: FOSTER PARENTS OF CANADA

A nonprofit organization's primary objective is something other than returning a dollar to its owners. Charitable organizations such as Foster Parents of Canada are heavily involved in nonprofit marketing. Examine the ad on Foster Parents and answer the following questions:

Questions

1. Evaluate the ad. What message is being presented? Do you think ads of this type by charitable organizations are effective in getting their message out to likely contributors? Is it possible to identify the type of person (target market) who would become a foster parent?
2. Pricing is a very important element in the marketing program of a nonprofit organization. From the ad, speculate on the pricing strategy employed. Read the bottom left-hand side of the ad. How is the money used by Foster Parents? Also, the organization states that financial statements are available upon request; does this statement strengthen the credibility of the ad?
3. Can you identify the distribution channels for this nonprofit service organization?
4. Can you think of other promotional techniques employed by Foster Parents to present its message? Discuss.

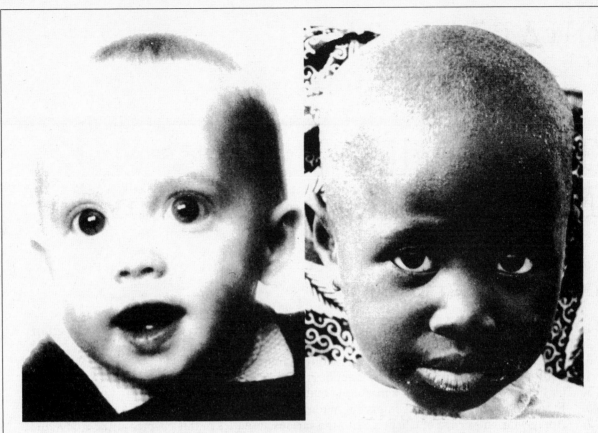

Open & shut.
Two views of the future.

Jordan and Monzon are two years old. Their futures stretch ahead of them, as yet unshaped. But while one boy faces an easy path, the other will endure a more tortuous trail. Jordan is the lucky one. Living here in Canada his potential will have every opportunity to shine – his future is an open book. But Monzon is a child of the developing world. He faces deprivation, hopelessness and even death – a life shut off before it really ever began. There shouldn't be a difference. There doesn't have to be. Your support through Foster Parents Plan can give a boy like Monzon an equal opportunity to shine. Less than a dollar a day can open closed doors to medical care, education, clean water and so much more. Please – won't you help one small child take his share of a bright tomorrow?

Call or write today.

We at Foster Parents Plan are proud of the handling of our funds. 86% of all contributions goes directly toward child and family material aid and services, with 8.2% used for administration costs, and 5.8% for promotion. We are non-profit, non-sectarian and non-political and we are officially registered as a Canadian Charitable Organization by the Federal Government (Reg. No. 0249896-09-13). Complete financial statements are available on request.

IMAGINE

CALL TOLL-FREE ANYTIME 1-(800)-268-7174

PLAN **FOSTER PARENTS PLAN OF CANADA**
(An International human development agency)
153 ST. CLAIR AVENUE WEST, TORONTO, CANADA M4V 1P8

I want to be a Foster Parent of a boy ☐   girl ☐   age _____ country _____
or where the need is greatest ☐   Please correspond in English ☐   French ☐
I enclose my first payment of $27 monthly ☐ $81 quarterly ☐ $162 semi-ann.☐
$324 annually ☐ I can't be a Foster Parent now, but enclose contribution of $ _____
Please send me more information ☐   your free-loan video ☐   VHS ☐   Beta ☐
Mr. ☐   Mrs. ☐   Ms. ☐ _____
Address _____
City_____ Prov. _____ Code _____
Phone Home ( )_____ Bus. ( )_____

PLAN operates in Bolivia, Burkina Faso, Colombia, Dominican Republic, Ecuador, Egypt, El Salvador, Guatemala, Guinea, Haiti, Honduras, India, Indonesia, Kenya, Liberia, Mali, Nepal, the Philippines, Senegal, Sierra Leone, Sri Lanka, the Sudan, Thailand, Togo and Zimbabwe. PLAN is officially registered as a Canadian Charitable Organization by the federal government. All donations eligible for tax credits.
6/30/90   MA905 111990

CHAPTER 21

Total Quality Management in Marketing

CHAPTER OBJECTIVES

1. Show the importance of establishing a process of reviewing the results of the marketing effort.
2. Review the importance of customer satisfaction in marketing planning.
3. Relate the concept of control to the marketing planning process.
4. Show how total quality management applies to marketing.
5. Outline the steps involved in a marketing audit.
6. Evaluate some aspects of the impact of marketing on society.
7. Apply your knowledge of Chapter 21 to the various activities in this chapter of the study guide.

VOCABULARY AND KEY TERMS

From the lettered terms listed below, select the one that best matches the meaning of each of the numbered statements that follows. Write the letter of that choice in the space provided.

a) total quality management
b) evaluation and control
c) marketing audit
d) customer satisfaction
e) social responsibility
f) marketing ethics

1. _____ The marketer's acceptance of the obligation to consider profit, consumer satisfaction, and the well-being of society of equal value in evaluating the performance of a firm
2. _____ The marketer's standards of conduct and moral values
3. _____ The various assessments that marketers employ to determine whether all phases of a marketing program have been effective
4. _____ A thorough, objective evaluation of an organization's marketing philosophy, goals, policies, procedures, practices, and results
5. _____ The ability to satisfy one's customers
6. _____ The premise that at every stage of production nothing less than total quality is acceptable

PRACTICE TEST

True-False: In the space to the right of each statement, check the appropriate line to indicate whether the statement is true or false.

		True	False
1.	The final aspect of the marketing planning process is control.	_____	_____
2.	Only after a systematic review of the outcome of the planning process can improvements be made in the marketing plan.	_____	_____
3.	A recent survey of marketing planning practices found that over 75 percent of firms developed a marketing plan.	_____	_____
4.	The first step in the marketing planning process is to determine marketing objectives for the firm.	_____	_____
5.	The last step in the planning process is to develop marketing strategies.	_____	_____
6.	The control aspects of marketing are part of the question, "Where do we want to go?"	_____	_____
7.	The customer doesn't care about systems; the customer cares about having problems handled.	_____	_____
8.	The H-P customer satisfaction program includes three programs — customer feedback input, total quality control, and marketing ethics.	_____	_____
9.	According to survey results, worldwide customer satisfaction has fallen off by 5 percent since 1989.	_____	_____
10.	The Japanese product invasion throughout the world has created a growing recognition of the importance of quality products.	_____	_____
11.	Quality is the responsibility of the production department within the organization.	_____	_____
12.	Total quality management applies not only to the products that are marketed, but also to the marketing management process.	_____	_____
13.	Total quality means that a good or service totally conforms to the customer's requirements.	_____	_____
14.	An integrated marketing organization is one of the five activities of the marketing audit.	_____	_____
15.	Social responsibility is not an important issue in business today.	_____	_____
16.	Marketing ethics are the marketer's standards of conduct and moral values.	_____	_____
17.	The professional association to which most marketers belong is the American Management Association.	_____	_____
18.	Total quality management is necessary not only for products and management practices, but also in the ethical approaches to doing business.	_____	_____
19.	In a marketing plan, situation analysis should follow the company's determining its marketing strategies.	_____	_____

20.   This chapter concentrates on the control aspects of strategy
      within the marketing plan.   _____   _____

Multiple Choice: Choose the expression that best answers the question or best completes the sentence.

21.   The final aspect of the marketing planning process is
a.   the situation analysis
b.   financial considerations
c.   control
d.   determining whether the objective of achieving customer satisfaction has been met
e.   c and d

22.   In a recent study of the marketing planning practices of the top 500 Canadian firms, Dale Beckman
      found that a written marketing plan was developed by
a.   75 percent of the firms
b.   57.8 percent of the firms
c.   25 percent of the firms
d.   90 percent of the firms
e.   65.7 percent of the firms

23.   In the above study, Beckman found that a post mortem of the past year's results in their current
      marketing plan was included by
a.   10.9 percent
b.   25.4 percent
c.   58.4 percent
d.   35.5 percent
e.   45.7 percent

24.   The marketing planning process covers all of the following except
a.   situation analysis
b.   marketing objectives
c.   marketing strategies
d.   quality marketing management

25.   Hewlett-Packard has established three programs to obtain customer feedback, in order to provide
      the kind of service that will make a difference. These three programs are
a.   customer feedback, learning resources, and customer surveys
b.   customer feedback, customer surveys, and management criteria
c.   customer feedback input, customer satisfaction surveys, and total quality control
d.   customer feedback input, total quality control, and management criteria

26.   According to worldwide "relationship" survey results, worldwide customer satisfaction has
a.   improved 3 percentage points over last year
b.   improved 5 percentage points over last year
c.   fallen off 5 percentage points over last year
d.   fallen off 10 percentage points over last year

27.   What country has led the way in creating a growing recognition of the importance of quality
      control?
a.   Canada
b.   the United States
c.   Germany
d.   Japan
e.   Cuba

28. Quality must be defined
  a. from an internal, customer-based viewpoint
  b. in terms of its relationships with people
  c. from an external, customer-based viewpoint
  d. from the point of view of the engineer
  e. from the point of view of the cost accountant

29. Which of the following is the best definition of total quality management?
  a. TQM is the absolute responsibility of every person in the organization.
  b. TQM is the production and marketing of quality products to meet the needs of customers.
  c. TQM is the economic and social justification of a firm's existence.
  d. TQM emphasizes that at every stage of production nothing less than total quality is acceptable.

30. Total quality management applies not only to the products that are marketed but also to
  a. the marketing management process
  b. the production process
  c. all aspects of engineering
  d. the management and control of the process
  e. consumer responsibility

31. All of the following are necessary to take quality from slogan to substance, except
  a. realization that the quality of the good or service must be the overriding goal
  b. communicating quality goals and standards to all employees, whether or not they interface with the public
  c. training all employees in a voluntary, co-operative atmosphere
  d. assurance that cost control measures are never sacrificed
  e. rewards for those whose involvement leads to quality improvements and real cost savings

32. Which of the following is a variable in the marketing audit?
  a. customer philosophy
  b. integrated marketing organization
  c. adequate marketing information
  d. strategic orientation
  e. all of the above

33. To which marketing variable does this question relate: Does marketing management generate innovative strategies and plans for long-run growth and profitability?
  a. customer philosophy
  b. integrated marketing organization
  c. adequate marketing information
  d. strategic orientation
  e. operational efficiency

34. To which marketing audit variable does this question relate: Does management acknowledge the primacy of the marketplace and of customer needs and wants in shaping plans and operations?
  a. customer philosophy
  b. integrated marketing organization
  c. adequate marketing information
  d. strategic orientation
  e. operational efficiency

35. To which marketing audit variable does this question relate: Are marketing plans implemented in a cost-effective manner, and are the results monitored for rapid corrective action?
  a. customer philosophy

b. integrated marketing organization
c. adequate marketing information
d. strategic orientation
e. operational efficiency

36. To which marketing audit variable does this question relate: Is the organization staffed so that it will be able to carry out marketing analysis, planning, and implementation and control?
a. customer philosophy
b. integrated marketing organization
c. adequate marketing information
d. strategic orientation
e. operational efficiency

37. To which marketing audit variable does this question relate: Does management receive the kind and quality of information needed to conduct effective marketing?
a. customer philosophy
b. integrated marketing organization
c. adequate marketing information
d. strategic orientation
e. operational efficiency

38. The types of ethics mentioned in the text include all of the following except
a. individual ethic
b. organizational ethic
c. religious ethic
d. professional ethic
e. All of the above are mentioned.

39. The type of ethic that transcends both other types of ethics is the
a. individual ethic
b. organizational ethic
c. religious ethic
d. professional ethic

40. Social responsibility is the marketer's acceptance of the obligation to consider of equal value in evaluating the performance of the firm profit, consumer satisfaction, and
a. the government
b. total quality-control management
c. the well-being of society
d. employee satisfaction
e. company objectives

ANSWER KEY: CHAPTER 21

Vocabulary and Key Terms	True-False	Multiple Choice
1. e	1. T	21. e
2. f	2. T	22. b
3. b	3. F	23. b
4. c	4. F	24. d
5. d	5. T	25. c
6. a	6. F	26. a
	7. T	27. d
	8. F	28. c
	9. F	29. d
	10. T	30. a
	11. F	31. d
	12. T	32. e
	13. T	33. d
	14. T	34. a
	15. F	35. e
	16. T	36. b
	17. F	37. c
	18. T	38. c
	19. F	39. d
	20. T	40. c

EXERCISE 21.1: THE URBAN FOREST

An increasing number of ads focusing on the environment have been placed in magazines by industry. Shown here is an advertisement created by the pulp and paper industry of Canada. Read it and answer these questions.

Questions

1. What message is presented by this ad? Is this ad effective?
2. The recycling of waste paper is a major ecological issue. From reading this ad and other material in the text on recycling, what would you say are the major problems involved in recycling? As you discuss the last question, tie it into the following questions: What distribution problems are presented by the recycling of waste paper? Who will buy recycled paper? What use can be made of recycled paper? Is recycled paper likely to be less expensive than nonrecycled paper?
3. Should consumers be concerned about the recycling of paper? Why?

THE URBAN FOREST

Recycling: an environmental idea that makes good business sense

It is not only with virgin fibre that Canada's papermakers do their work. **More than 40 of Canada's 145 pulp, paper, and paper board mills recycle waste papers for all or part of their raw material needs.** Some have been doing so for more than 50 years.

The pulp and paper industry welcomes additional supplies of high-quality waste papers to meet its fibre needs. In fact, the quantity of recyclable papers has been increasing steadily: in 1980, 1 200 000 tonnes of waste paper were used; in 1990, that figure will exceed 1.9 million tonnes.

Growth of waste recovery

Nearly 25 percent of the paper and paperboard used in Canada is collected for recycling. Recovering papers from a variety of sources, once the province of small entrepreneurs, community groups, and service clubs, has also become the domain of businesses of significant size.

Market forces and environmental

considerations will continue to shape the recycling business. For one thing, people are asking for recycled content in the products they buy. For another, landfill sites are becoming more difficult to find. Recycling enables the industry to respond to the recycling ethic and to ease the environmental burden created by increasing municipal solid waste.

Industry research

As research solves the technological problems that today constitute barriers; as supplies of recyclable papers become reliable; **and as more markets open for recycled papers, Canadian mills will use greater quantities of waste paper.**

In keeping with the spirit of its **Environmental Statement,** the pulp and paper industry is resolved to strike a balance between its business opportunities and its responsibilities to the environment.

Recycling is an expression of that resolve.

FOR MORE INFORMATION:
Public Information Office
Canadian Pulp and Paper
Association
Sun Life Building, 19th Floor
1155 Metcalfe Street
Montreal, Québec   H3B 4T6

The Pulp and Paper Industry of Canada
—— Committed to renewal ——

Case 15

LIVE AID

On July 13, 1985, the world witnessed a televised spectacle of a size that had previously been associated mostly with sporting events. On that day 14 satellites telecast 63 rock acts from London and Philadelphia to 150 countries for a total of 16 hours. The concert was known, of course, as Live Aid, and it raised millions for Ethiopian famine relief.

Irish singer Bob Geldof conceived of the fundraising event, which was then organized and executed by Michael Mitchell. Mitchell had been a logistics planner for the 1984 Los Angeles Olympics. Early in 1985 he and a number of other staffers from the Olympics formed what they called Worldwide Sports & Entertainment, a company created specifically to organize more large-scale globally televised "mega-events" like Live Aid.

Because services at the Live Aid concert were mostly provided free or at cost, 100% of donations were allowed to go to famine relief. The estimated $20 million concert expenses were reduced to about $4.5 million, an amount easily covered by the $12 million ticket sales, sponsorships, and broadcast rights. But Mitchell conceived of Live Aid not just as a charity event but also a vehicle for advertising and as a means of promotion for future mega-events. Some critics have suggested that there may be basic incompatibility between corporate sponsorship and such charity events.

The sponsors of Live Aid — Eastman Kodak Co., PepsiCo Inc., AT&T, and GM's Chevrolet division — each donated $750 000, but in return received dozens of commercial spots during the telethon. They received additional advertising benefits through such things as having performers use Pepsi drinking cups on-camera.

Also, ABC, which carried the broadcast, paid a $1.5 million licensing fee, but earned about $6 million from commercials. Critics of the sponsors' motives for participating in the concert ask why, for example, various labourers should have worked cheap for the concert when a corporation like ABC made such huge profits.

In response, the concert promoters contend that a major network was needed to lend credibility to the event and to make the event possible in the first place. No event, no funds for famine relief; no profits for sponsors, no event. Also, the promoters reason that if large corporations can reap profits from these charity events they will be more likely to participate in future events.

Despite questions of the compatibility of advertising and social concerns, Worldwide and other groups are already planning future mega-events. The success of these events may depend less on corporate sponsorship than on whether the public will continue to show an interest in more such massive entertainments.

Questions

1. Assess the motives of the Live Aid sponsors. Can advertising have a socially responsible purpose? Discuss.
2. If you were responsible for the advertising of a major firm, would you become a sponsor of a charity telethon? Why, or why not?
3. Discuss the marketing success or failure of other charity telethons. Can any generalizations be drawn about the factors associated with successful events?

Source: Jeffrey Zaslow, "Next from the Live Aid Team: Global Charity Telethon for Profit," *The Wall Street Journal*, 9 August 1989, p. 19. Reprinted by permission.

Case 16

KELLOGG'S CORN FLAKES

Kellogg Company is a leading food products manufacturing company based in Battle Creek, Michigan (1989 sales were over $4.5 billion). The company produces a wide variety of ready-to-eat cereals and other food products, including toaster pastries, frozen waffles, soups, dessert mixes, Salada tea, snack items, and other convenience foods. The company also engages in supporting activities such as grain milling and carton printing in a number of countries where principal manufacturing operations exist.

Kellogg International handles the company business outside the United States and Canada. Sales outside the United States account for one-third of the total. Kellogg has 22 manufacturing locations on six continents, with Europe and Latin America accounting for most of them. Japan and Australia are also good markets.

Kellogg Company markets through its own salesforce in major world markets and through broker and distributor arrangements in less developed market areas.

A basic thrust of the company's advertising and promotion is designed to further consumer knowledge regarding the nutritional worth of Kellogg's products. Both advertising and packaging are oriented to the theme of health and nutrition information (see Figure C16-1).

Kellogg's Corn Flakes is the company's most famous product. It is sold in many world markets.

Questions

Putting yourself in the position of international brand manager for Kellogg's Corn Flakes, make brief recommendations on the following:

1. Should the product itself (cornflakes) be standardized or adapted for world markets?
2. Should the brand and trademark Kellogg's Corn Flakes and the familiar red script be uniform in all markets?
3. What is the appropriate packaging for foreign markets?
4. What is an appropriate labelling strategy for world markets?

Source: Vern Terpstra and Ravi Sarathy, *International Marketing* (Chicago, Ill.: The Dryden Press, 1991), pp. 297–98.

FIGURE C16-1 WHAT'S ON THE NUTRITION LABEL?

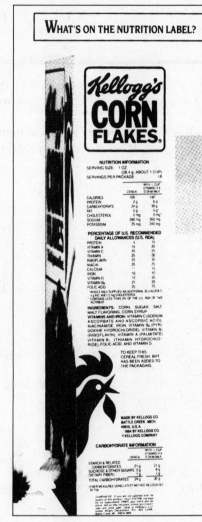

WHAT'S ON THE NUTRITION LABEL?	LET'S TAKE A CLOSER LOOK

When nutrition labeling is practiced then the package must conform to the following format under the heading "Nutrition Information."

1. Serving size may be in ounces, grams or cup measures. A standard serving of KELLOGG'S® ready-to-eat cereal without added fruit is one-ounce.

2. Provides per serving, the amount of calories, protein, carbohydrates and fat in grams (g); and sodium and cholesterol in milligrams (mg).
The potassium and cholesterol information in this section is voluntarily provided by Kellogg Company because some consumers may need this information.

3. The amount of protein, vitamins and minerals per serving, expressed as a percentage of the U.S. Recommended Daily Allowances (U.S. RDA). The FDA requires that the label must provide information only on the first eight nutrients listed.

If a food contains less than two percent of the U.S. RDA of a nutrient, an asterisk or a zero may be used to indicate that fact.

4. Ingredients are listed by their common or usual name, in order of the amount contained in the product by weight. For example, if corn is listed first, the product contains more corn by weight that any other ingredient listed.

5. The FDA requires that the label must provide the name and address of the manufacturer, packer or distributor.

6. Information in this section is provided voluntarily by Kellogg Company to inform consumers about the complex carbohydrate and fiber content of our products. There is no U.S. RDA for carbohydrates, however, the U.S. Surgeon General and the National Cancer Institute (NCI) recommend that Americans should increase intake of complex carbohydrates eg., starch and fiber.

To the Owner of This Book:

We are interested in your reaction to Study Guide to accompany *Foundations of Marketing* by C.E. Greene. With your comments, we can improve this book in future editions. Please help us by completing this questionnaire.

1. What was your reason for using this book?
   _____ university course
   _____ college course
   _____ continuing education course
   _____ personal interest
   _____ other (specify)

2. If you used this text for a program, what was the name of that program?

3. Which school do you attend?

4. Approximately how much of the book did you use?
   _____ ¼   _____ ½   _____ ¾   _____ all

5. Which chapters or sections were omitted from your course?

6. What is the best aspect of this book?

7. Is there anything that should be added?

8. Please add any comments or suggestions.

(fold here)

(fold here and tape shut)

0116870399-M8Z4X6-BR01